A DIPLOMAT IN SIAM

ITINERARIA ASIATICA

THAILAND   LA THAILANDE

Volume VIII   *Tome VIII*

ORCHID PRESS

Bangkok 2000

A DIPLOMAT IN SIAM

H.B.M. Minister-Resident,
Bangkok, 1885-88

Ernest Satow C.M.G.

Introduced and Edited by
Nigel Brailey

Originally published in 1994

Ernest Satow C.M.G.
A DIPLOMAT IN SIAM

First published: 1994
Revised edition: 2000

Published by
ORCHID PRESS
P.O. Box 19
Yuttitham Post Office,
Bangkok 10907, Thailand

Printed in Thailand

ITINERARIA ASIATICA est une série de réimpressions d'ouvrages
contenant des descriptions et récits de voyageurs en Asie

ITINERARIA ASIATICA is a series of reprints of books
containing first-hand descriptions and narratives by travellers in
Asia

This book is printed on acid-free long-life paper which meets the
specifications of ISO 9706/1994

ISBN 974-8304-73-6

Ernest Satow C.M.G.

Contents

Introduction by Nigel Brailey

The title given the original manuscript of this book by Sir Ernest Satow was merely 'Diary of a Journey from Bangkok to Chiengmai and Back, 1885-86', or alternatively 'Travels in Siam'. But it contains a number of comments inserted by the author into the amended version of his original diary expressive of his experiences in 'Old Siam' more generally. What is more, after his promotion to Minister Resident in February 1885, Satow *was* a genuine diplomat, which was not at all the case at the time of the experiences he describes in his well-known *Diplomat in Japan*. Back in the 1860s, he had been merely a student interpreter and Legation language secretary, and while already politically active beyond his years, that book too was essentially an elaboration on a diary. [1]

A Diplomat in Siam involves probably a rather more jaundiced view of the country than the diary on which it is based. Satow evidently strove to exclude almost everything of political significance, even scoring out in the manuscript a number of paragraphs which could have been of considerable interest. And few individuals are mentioned by name. But this does not prevent him indulging in a variety of negative comments about 'Siam' and the 'Siamese' more generally.

Undoubtedly the journey was of great importance to him, and arguably also to his Foreign Office masters in London whom he continued to advise almost continuously through to 1906, when he retired as British Minister in Peking. In effect, by various means, it seems to have thrown into at least temporary question some of the most fundamental ideas and principles by which he had come to live over the previous two decades; i.e. since his original arrival in Eastern Asia as an eighteen-year old in 1862. It also threw into doubt whether he would ever achieve what he finally did manage in 1895, a return to Tokyo as British Minister in Japan.[2]

One point is that it damaged his health seriously, if temporarily. His first year in Siam, 1884-85, had not been illness-free, but he returned from Chiangmai to Bangkok in March 1886 suffering severely from malaria. In April, he took a week's sick-leave at his seaside home on Sichang Island for which his diary entries are rather desperate, although it was also at this time that he was beginning to write up his Chiangmai journal. On his further return to Bangkok he was able to do little work.

In June, he took three months' leave for a trip to Japan, but was still forced to divert to Singapore for a couple of weeks of medical treatment before returning to Bangkok at the end of September with the journal completed in its original form on the 24th, just prior to catching the steamer up. His final spell of seven and a half months in Bangkok was marred by special official difficulties with both the Siamese Government and sections of the expatriate British community, and by February 1887, he was anyhow appealing for recuperative leave in England. He arrived there in June weighing, as a six-footer, less than ten stone, and not until October 1888, did the Foreign Office finally decide what to do with him. He was then sent to the delightful Montevideo in Uruguay, apparently for fear that his health was permanently damaged. It seems the Chiangmai journal had been reproduced by typists during the autumn of 1887.

But if this Chiangmai journey can certainly be held directly responsible for the abbreviation of Satow's tenure in Siam, it did also call into question the fundamental principles which he had been attempting to apply as Minister there.

No record seems to have survived of any explicit instructions given him by the Foreign Office on his departure for Bangkok in January 1884. He had been shown files of recent correspondence with his predecessor, W. Gifford Palgrave, and the subsequent acting British representative, W.H. Newman, but not even his private diaries make reference to anything more. As an indication of what might have been said to him we have only a letter of his of June 1884 to Sir Philip Currie, the under-secretary to whom he reported directly at the Foreign Office. In this he acknowledged the concern in London to sustain the independence of Siam, at least as a buffer between the Asian empires of Britain and France. This was a policy originally formulated in the early 1860s by the then British Consul in Bangkok, Sir Robert Schomburgk, referred to by Satow in his preface below.

However, the Satow papers also comprise a lengthy memorandum by their progenitor, undated, but apparently deriving from the latter part of 1884, when he was paying an earlier visit to Japan. This may originally have been intended for submission to London, but ultimately developed so forceful a coloration that Satow must have thought better of such action, and retained it simply for his own reference. Its concluding and key section is a declaration that 'Diplomatic communications [are] to be conducted as far as possible in accordance with the tone & character which characterize [mark?] such communication with European & American states, and generally [we are] to endeavour to place our relations with Siam on the basis recognized by universal international law, rather than to regard them as necessarily limited by the exceptional conditions arising out of extra-territoriality.'

This memorandum follows on naturally from another, much longer memorandum, drawn up by Satow when in England in September 1883. In this, which had specific respect to Japan, as he noted later, he had urged that notwithstanding extraterritoriality, local Asian laws 'should be accepted by us without demur, and enforced ag[ain]st our people'. Moreover, in May 1886, albeit sick at the time as indicated above, Satow had been willing privately to criticize quite vehemently the British annexation of Upper Burma at the beginning of the year. Thus until perhaps the summer of 1886, he was in many respects an *anti*-imperialist, by no means in line with the inclinations of many of the people back in England whom he served.

As for Siam specifically, as the memorandum of late 1884 indicates, Satow had hoped to exploit the 1883 Anglo-Siamese Chiangmai Treaty to diminish extra-territoriality as such. The treaty itself, predating his arrival, was concerned mainly with the rights of the large number of British Indian and Burmese subjects in the Chiangmai region. In deference to the wishes of the government in Calcutta which feared endless trouble in pursuing them, it had instead deprived them of extra-territorial consular protection of the sort enjoyed under the Anglo-Siamese (Bowring) treaty of 1855 by British subjects in 'Siam Proper'. Satow's hope, apparently, had been that the administration of Siamese justice in Chiangmai might prove so successful that objections to the abolition of extraterritoriality in Siam Proper too might be steadily worn down and ultimately defeated, and Siam regain its sovereignty in this most important area.

But Satow's conclusions from his trip to Chiangmai were that his hopes had proved wholly false. Admittedly, he had spent only some four weeks in and around the city, weeks for which his diary is inexplicably thin. And the journal seems to indicate a peak of elation on initially entering the glorious Chiangmai valley, but a steady loss of spirit on the long boat journey back, that may have continued to afflict him right up to the point at which he left the country for good in April

1887. On his return to Bangkok, with fever setting in, his first reaction
seems to have been to blame mainly the first, trial British Vice-Consul
at Chiangmai, E.B. Gould, who he had already decided to withdraw
and replace, for the huge backlog of unsettled lawsuits involving British
subjects. But other comments in his diaries and correspondence through
1886 and into 1887, indicate that he was himself steadily losing faith
in the chances of the Siamese judicial system being improved. The
experiences of the replacement Vice-Consul in Chiangmai, W.J. Archer,
apparently persuaded him that after all the trouble had been with the
system, not the personality of his predecessor. When, during his leave
in England in 1887-88, Satow was called on to comment on the powers
to be given to a similar vice-consular appointee in the Siamese Malay
States, he firmly opposed the idea that he should have the same as his
Chiangmai colleague.

By this time, himself seeking as he was to avoid being sent back to
Bangkok, Satow was actively projecting to the Foreign Office the bogey
of a Siam striving to regain judicial sovereignty against British (and
other Western) wishes. And he was even arguing against making con-
cessions to Japan precisely for this reason, for fear of thereby creating a
bandwagon effect from which Siam could benefit, quite as much as
new-found reservations with respect to Japan itself. It is unlikely that
his Foreign Office masters were in any real sense persuaded; rather that
where he was concerned, they prepared themselves to await the recovery
in his spirits and health out in Uruguay that duly eventuated in 1893.
Thereupon, they despatched him to Morocco for two years, itself a cockpit
of Western imperial rivalry. And by the time they returned him to
Japan as Envoy Extraordinary and Minister Plenipotentiary in August
1895, it was to build upon the first major breach in the system of
extraterritorial jurisdiction and 'unequal treaties' that bolstered Western
hegemony in Eastern Asia, the 1894 Anglo-Japanese Kimberley-Aoki
treaty, that was already firmly in effect. [3]

Satow thus returned with renewed enthusiasm for Japan and the
Japanese, as in his view a country and people generally representative of Eastern Asia as a whole through the pan-Asianist movement. However, he at once found himself consigned to the sidelines
by the last Salisbury administration which had already succeeded
to power in England. He was nonetheless to contribute much during
the subsequent few years in setting the scene for the 1902 Anglo-

Japanese Alliance.

As for Siam, it had little chance now of climbing on the Japanese bandwagon, being direly threatened for most of the 1890s with a French takeover or, even worse, Anglo-French partition. But after the 1914-18 War, the Japanese were to make a contribution to the restoration of Thai sovereignty through a new equal-handed Siam-Japan treaty in 1922.[4] Things also began to move with the Western powers, and Siam ultimately regained full legal sovereignty as envisaged by Satow in a series of treaties in 1936-37.

In large measure, the above circumstances also serve to explain why this journal was never previously published in full. A section did appear as 'A Journey in Siam, 1885-6,' in *The Arrow* of Buenos Aires about 1892, while Satow was serving across the River Plate as Minister to Uruguay. And other sections had been published in *The Journal of the Society of Arts*, XL (1892), 182-197, 849-856, as a consequence of encouragement from his Foreign Office masters on a home leave visit to London.[5] Satow's preface below anyhow suggests some diffidence on his part even in 1888 about proceeding with publication of what he found himself describing, very questionably, as a 'twice told tale'.[6] But it would appear that while taking the typescript away for correction on his tour of France, Italy, Spain and Portugal in the spring of 1888, the purpose of that tour, collection of material for his volume on *The Jesuit Mission Press in Japan*, published later in the year,[7] quickly ousted it from his mind, along with the original manuscript for *A Diplomat in Japan*, completed during the earlier stages of his term in Bangkok. Only the earlier chapters of the present book were properly corrected by him, and it has been left to the present editor in retrieving it from the obscurity in which it has for so long lain, to deal with the rest. It is currently held amongst the Satow Papers as PRO 30/33/20/1 at the Public Record Office, Kew. I am specially grateful to Mrs Mary Tosh for her efforts in retyping it out. In all cases, Satow's own preferred spellings have been retained, as have the original line-drawings after the model of Carl Bock in his *Temples and Elephants*, albeit reduced in size.

N J B
June 1998

Notes

[1] Satow explains that he only began to write *A Diplomat in Japan* while in Bangkok in the 1880s, and it was not to be published until 1921, when he had already been fifteen years in retirement. He was not knighted until 1895. Before leaving Japan in 1883, he had compiled with A.G. Hawes a somewhat turgid pioneering guidebook to that country.

[2] The transfer had been under consideration in London in early 1885 at about the same time as Satow received his promotion as Minister in Bangkok, but was blocked by Sir Francis Plunkett's refusal to move from Tokyo to Peking to succeed the deceased Sir Harry Parkes.

[3] Not, however, with the full-hearted support of the current British Ministers in Tokyo and Peking, Le Poer Trench and N. O'Conor. For an overview of Satow's career as a whole, see my 'Sir Ernest Satow, Japan and Asia: The Trials of a Diplomat in the Age of High Imperialism'. Cambridge *Historical Journal* 35, 1 (1992), 115-150.

[4] If it is ever really legitimate to use the alien name 'Siam' forced on the country by Westerners in the nineteenth century, with the onset of modern 'Thai' nationalism during the reign of King Wachirawut (Rama VI), 1910-25, it becomes increasingly necessary at least to alternate the use of the word 'Thai', well in advance of the official proclamation of the name 'Thailand' in 1939.

[5] It was originally presented as a lecture to the society in January 1892. It is unclear whether these officials were motivated by a desire to bolster Satow's current low morale, or to extend general interest in Siam at a time when its future was seeming increasingly uncertain in face of Western (i.e. Anglo-French) imperial rivalry.

[6] Unlike Schomburgk and Bock, in addition to making his visits to Sachanalai/Sukhothai and Sawankhalok, Satow also traversed most of the Menam Pho tributary of the Bangkok river, visiting the towns of Phichit, Phitsanulok, Uttaradit and Phichai, and the Lao town of Phre on the Me Yom.

[7] See my 'To Rome and Lisbon: Ernest Satow's diary of a bibliographical quest in 1888', forthcoming.

Preface

The northern and eastern portions of the dominions which acknowl-
edge the sway of the Siamese King are known to geographers as the
Laos, from the Siamese names of their inhabitants. Along the banks of
the Me-khong or Cambodia River these populations, though governed
by officials of their own race, are directly subject to Bangkok, but in the
north they are divided into six states, ruled over by their hereditary
chiefs, and thus are semi-independent. These six states are Chiengmai,
Lamphun, Lakhon, Nan, Phrë and Luang Phrabang. In the first five,
Asiatic subjects of the Queen, chiefly natives of Burma, have for many
years carried on an extensive trade in teak-timber, taking leases of forests from the chiefs and other owners.

Almost from the very commencement of the diplomatic relations
with Siam which followed upon the conclusion in 1855 of Sir John
Bowring's Treaty of Commerce, disputes and lawsuits began to arise in
connection with the rights thus obtained. In 1874 a treaty was negotiated between the two Kings of Siam and the Viceroy of India which had
for its principal object the establishment on the spot, of tribunals for the
determination of such disputes, but having failed in completely securing the objects aimed at, it was superseded in 1883 by a fresh treaty
concluded between Great Britain and Siam. Under the new Treaty a
native court was created at Chiengmai for the trial of all cases, both
civil and criminal, in which British subjects were either plaintiffs or
defendants, and a Vice-Consul was appointed to reside there to watch
over the execution of the provisions and to protect the interests of Her
Majesty's subjects. The judges of the Court were Siamese, and a Commissioner was in addition appointed by the King of Siam, to discharge
functions similar to those of the British Resident at a Native Court in
India. At first the Treaty applied only to Chiengmai, Lamphun and
Lakhon, but its operation was afterwards extended to Nan and Phrë.

The arrangements looked well on paper, but owing to the vast amount
of arrears which had accumulated in consequence of the failure of the
Treaty of 1874, they did not work smoothly, so that it became advisable
for me to pay a visit to Chiengmai in order to make myself acquainted
with the causes which impeded the settlement of the outstanding claims,
and to gain personal insight into the circumstances and conditions of
the teak trade. Having obtained the sanction of Her Majesty's Secre-

State for Foreign Affairs, I started on my journey towards the end of 1885, and spent nearly three months in travelling through regions which have seldom been traversed by Europeans, and still more seldom been described. Sir Robert Schomburgk had visited Chiengmai in 186[0], and after his return published a short record of his experiences. [1] In 1882 Mr Carl Bock, a Norwegian naturalist, travelled in Siam, and an account of his journey up the Menam River and through the three western Lao States was brought out in 1884 under the title of "Temples and Elephants". [2] The following pages have no pretence to offer more than a narrative from day to day of personal observation and of incidents of travel in a country little explored and entirely deficient in the conveniences with which the tourist in Europe is so abundantly provided. I profited by the opportunity to visit the sites of two ancient Siamese capital cities, now lying in ruins and half buried in the jungle, which had not, to my knowledge, been examined by any preceding traveller, and I hope that the albeit imperfect descriptions of Sachanalai and Sawankhalok, which will be found in their proper places, may in some measure atone for the commonplace for what is to a great extent a twice-told tale. It should be premised that the tale was written for the perusal of members of my own family, and not for publication.

My companion as far as Chiengmai was Mr W.J. Archer, endowed with exceptional linguistic aptitude, and one of the most promising of the younger members of our own Consular Service in Eastern Asia. [3]

[EMS]
January 1888

Notes

[1] 'A Visit to Xiengmai, the principal City of the Laos or Shan States.' *Journal of the Asiatic Society of Bengal* 32, no. 292 (1863), 387-399. However, he was four times preceded by Dr. David Richardson representing the British Commissioner at Moulmein in British Burma, in 1829, 1834, 1835, and 1839-40. Richardson's last journey, via Bangkok, was partially described by him in the *JASB* VIII (1839) and IX (1840). The 1837 account of another visitor from Moulmein, Lt. W.C. McLeod, was printed up in British Parliamentary Accounts and Papers C, vol. 50. 1867.

[2] Recently reprinted, 1986, by Oxford University Press.

[3] A 12,000 word report on this journey as far as Chiangmai by Archer, dated 3 April 1886, appears in FO 69/109 with a copy amongst the Satow Papers at PRO 30/33/1/8. The map on pp 16-17 derives from this source.

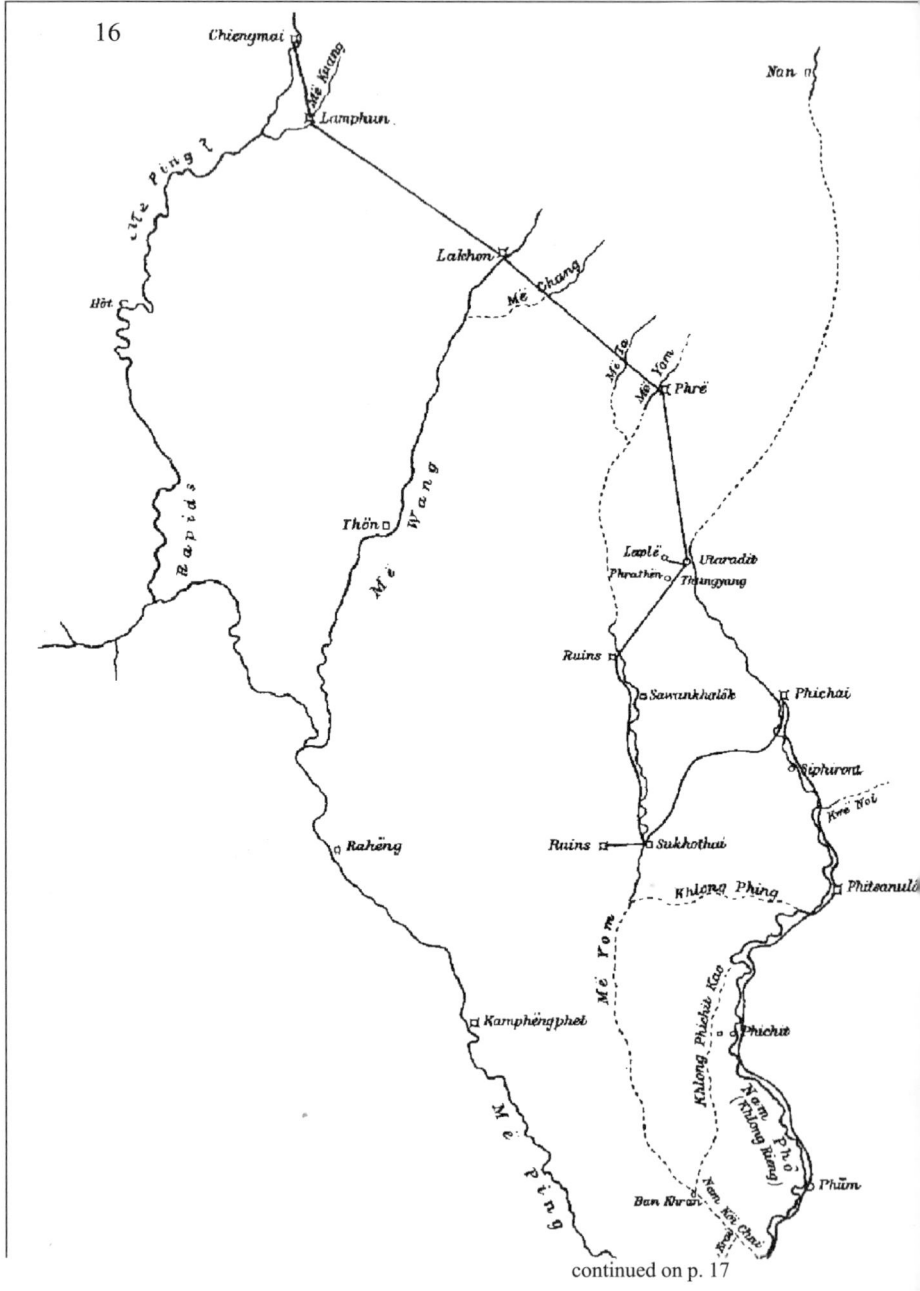

16

continued on p. 17

Satow's route to Chiang Mai and the river by which he returned

continued from p.16

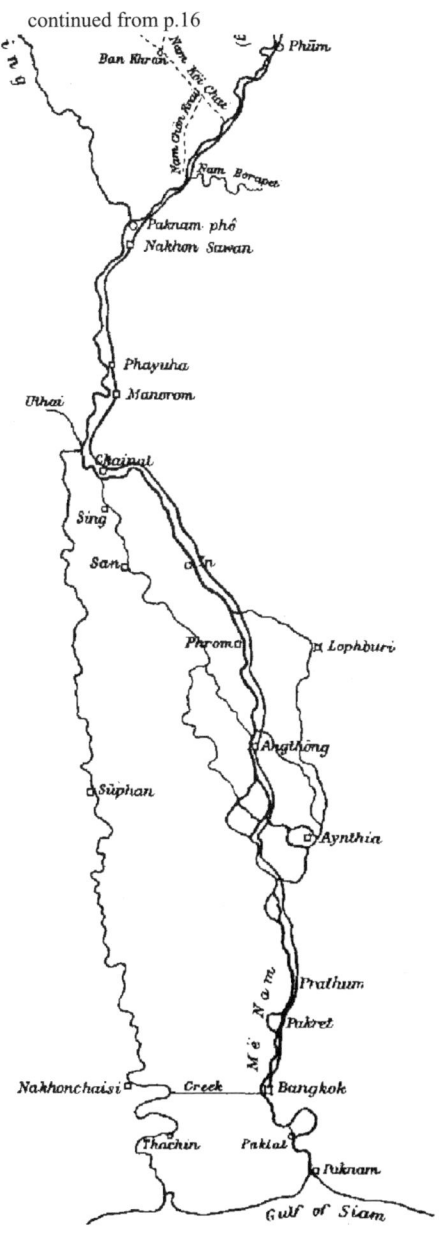

Route ——————

Capital of province □ (Walled town ⊠

  "   " sub-province or village ○

SATOW WITH A FAVOURITE HORSE

PART 1

BANGKOK TO PHICHHAI

December 1, 1885. I started at 9.15 with Archer in a large boat lent for the journey by a Lao noble who resides at Bangkok. He says it is the largest of its kind in the whole of Siam. It is fifty-two feet long and nine feet wide, not including a gangway eighteen inches in width which runs along each side amidships. The stern is formed into a square chamber having a high waggon roof and windows all along the sides and back. On one side of this "state room" the steersmen, of whom there are two, stand on a couple of large short-legged square stools, in charge of a massive spatula-shaped oar that projects behind the boat, its shank being passed through a circular hole on the port side of the rear bulk-head. When the stream becomes very strong, as for instance at a sudden bend in the river, both men's efforts are required for the management of this huge rudder-oar. Probably the first rudders in Europe were simply oars, for our English word is evidently the German "ruder".

The central portion of the boat is occupied by a long waggon-roofed cabin, the top of which is only four and a half feet above the deck, and over it the steersman looks out ahead to see where we are going. Here our luggage and stores were deposited, the planks of the deck being taken up so as to leave more space. A flag was thrown over the gap left by the difference in height of the two roofs to protect us against the "blacks" emitted from the funnel of the steam-launch which towed us upstream. The front of the boat is covered at night by a movable waggon-roof which during the day is telescoped back onto the central part. Here live the crew of five boatmen whose services will be required when the river becomes too shallow to admit of the launch going any further; and here too the Chinese cook prepares our food on one of the native shoe-shaped portable fireplaces of terracotta. The bow is formed by a broad piece of wood projecting like the bill of a duck, while at the stern another solid piece curls backwards and upwards like the tail of a fish. Here is a rough sketch of the boat, taken one evening from the river bank, with the shutters of the stern cabin propped up to let in the air and the covering drawn over the fore-castle. Add a small union jack flying at a tiny staff tied on to the "fishtail", let your imagination pro-

vide a steam-launch towing her ahead, and you have our boat as she appeared on the waters of the Menam. The cabin is nine feet wide and twelve in length, so that there is plenty of room for a table and two or three chairs. In fact, four persons can dine in it with a comfortable amount of elbow room. Above the windows runs a shelf, which was speedily furnished with books, chessboard, plates and glasses, and all the other small articles needed on a journey in a country where there are no inns. Our party consisted, besides ourselves, of Saburo my Japanese "boy", a Chinese cook, Archer's "boy", the offspring of a Chinaman and a Siamese woman, and three Siamese boatmen, who were supposed to make themselves generally useful.

As we passed the pagoda of Wat Chëng, the owner of the boat came out from the shore to wish us good speed and deliver a letter for a Siamese official who had preceded us up the river to provide elephants and ponies for the overland journey from Utaradit to Chiengmai. The usual route to Chiengmai is up the western tributary of the Menam to Rahëng and thence by elephant through Lakhon, or by boat up the 'rapids'. But I had been told, on what seemed to be excellent authority, that the voyage up the eastern branch to Utaradit, and thence by land through Phrë, Lakhon and Lamphun was really much shorter, which doubtless is true when there is plenty of water in the river, and if one travels right through without stopping. This year, however, the water had fallen below its usual level, or rather had never attained it during the rainy season, so that the launch could not get as far as Utaradit, and for the latter portion of the way we had to pole our heavy boat against the current. Still, no-one in Siam wants to travel at express speed, and there is so much to be seen by the way that the traveller may easily be seduced into spending more time in his journey than he originally intended. My plan was to reach Chiengmai in three weeks - I took over six.

My visitor sat talking for some time, so that we did not get fairly away from Bangkok till past ten. At 11.20 we passed Ban Mò (Pot

village) on the left bank, where cooking vessels of terracotta are produced in large numbers, and exposed for sale piled up in tiers in front
of the houses. Under other circumstances I should have landed to visit
the potters at their work, and learn the secret of the curiously irregular
incised patterns which cover some of these jars. But at the beginning
of a long journey against time the natural impulse is to hasten onwards,
and so the opportunity of learning something precise about one of the
few domestic manufactures of Siam was lost.

Samkok, the next village reached, lies on the right bank, and is
apparently not a very important place, though shown large on the map.
From this point onwards, for some hours, we are seldom out of sight of
houses, as they lie scattered along the riverside in small clusters. Sometimes groves of large trees line the banks, succeeded by bare flat country rising but a few feet above high water mark. About half-past five
the boat leaves the main stream, and turns into a canal called the
Bangsai creek when you ascend, and Sikok creek when you descend,
from the two villages which mark its lower and upper junctions with
the Mënam. The word canal, I am afraid, will hardly convey an exact
idea of the real nature of this water course. It is not straight, nor
narrow, nor has it locks. On the contrary, owing to the swift current
and the loose character of the alluvial soil through which it flows, its
width is by no means contemptible and its windings are innumerable.
It probably started in life as a ditch intended to give access to the
fertile plain west of the Mënam, and having gradually increased in
size and depth, has finally replaced as a national thoroughfare the
original river on whose banks stand the ruins of Ayuthia, the former
capital of Siam, where ocean-going ships used to lie a couple of centuries
ago. Now-a-days it is as much as a fair-sized barge can do to reach the
modern town that has risen not far from the site of the great city laid
waste in 1767 by the Burmans. But this is only hearsay, and I mean to
confine myself to what I have seen with my own eyes, or learnt, with
Archer's assistance, from the lips of natives we met with during the
journey.

A handsome *phra-chedi**or pagoda stands in the angle formed by
the junction of the river and canal. You must pronounce the first syllable as if it were spelt *prah* with a strong *h* after the *p*. It is a tall

* This is a corruption of two Pali words meaning Excellent Relic-shrine.

spiral building with a square pedestal, built of brick and covered with the hard stucco called chunam in India, originally white, but now agreeably discoloured by the action of the weather. Such shrines were in the beginning meant to cover relics of the founder of the Buddhist religion, but apparently have lost their original significance. Nowadays they are built by pious people as a means of securing happiness in the next stage of transmigration, for the Buddhists believe that according to the character of their actions as men, they may after death have to pass through a long series of other forms, till at last they attain to perfect bliss, which consists in being exempt from any of the sensations that in this life are the source of such profound misery. When people tell you that Buddhists believe in annihilation of the thinking substance, do not be persuaded. What they believe in is the ultimate annihilation of pain and grief. Perhaps it comes to the same thing in the end, but you must not force people to adopt all the possible inferences from a formulated creed, if you wish them to have any religion at all.

At seven o'clock it was already too dark to go further, and we stopped opposite a rather dirty monastery (*wat* in Siamese). The crew went ashore to sleep, but I preferred remaining in the boat, which if not very spacious was at least clean, and there was quite room enough to spread two mattresses on its deck.

December 2. We got away about 6 o'clock, but after passing a couple of curves in the canal we stopped to take a walk. The bank is lined by a bamboo thicket, in which the peasants' houses lie concealed, and behind this the muddy plain stretches away for miles. The mud however is quite dry at this season. When the rains come on it will be sown broadcast with rice, and in a very short time be covered by a huge green carpet. The last season's crop had not yet been completely cleared off the ground, and at this early hour of the day there were numbers of women and children busily engaged in scaring away the birds with bamboo clappers. Here and there we saw stationary scarecrows made to represent kites (not toys but carnivorous birds), and I dare say they fulfilled their destined purpose. Returning to the boat we pursued our way along the winding channel until at 10.15 we got back into the main river at a place called Sikok, and saw far away to the east the peculiarly abrupt outline of some hills, amongst which lies the sacred temple of Phra bat, the Excellent Footstep of Buddha. The mountain that goes by this name stands up conspicuously from the rest in the form of a huge truncated cone. Such "footsteps" abound in Siam. Sometimes they are double, but quite as often single footprints, many of them six feet in length and proportionately broad. Of course they have been carved by human hands, but it would be sacrilege in the ears of devout Buddhists to suggest that they are artificial. Immense numbers of pilgrims visit this particular Phrabat every winter, and the temple which covers it is said to be a most gorgeous edifice. Palgrave described it a few years ago in Macmillan's Magazine. *

Shortly afterwards a low-looking distant range appeared on the same horizon, but further to the north, being probably the line of mountains that divides this valley from the province of Khorat, which lies at a great elevation some distance to the west of the Mëkong River. About here I noticed large flocks of a bird of prey somewhat resembling a kite. Some had rusty red feathers, white heads and breasts, others were covered with pepper-and-salt plumage. They were feeding on the banks, or washing their feet in shallow places. Wide gaps now occurred between the bamboo clumps at the water's edge, affording an extensive view of nothing but flat rice-field plains.

At 3.30 the boat reached Angthong, the capital of a large province, and after a short exploration towards the rice fields which lay behind the fringe of trees lining the bank, we proceeded to pay a visit to the governor, a good-looking strongly-built man of middle age. The room in which he received us was furnished with a few European chairs and tables, a dingy mirror or two, and a four-post bedstead. Dishes of curry and sweetmeat, which were in readiness to be given as presents, were exhibited to me, and sent away on board the boat. They did not look particularly inviting, but I thought it a duty to taste them afterwards by way of requital for his hospitable intent, and the boatmen probably consumed what was left. The Governor informed me that the population of his province, which is of great extent, was returned in 1868 at 10,000 able-bodied men,

* [W.G. Palgrave, 'Phra-Bat', *Macmillan's* 45 (1882), pp. 20-36. It was republished in his *Ulysses, or Scenes and Studies in Many Lands* (London, 1887). Palgrave, the Arabian explorer, was Satow's predecessor as Agent and Consul-General in Bangkok, 1880-83, and also as Minister Resident in Montevideo, 1884-88. Ed.]

and it might have increased since. *

He added that the rice-crop had been short this year owing to the want of rain. The showers we had yesterday and today were an unusual phenomenon at this season. The river had overflowed its banks twice only during the past ten years, but the water usually came up to within a hand's breadth of the margin every year during the highest floods. The banks being however everywhere higher than the interior, the whole country was flooded for a considerable time, and the shallow creeks that intersected it in every direction then became navigable for small boats. A good many ponies were bred in the province, and were mostly sent to Bangkok for sale. About 400 Chinese lived within his jurisdiction but he was seldom visited by Burmese British subjects. After a cup of tea and a cigar, I took my leave of this hospitable official, and re-embarked. The town is divided by the river into two portions, that which lies on the right bank opposite to the governor's house being the most extensive. Owing to the lowness of the water throughout the journey we were obliged to have a pilot in order to avoid running ashore. Here we dismissed the man whom we had brought from Bangkok, and shipping a fresh one got under way again, after an hour's stay. At 6.30 we tied up close to a *wat* on the right bank, near a village called Bo-nam (well). As soon as the lamps were lighted a cloud of white-winged insects like day flies filled the cabin, being attracted by the unusual glare. They flew up against the globes, and fell motionless on the table, or buzzed round within a short distance in a distracted manner that seemed to react on one's own nerves. It is easy under such circumstances to form an idea of what a "plague of flies" means. But they subsided in about an hour, owing very likely to the local supply having at last come to an end. To know that the numbers of such a pest are not unlimited is some comfort at least.

December 3 On getting up we discovered that the engineer had overslept himself, and was just beginning to light the fires. As he could not possibly be ready for at least half an hour we started for a walk on the plain behind the trees that hid the bank, and found nearly all the popu-

---

* What the proportion of enrolled men is to the whole population no-one can tell. Probably it is over a tenth and under a fifth, but it must also be remembered that a good many find means to evade enrolment. Perhaps one would not be far wrong in putting the population of the province of Ang-thong at from 80,000 to 100,000.

lation out in the rice field engaged in scaring birds, and making a tre-
mendous noise about the business. Here, as elsewhere, they said the
crop had been short, as the water had not risen high enough to cover
the upper fields. These so-called "upper fields", which I supposed to be
situated in elevated places on hillsides, as they are in Japan, turned out
on inquiry to be merely the upper surfaces of the extremely gentle un-
dulations that occur here and there. At first the plain had appeared like
the drained bottom of a vast uninterrupted swamp, but in looking closer,
I saw the remains of the "bunds" which are used for retaining the water
when it begins to subside. The villagers seemed well-to-do, and their
houses well-built. We observed plenty of buffaloes and well-shaped
little bullocks, from which we inferred that the district must be a fine
ground for cattle-thieving, which however report says is pursued rather
as an occasional pastime than as a profession.

We got off at half past seven, and soon found the river widen out
considerably, the banks being at first almost perpendicular. Then we
got into long, straight reaches, where the banks slope down to the
water's edge, and in the dry season are utilized for planting tobacco in
large quantities, with a small proportion of beans and sweet potatoes.
This practice no doubt contributes to the constant tendency of the river
to widen out, get shallower and take ever-increasing curves, for the culti-
vators are in the habit of cutting down the more solid portions of the bank
to get additional space for planting and the soft soil thus created is easily
washed away by the floods of the following year. No supervision of any
kind is exercised by the government, and no attempt is made to prevent
the navigation of the river becoming worse and worse as time goes on.

The region we are passing through is very populous, if one may
judge from the number of trading boats that we meet. About two o'clock
we reached an insignificant village on the right bank where the governor
of the province of Phrom resides. The most remarkable striking object
that presented itself was a red post-office box occupying a prominent
position in the open shed which is used as a court-house. In a tropical
country however one must not be surprised to find public buildings
presenting a shabby appearance. Walls, and the consequent doors and
windows, would not allow sufficient ventilation, and they are therefore
almost entirely dispensed with, and as the custom of the country is to
squat or lie on the floor no furniture is needed. Sitting upright in a
chair is regarded by the natives in a hot climate as a fatiguing form of

physical exercise. The post-office box is a sign of the times. I did not see the governor, but went off for a walk behind the houses, while search was being made for a pilot. The country was much the same as before, flat as far as the eye could see, and only partially cultivated. The only wild flower we came across was a small pink mallow-like plant, about three feet high, but the bastard tamarind, * of which we make hedges in Bangkok, seemed pretty common. When left to itself it grows to be a good-sized tree, and bears bunches of beautiful crimson berries of which the birds are very fond.

At three o'clock the pilot made his appearance, and we steamed on for another four hours, arriving after dark in front of a monastery called Wat Banlai. As soon as the lamps were lighted a swarm of malodorous little beetles filled the cabin, and scorching their wing-cases as they flew up against the heated globes, fell on the table, where they spun round and round on their backs with incredible velocity, diffusing their offensive effluvium through the air. It was of no use to tell a servant to sweep them away; they were succeeded by fresh swarms, until at last in self-defence we were driven ashore to dine in the *sala* or traveller's rest-house of the monastery. Or rather it was the Kan-burien, or preaching hall, the only distinction between the two being the presence of a very rickety pulpit in the latter. As far as architecture is concerned there is no difference, the open-sided shed being the type of all these subordinate buildings of a *wat*. But the real temple, called *Wihan*, is very different. This is usually of brick, with solid walls sometimes pierced with windows, and often decorated with frescoes on the inside, and a finely carved gable at the front. The altar stands at the further end of the interior, and is usually occupied by a sitting image of Gautama, the founder of Buddhism. Sometimes he is faced by erect statues of his two principal disciples, whom the Siamese call Mokalâ and Sariphut, ** and the altar is covered with innumerable little idols offered up by believers as the price of their intercession. A many-branched candlestick usually stands in front of the altar. The best *wats* usually possess a collection of sacred books, written in the Pali language on palm leaves, which are kept in handsome boxes in a special building raised on piles to protect its contents from floods and white-ants. After dinner we

* This is the Pithecolobium dulce, called Madras thorn in India.

** Maudgalyâyana and Sâriputra.

returned to the boat, from which by this time our insect pests had retired, not without leaving behind them a faint reminder of their unpleasant emanations.

December 4. This morning we made an early start, and in an hour and a half reached a small island adorned by a rather pretty *phra-chedi*. Three quarters of an hour more, and we arrived at the residence of another governor, a paralytic old man who from his dirty mattress in a dilapidated cottage rules over the province of In. It was necessary to apply to him for a pilot, and having done this we proceeded to inspect the fields at the back of the house, where beans, sugar-cane, sesame and a sort of thyme are cultivated on a fairly large scale. Sesame or til seed, is exported in large quantities from India as well as from Siam for the manufacture of olive-oil in France. Further on in the lower ground are the rice-fields. Just as in Egypt, the banks of the river are the highest portion of the delta, owing to the greater part of the river mud being deposited there when the water overflows its banks. During the heavy squalls of the southwest monsoon the rain-water collects between the hills and the river, converting the country into a swamp, which towards October or November becomes a vast lake during a few days only. The course of the river is then entirely hidden, and the boats can traverse the submerged plain in all directions. In this point Siam closely resembles Lower Burma, but in no other.

Beyond In we pass a fine temple standing in a grove of magnificent trees, and seven hours steaming brings us to Chhainat, an important seat of government on the left bank, where the inland duty is collected on the teak rafts which come down from the forests of the upper provinces and the Lao States. Here it may be explained that Laos on our map is not properly the name of a Kingdom, but means the tribes inhabiting the country so marked out, who are governed by at least six chiefs or governors, entirely independent of each other, but all subject to the King of Siam. Lao is the old Portuguese spelling of the name given to these people by the Siamese, and is to be pronounced Low (ow as in "cow"). To this we have added the English plural *s*. So that to pronounce the word "Lay-oss", as we usually do, is a barbarism, of much less gravity however than the mistake of supposing that there is a country of that name ruled over by a single king. The Laos all speak a language which differs from Siamese to no greater extent than Lowland

Scotch does from English. Those who inhabit the country containing the different tributaries of the Më-nam river have the custom of tattooing themselves more or less completely from the waist down to the knees, and the Siamese therefore call them the 'black bellied Lao', while nearly all who are settled in the valley of the Më-khong abstain from the practice, and are in consequence known as the 'white bellied'. An account of the process of tattooing will be given elsewhere; it has been very carefully described by Carl Bock in his "Temples and Elephants".

The residences of the governor and other officials stand in separate compounds enclosed by neat bamboo fences. I went on shore to make a call and ask for a pilot, but found that the Governor and vice-governor were dead, and the other headmen absent. But nevertheless I got a pilot without difficulty from some of the subordinate officials.

This seems a suitable place for explaining the system of provincial organization. With the exception of Bangkok, the whole of the country is divided between three Ministers, who reside at the capital. One has the western provinces, including the Siamese part of the Malay peninsula, a second has the southern and southeastern provinces, while the third has jurisdiction over all the provinces of the north, which are more extensive perhaps than the other two portions added together. The number of provinces, which means those districts whose governors report direct to Bangkok, is variously stated, but seems to be about forty, and many of these are divided into sub-provinces. It differs from time to time, because a subordinate province every now and then is allowed to have direct relations with the minister. The local administration of a province is composed of a Governor, vice-governor and a judge, with a censor whose duty is supposed to be that of reporting any irregularities of which the others may be guilty. An admirable arrangement, no doubt, if it worked properly, but in practice the censor is an accomplice of the other three in plundering the people and embezzling the revenue. Only a portion of the latter comes to Bangkok. The officials have either no fixed salaries, or such as are merely nominal. On the other hand they are allowed to pocket all fees, without rendering an account. They generally obtain their appointments by bribing the minister or some other high official, and as they pay large sums for their places, it often requires years of extortion before they can recoup themselves. I have heard of a governor of a sub-province who had given a note of hand for a large amount to the official who negotiated his appointment, and who was threatened with imprisonment for debt because he had not contrived to redeem it within the stipulated time.

The principal legal revenue is obtained from the land tax, but every able-bodied man is bound to perform labour for the government during a portion of the year, said to be on the average three months. This he may commute by the payment of a fixed sum. After paying the exemption he is often forced to work all the same, and that too beyond the legal period. I have met a man who had abandoned his wife and children and gone into the priesthood in order to escape imposition of this kind. In another case a levy of 100 men had been ordered to accompany a military expedition against the Chinese who have been encroaching on the north-eastern frontier. The governor called out the whole male population, selected the number required, and made the others pay to get off being sent. Wherever one goes the cry of the people is that they are oppressed by the authorities. Of course a certain amount of unjustifiable grumbling there will always be even under the best of governments, especially where the people have no voice in their own affairs, but even making a considerable deduction on this head, there can be no doubt that oppression and extortion know no limits in Siam, except in the immediate neighbourhood of Bangkok, and the greater the distance from the capital, the worse the condition of the defenceless people. The difficulty of locomotion is one cause of this, and it is helped by the custom that seems to prevail of appointing the local officials from the local families, so that the chief offices may almost be said to be hereditary.

The forced labour system is one of the curses of Siam. Debt-slavery is a second, the appropriation of fees by the officials who levy them is a third, and the polygamy of the king is a fourth. In order to provide for his excessively numerous children as they grow up, he has to appoint them to offices which afford opportunities of squeezing the people. A fifth abuse is the practice of farming out the taxes which are imposed on nearly every article of daily use, and the farmers are almost exclusively Chinamen, who as they pay very highly for the monopoly of collecting the revenue, have often to take more than their lawful due in order to square their accounts. Perhaps there is no eastern country, certainly none of those which have regular diplomatic relations with Europe, where the administration is so utterly bad, for in China, in spite of the mandarins, the people have much greater freedom, and are not afraid to become rich, as in Siam. Here if a man makes money, his only way of keeping it is to purchase with bribes an appointment to some government office.

We got a pilot in half the usual time, and proceeded on our way. On rounding the corner just beyond Chhainat, I saw a boiler being hauled up the bank by the aid of shears under the superintendence of an European. It is no doubt intended for a sawmill. Owing to the recent succession of insufficient rainy seasons there was little timber lying at Chhainat, which boded ill for the steam saw-mills at Bangkok during the following year. At nightfall we tied up at a "floating-house" below a *wat*. (I do not think I have explained this term before.) Rivers and creeks being the highways and cross-roads of the country, the vast majority of people live along the banks in houses built on piles out of reach of the annual floods. No-one, unless he be of high rank, may have a staircase leading up to his front door, but must be content with a ladder. For those engaged in trade a ladder is somewhat inconvenient. So the shopkeepers live in small houses of two or three rooms built on wooden caissons or on thick rafts of bamboo, which being moored to posts planted near the bank, rise and fall with the water. At Bangkok the river is almost lined with these floating-houses on both banks for two or three miles. They present several advantages. People going shopping in their canoes or having goods to sell, can go close alongside. It is even more convenient than shopping in an European city in your carriage, because there is no pathway along the front of the houses and you paddle up alongside of the counter, as it were. The occupants of these houses require no drainage, for the river becomes the common sewer, and as natives do not mind dirt, they use it for their aqueduct and bathing-tub as well. If a fire breaks out, the householder unties his tenement and away it floats with stream or tide to a safe distance. I do not think this invention is used anywhere else than in Siam, so that the natives must be allowed the credit of some originality.

December 5. We make an early start, and see right ahead of us an isolated hill covered to its summit with wood; but just as we seem to be getting close to it, the river makes a sudden bend away to the left and we lose sight of it. It will be easily understood that after a prolonged residence in the flat alluvial region of southern Siam, the traveller's eye greets with satisfaction any hill, no matter how small, and our disappointment on this occasion when we were deprived of our tiny mountain's company after so short an acquaintance can be imagined without much exercise of the sympathetic faculty. The country is less populated than below Chhainat and at the same time less wooded. After an hour or two of steaming we got round the bend and came back to the hill, at the base of which stands a neat-looking whitewashed temple, which the Laos boatmen called Tera Mamun, but the Siamese probably by a different name. One might walk across the neck of land here in half an hour. On my way down in the following February it took me two hours and twenty minutes to tow round, even with the help of the current.

At 9.45 we reached the frontier of the province of Manorom, and had to change pilots again. I landed to explore the neighbourhood, intending to return to the boat at the place where I left her, but in a strange country it is easier, because more attractive, to go forward than to retrace one's steps. There is always the hope of making some interesting discovery as you go along. But on the present occasion that hope was not fulfilled. The province has I believe but few inhabitants, and might have gone on for centuries in subordination to a larger centre of population, but for the fact that some years ago one of those brick dust-coloured elephants which foreigners call "white" was discovered here, and Manorom received its independent status in honour of the auspicious event. Of course everyone is now aware that there is no such thing as a white elephant. The native term means "Albino", neither more nor less, and described the creature's appearance quite correctly. This absence of colour is unnatural, and one wonders at the honour which it is held to confer on the animal that thus differs from its fellows. The Siamese however do sometimes talk of the albino elephant's colour as "white", and I suppose foreigners have merely translated the word. Our proverbial use of the term arises from a story that the king of Siam, if he wished to ruin a prominent noble, would make him a present of one of these semi-sacred beasts, the cost of whose entertainment would in a short time reduce him to beggary. Pinto says in one of his letters that certain domestic utensils affected to the use of the elephant were of gold in his time and the rest of his stable furniture was no doubt equally expensive.* One of the Siamese king's titles is "lord of Albino elephants".

---

* [This is the famous sixteenth-century Fernao Mendes Pinto, author of the *Peregrinaçam*, always a special interest of Satow's. Ed.]

Our Queen might with equal reason be styled "Lady of the fat Hanoverian white coach-horses". A certain number of Albino elephants are kept at Bangkok in the Palace, or rather the Royal Mews, and these are exhibited to people at certain festivals. Last year a new one from one of the northern provinces was added to the collection, and there were great rejoicings, which lasted for several days and must have cost a great deal of money. A magniloquent title was given to the beast, who thereby was converted, so people say, into a nobleman of the third rank, or "Count".

Instead of returning to the boat I walked along the bank, high above the stream, for about an hour, to a village called Ban Mëkok, where it seemed advisable to sit down and wait for the boat. I noticed here for the first time a very common kind of fish-trap, which is used in the weirs that are planted here and there across the river when the floods have passed. It is made of a thick bamboo about six feet long split from one end to within a few inches of the other, and spread out so as to form the ribs of a basket, which are then bound with slips of interlacing bamboo, so as to leave large meshes. This basket lies on its side, and the open end is closed by a door of reeds which slides between two upright poles. Here is a rough sketch of it.

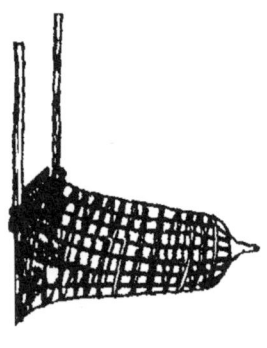

At this place I met a Burmese on his way down to Bangkok in a boat, evidently a man of some importance, or rather swagger, who gave himself airs until he learnt who I was. Then he changed his tone, and offered me a present in the shape of a lacquered box, which I did not accept. He was apparently one of the men who are engaged in the teak trade, and who by a lavish expenditure of the money they borrow from the Indian Bankers in Maulmain, create for themselves a great position in Siam. It would be more correct to speak of them as Peguans, since although natives of Burmah, they do not belong to the true Burmese race. After about an hour's waiting one of my native servants came up with an umbrella, which was very grateful (authority for this use of the word is to be found in the advertisements of Epp's cocoa), and shortly afterwards the launch made her appearance round a bend in the river. We bought some excellent fresh fish from a woman who came alongside. At 1.15 we arrived before Manorom, an insignificant village perched high up on the bank. The difference in the level of the river at the end of the dry season and during the floods must be at least 20 feet. A few minutes were spent in changing the pilot, and off we went again.

It is generally the *Kamnan* or village mayor who performs the duty of pilotage, but sometimes his wife replaces him, which is not to be wondered at, for in this country the women have quite as much intelligence as, and more "go" than, the opposite sex. But a mayor does not profess to be acquainted with any part of the river beyond the limits of his own little district, and hence the frequent changes. Sometimes we found it difficult to get the mayor, for as no payment is made for such services by Siamese government officials, and as the people have no means of discerning that an approaching boat contains a foreigner willing to pay, the whole male population decamps as soon as the steamer is heard coming along. I tried the plan of making small presents to a pilot, but did not find that it helped me over the difficulty. The same sort of thing happened afterwards with the guides who were impressed to show the way through the forests. The man would walk on briskly ahead at first, but would disappear round the first corner, or explain that he had to get some indispensable article from his hut, and seize the opportunity afforded by permission to go and fetch it, to run off in the opposite direction. It is not convenient to be left alone in the middle of an almost pathless jungle, but so long as the system continues of making the common people perform such services without remuneration, this sort of thing will constantly happen, even to native officials.

At 4 o'clock we reached Phayuha, where the governor came off to visit me. He was dressed simply in his *pha-nung*, a broad strip of cloth fastened round the waist, with its front edge drawn backwards between the legs and tucked in behind. This is the common costume of all the Siamese, both men and women, and its general effect is that of a rather baggy pair of knickerbockers. In the towns however a close-fitting white cotton jacket is usually added, and the higher officials wear a neat coat buttoned up to the throat, with white stockings and shoes when they are in full dress. Women often substitute for the jacket a silk scarf which is thrown loosely over the shoulders, or tied across the bosom. To a newcomer the Siamese woman's costume is not pleasing, as it gives her the look of a huge cochin-china hen, and the blacking brush style of short bristly hair, which deprives them of their most beautiful natural decoration, is at first revolting. But if you remain long enough in the country you become accustomed to it all, and there are men to be found who will maintain that a Siamese woman is the most graceful and attractive of her sex.

But to return to our Governor. From his habit of wearing only the *pha-nung*, his body and legs had become of a fine mahogany colour, French-polished. He said the rice-crop had been much below the average. In an ordinary year the tax collected on the rice-fields of his province amounts to £600 or £700. There were 2,000 able-bodied men on the registers, which may mean a population of from 10,000 to 20,000 according to the fancy of the calculator, for no-one yet is in a position to say what proportion of the inhabitants are enrolled. Besides rice, the province produces tobacco, beans and bananas, but no cotton, as the country is subject to heavy floods. The river has been rising again within the last few days, but at present it is 160 inches below its usual level at this time of year. It overflows the banks but rarely. Carts are used to carry produce from the interior, but the roads are mere tracks through the jungle. I noticed here a remarkable kind of bucket, made of bamboo basket-work, smeared over with resin, which renders it perfectly water-tight. These buckets are in use all over the northern part of Siam, and I think also in the provinces on the gulf. This particular kind of resin is obtainable in large quantities, and might, I imagine, be a valuable article of export. The village of Phayuha stands on the left bank, a short distance above the governor's residence, and seems to be entirely surrounded by jungle, but probably there are rice-fields at no great distance inland, as has proved to be the case everywhere else on the journey, especially since we passed Angthong. The banks being higher than the general level of the country, are in most places scarcely capable of cultivation, except by means of artificial irrigation.

We left again at five. Beyond Phayuha the sloping banks were planted with beans and tobacco. The river is full of fish - large ones which jump out of the water and fall back again with a sudden splash, and shoals of little ones near the shore. The hills about Nakhon-Sawan, which have been more or less visible all day, now grow more distinct, and at 7 we reached a village named Ban Yang-masi, standing in thick jungle on the right bank. I landed as usual, hoping to get into the open country, but it was too dark to see anything, and the people said the distance to the rice-fields was considerable. But that may not have been true. My experience has always been that if a foreigner proposes to go anywhere, especially on foot, he is immediately told that it is a long day's journey, even when it may be only half an hour's walk. That is their way of putting it. A charitable explanation is that as Siamese of the ruling classes cannot walk, say a mile, without being completely fatigued, they naturally suppose Europeans to be equally feeble. One can hardly be surprised that a people whose usual means of locomotion is a boat should not be particularly good on their legs.

December 6. Started at twenty minutes to seven. Yesterday we met four rafts of teak logs and today fourteen. They come down chiefly, I believe, from the forests on the eastern branch of the river. Owing to the deficient rainfall of the last two summers the foresters have not been able to float out an average quantity of timber, and must be getting hard-up, as they mostly work on borrowed capital, on which they are bound to pay interest at the rate of 36 to 48 per cent per annum, besides being in debt to the owners of the forests for arrears of royalties on which a similar interest has to be paid. It is a highly speculative business, in which failure or success entirely depends upon the chances of the seasons, and one does not hear of any forester making a fortune out of it. The foreign merchants at Bangkok, who obtain supplies of teak for exportation by giving advances to native buyers up country, are exposed to sudden and violent fluctuations in the price of teak at home. The profits of one year are eaten up by the losses of the next, if one is to believe what they tell you.

Clocks and measured distances are unknown in the country districts. To the question "how far is it to - ", the usual reply is "so many bends of the river", in entire contempt of the fact that the bends vary in length. The information, if exact, is only of value as assisting you to conjecture that you have reached the place you are bound for, after you have accomplished the stated number of windings and see a collection of houses before you. I do now know however that it would be of much use if we were able to foretell how long it will take to reach a given point. We have to get there some day or other, and an exact knowledge of the time required cannot shorten the distance. The difference between the European and Asiatic is that the one has a habit of enquiry, with or without the prospect of a resulting advantage, while the other resigns himself to a contented ignorance, that almost resembles fatalism. If you vary the question by asking when shall we get there, the native points to the sky, and says "when the sun is over there", as if your eye were at the end of his finger, and you carried on it an imaginary circle divided into hours. The second process is of little more value than the method of calculating how many miles a number of bends of varying length may come to when you do not know their average. Hereabouts the banks are mostly precipitous and crowned with jungle, in which the tall white dammar-oil tree is a conspicuous and frequent object. Now and then a plantation of bananas seems to indicate the proximity of some small hamlet. At ten we landed at a village called Ban Tukpha to get a little exercise while the boatmen went in search of a fresh pilot, but on returning from a twenty minutes walk into the jungle, we found that all the inhabitants had taken to their heels, and that the man we brought from Phayuha had also disappeared. Broad cart-tracks traverse the forest in every direction, and seem to imply the existence of cultivation further inland from the river. From its being covered with clumps of thorny bamboo as far as we penetrated, the inference would be that it is subject to floods, and is therefore unfit for dry crops or timber trees. But near the village we came across a small field of cotton that had been allowed to run to waste, till the plants were as much as seven or eight feet high. Inquiries made at various places appeared to result in the conclusion that there are two varieties of the cotton plant, one a low herbaceous large-leaved kind, growing thickly together, the other taller having a woody stem and bearing much smaller leaves. But I doubt the accuracy of the information. Where the taller plants were met with, the fields had always a neglected appearance. The size of the leaves is not necessarily evidence of a difference in variety, for the leaves of many woody plants diminish in size as the plant grows older. Having been unsuccessful here in our search for a pilot, we went on boldly without one to the next village, called Banphra, where after much delay we hired a man for about 4 shillings to take us as far as the next mayor's place.

After lunch we landed at Banköh, and visited the village, which lies five minutes' walk from the bank and is picturesquely situated on the border of the forest, in the vicinity of banana plantations and fields of sweet potatoes. For the first time, I noticed that the houses were thatched with grass instead of the leaves of the Nipa palm, which is used at Bangkok and in its vicinity. Probably the change from the palm frond to grass begins much lower down the river. But this thatch is quite different in appearance from ours. The grass is doubled over a slender strip of bamboo about three feet long and threaded together with some undressed fibrous plant exactly in the same manner as the ataps familiar to travellers in the Malay countries, so as to form a sort of mat, which is laid on like tiles, and the whole thickness of roofing thus obtained cannot be more than a couple of inches even where these "tiles" overlap. Compare that with the deep thatch of an English cottage of the olden style. Yet it seems to form a perfectly water-tight covering, and this is all the more remarkable because of the heavy fall of rain, sometimes three inches in six hours, which you get in these countries. Two men were playing at a sort of backgammon. Each player in turn takes five cowries which he slides into the bamboo tube that serves for a dice box, and pours them out through a drum (marked A) furnished with three sets of cross sticks, which entirely prevent the player from controlling the manner in which the cowries shall fall - whether on their backs or faces - and the coins on the board are moved in accordance with the number which fall on their faces. What brings the game to an end I was not able to learn, owing to my ignorance of the language.

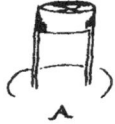  

We persuaded the mayor to come as pilot, and at a quarter past four we reached Nakhon-Sawan, which seems to mean the "City of Heaven". Perhaps there were more reasons at the time of its foundation for giving it this high-sounding name than exist at present, but now-a-days it is certainly in no way superior to any other country townlet in Siam. Most of the provincial capitals (which you must understand are something far below an English country town in importance and immeasurably inferior in outward respectability) have names taken from the Sanskrit or Pali, and perhaps it is only a sort of brag that induced the early Siamese to bestow such magnificent appellations on their collections of dirty hovels. For instance, the official name of the capital, vulgarly called Bangkok, is "the invincible city, the great city of the angels", which is only to be equalled in absurdity and inappropriateness by the expression "Venice of the East" given to it by foreigners, the sole point of resemblance being the existence of stinking canals in both. A gang of fellows seated in a shed high up on the bank beat a gong vigorously, to summon us ashore to pay taxes, but we ignored them and went on further to the house of the governor, who as usual turned out to be a decrepit old man, quite blind. There was a lively market going on, and women came alongside in canoes to sell food to our men. The existence of a market where he can procure the elements of his daily curry and the concomitants of his "betel" is an important element in the happiness of a Siamese. An English friend once proposing to spend a few days at the island where I have my "villa by the seaside" and acquainting his servant, an urchin of fourteen, with his intention, was met with a plaintive remonstrance. "I can't go there, I should die". "Die? What do you mean?" "There's no market there (with a tear in his voice). The fact is, the Siamese are cockneys at heart, one and all.

We left about five o'clock, passing at the upper end of a rather pretty *phra-chedi*. It stood on a square base, a series of steps to an oval  body surrounded by a moulding of petals, and terminating in a slender gilded spire, something like the accompanying sketch, the roughness of which must be excused as it was taken while we were passing at full speed. Some twenty minutes further we came to a low hill crowned by a neat-looking temple, from which there is said to be an extensive view of the surrounding country, but I was in a hurry to reach the confluence of the two rivers before night, and so consoled myself with the formation of a resolution to visit it on my return to Bangkok. An unwise procrastination, for on my way down the river, the water had fallen so much that the boat could not get near the bank, and I was unable to land.

As the sun sets we come in sight of a channel leading away to the left, in front of which lies a string of boats, and shortly afterwards catch the first glimpse of the houses of Paknam Phô. The river now widens out almost to the dimensions of a lake, and we bend away to the right to avoid a bank of sand which lies high and dry. The gloom of evening falls upon us rapidly and lights begin to twinkle along the shore, which are almost the only objects we can distinguish besides the dim outline of hills and trees to the west and southwest. At a quarter past six we suddenly turn a corner into the river Phô, and come to a stop for the night in front of a *wat*. By this time it is quite dark.

The coal we brought from Bangkok being almost exhausted, the question arose how to procure fuel for the rest of the journey. Luckily there was plenty of firewood lying here which had been stored for the use of the expedition sent up northwards against Chinese encroachers on the frontier, about a month before my own departure from the capital. A polite and willing official, to whom my circular letter of introduction from the government had been duly exhibited, offered to supply any quantity that might be needed. The engineer of the launch, on being referred to, said that 500 pieces would be sufficient, and orders were given at once to cut that number into lengths short enough for the furnace. Men were set to work at once with saw and hatchet, and the officer promised that all should be ready for a start at twelve o'clock tomorrow.

Paknam Phô means "Mouth of the river Phô" (pronounced Po with an aspirate after the P), and the town which has recently grown up there takes its name from the topographical fact. The houses are neither numerous nor beautiful, in fact they might be classed as shanties, with the exception of a Chinese temple dedicated no doubt to some god of riches, and a gambling establishment, as big as a goodsized barn, which is intended for the benefit or perdition of some three hundred Chinese who here inhabit. The Chinaman is an excellent person from certain points of view, industrious and frugal, always ready to work for hire and able to put his hand to any kind of job. But there are three things which he cannot or will not do without: opium, spirits, and gambling. His propensities are taken advantage of by the Siamese government to extract out of him in the shape of indirect taxes the revenue they do not venture to levy by a direct impost. Chinamen are subject to a triennial poll tax of twelve shillings, which is nearly twelve times less than the lowest legal rate of commutation for forced labour that the native Siamese have to pay. Suppression of these three forms of indulgence of physical and mental appetites would be impossible, even if the Siamese government had arrived at the advanced conviction that it was their duty to care for the moral well-being of these aliens to the soil, and under the circumstances they cannot be severely blamed for the adoption of a prudent expedient for the regulation of these matters while at the same time profit accrues to the royal Treasury. So the licence to keep public hells, opium-dens and drinking shops is farmed out - to Chinamen - with full authority to suppress all illicit establishments that competition might venture on. Chinamen make a great deal of money in the country, and it is only fair - argue the Siamese - that they should let the King share in their profits.

December 7. Next morning I went down to the confluence of the two rivers, the Më Ping which comes from above Chiengmai, and the Mënam Phô up which my journey is to be prosecuted. A sharp tongue of land divides the two streams. We get round the sand bank that projects at this point into the combined river, and try to row up the Më Ping, but it is hard work to make any progress with a couple of sculls against the strong current. The word "sculls" must not be understood to mean such as we use in England. The Siamese propel their boats either by sitting down in the bottom and using short paddles like those of the North American Indians (as described in Cooper's novels), or by standing up and pushing the boat through the water in the same manner as the Venetian gondoliers. In either case the boatmen have their faces towards the bow, and see where they are going. In paddling no steersman is required, but in the other boats there is a rudder which the rearmost sculler guides by pressing his foot against the helm. The variety of boats and canoes on the rivers in Siam is enormous. The latter are nearly always scooped out of a single trunk, which is then expanded in width by roasting it over a wood-fire, and are of diverse lengths from six to over twenty feet. Boats in all cases are constructed of a single log at the bottom, on which the sides are built up with planks, fastened together with rattan, and well-caulked with resin. Some are broad and deep like a Dutch hoy, others long and pointed like an American "double-ender". Generally they have a waggon-roofed house in the centre, and perhaps a square cabin at the stern, while other arrangements at the bow enable the crew to make a comfortable sleeping place with the aid of stiff woven bamboo mats. At this time of the year you find the larger trading boats "laid up" at convenient points on the river, where they carry on their petty commerce, selling foreign goods by retail and buying small parcels of native produce, which later on they will carry down to Bangkok. The tobacco planters, of whose operations along the sloping banks I have already told you, come up the river at the commencement of the dry season, sow their seed, and remain alongside in their boats till it is time to gather the crop. That done, and the boats loaded, they pull up their stakes, and depart again downstream. Many of the larger boats at Paknam Phô and such places are hardly distinguishable from the inferior class of floating houses. Altogether there must be a considerable percentage of the inhabitants of Siam who never sleep in a house on shore.

We managed to make a start about ten o'clock. The Mënam Phô contrasts in a marked manner with the Mënam, being narrow, deep and slow, although winding as much as if its current were more rapid. The bank on the left hand is covered with dense forest, on the right by equally dense grass high enough to conceal a horse and his rider. In three-quarters of an hour we came to a good-sized village named Paknam Borapet, from its situation at the mouth of a stream which is probably called the Mënam Borapet. I will spare you some notes destined to clear up certain obscure points relating to the streams which join the river on its right bank. It is a fact that no decent map of Siam is yet in existence, * and that no scientific exploration of the country has been made. Travellers are influenced by fashion, like other people, and men who want to gain a name go to Africa, or cross from India to China. A wide field remains for any man who has sufficient disinterested persistence to make a thorough knowledge of Siam the purpose of his life. Among the multitudinous crowd who write books of travel how few are real travellers. In the far east perhaps never a one but Bastian, and his object was quite other than geography. Wallace was a naturalist - hardly a traveller in the proper sense of the word. **

Kingfishers with black and white plumage flit along the surface of the stream in bands of three or four, uttering a harsh cry as they go, and every now and then darting at a fish which they do not catch. White herons, and white-bodied cranes with black wings, flap their way lazily across from bank to bank, or stand in vacant meditation on a dry patch of sand near the water's edge. Grey monkeys come down to the brink

* This is no longer the case, since the publication of Mr. J. McCarthy's excellent map in the Proceedings of the Royal Geographical Society, for April 1888.

** [Cf. A. Bastian, *Reisen in Siam* (Jena, 1867), A.R. Wallace, *The Malay Archipelago* (London, 1869). Wallace was a contemporary of Charles Darwin. Ed.].

to quench their thirst or curiosity as the noisy smoking launch passes by, whole families of them, father, mother, grown-up sons and daughters, and babies not six inches high. We hardly meet a single boat, but four narrow rafts tell of teak forests higher up near the source. No mountains are visible, and the high banks close us in from the outer world. Scarcely a hut anywhere all day. Surely it must have been the end of inhabited Siam, that we left behind us this morning. At sunset we reached a tiny settlement formed by two or three families engaged in cultivating the banana and in drying on hurdles over a wood-fire the big fish that they catch abundantly in the river. As a matter of course I go ashore to explore, but the tall grass hinders the view on every side, and besides the night is at hand. This is not travelling - hastening along the aquatic highways of Siam, without stopping for a moment to see what lies to the right or the left. But when tongue to ask and ear to hear are both useless, eye alone cannot get much information worth having.

December 8. Just after we started this morning we met a foreign-built boat belonging apparently to some Siamese of rank, which was return-ing southwards without its master. The crew of four men looked the picture of misery, as they squatted on the deck, or below it, muffled in dirty blankets and drifting along with the stream, too indolent to row or even steer. For it was a cold morning, and a thick mist was still hanging on the surface of the water.

We passed one or two small villages, and at a quarter past nine reached a place called Ban Khinak, the port, if it may be dignified by such a name, of Mu'ang Phûm, a town said to be half a day's journey inland to the east. (Pronounce Phûm like the English "whom", taking care to put a P in front of it.) Here the necessity arose of stopping to obtain fuel, for by a mistake at Paknam Phô we had taken on board only one-third of the intended quantity. While waiting for a fresh supply I walked away from the bank for some ten minutes. The country was flat, and covered with dense, tall grass, alternating with patches of an extremely slim bamboo. The people say that from here down to Paknam Phô the annual floods are so deep that cultivation is impossible. A theory that may possibly account for the prevalence of this long grass is that it has sprung up over tracts of country that were once the home of a busy agricultural population, for it is seldom found growing in great luxuriance under trees, and forest is a more natural condition of the primeval waste than any other kind of vegetation. But how long ago these grass-grown tracts lapsed into their present state I would not undertake to say, perhaps hundreds or even thousands of years.

Late in the afternoon we ascended a rocky shoal, where the water is shallow at this season, and the current strong. The Siamese call it Taphan-Hin, the Bridge of stone. During the rainy season it doubtless completely disappears, and causes no trouble to the boatmen. The usual difficulties about a pilot occurred at a village just beyond, and we had to tie up earlier than usual. Rank grass, ten to twelve feet high and thick-stemmed in proportion, made it impossible to get more than a few yards from the bank. During the night the big fish were more obstreperous than ever, jumping and splashing about close to the windows of the boat. I got up once to see what the noise was about, and found them as it were crawling on the top of the water and feeding on a patch of floating weed, just like so many cows. Or was it only fancy. Anyhow large numbers are caught and smoke-dried to be sent up north by caravans of cattle, which come from over a hundred miles distance with empty panniers to buy them. So you see the profit must be considerable, as there is double carriage to pay.

December 9. This morning at six the thermometer marked 69°, which shows that we have got a considerable distance north of Bangkok. What in England is considered an uncomfortable degree of heat, requiring doors and windows to be set wide open, produces quite contrary sensations in the inhabitant of the tropics, and makes him wish he could interpose some continuous barrier between his rooms and the outer air.

At eight we passed the Khlong Nongkan, a small river falling in on the left bank, deep enough even now for boats. Teak forests of no great importance are said to be worked near its source by some British subjects from Burma. We now pass some very short and abrupt turnings, at one of which the current took charge of the launch, and we were on shore for a minute or two. I mention this unimportant incident by way of contrasts, our luck in navigation having been hitherto all unclouded. A little further on the current again put forth its power, so that we had to get out our sculls, and the steersmen became very excited, even to redness of the face. Much cry and little wool, but the engineer screwed up a nut, or held down the safety valve, or put on more wood, or adopted some other expedient which enabled the launch to go ahead again to

Wang Taphâ. Here we again had to stop for firewood.

Away to the eastward appeared a long range of blue mountains, be-yond which, said the villagers, lies the Lao town of Lôm. The country right away to their base seemed one unbroken plain, with not a sign of habitation or cultivation, except on the bank of the river just in front of us. Behind the village are some fields of cotton, sweet potatoes, mus-tard (grown for its leaf which is eaten as salad) and sesame. Some of the villagers were engaged in twisting yarn into cord for nets, just as ropes are made, and in reeling yarns made from the cotton grown here. To judge by appearances the country must be well suited for the cultiva-tion of cotton, but owing to the fall in prices, it is no longer planted as largely as in former times. From the time when the seed is sown till the pods are ripe takes about five to six months. The river then becomes crowded with the boats of the Chinese and Siamese-Peguan traders who come to buy it from the growers. This information you will understand was not procured by the exercise of the observing faculty, but was obtained through Archer, who speaks Siamese admirably.

The people here say that the river annually overflows its banks; the cotton is sown after the waters have retired, and comes to maturity in the end of the dry season. I suspect that what we were elsewhere told about the dampness of the soil being a hindrance to cultivation was mere nonsense; laziness, or some other non-natural cause prevents it. The banks are quite twenty feet above the present level of the river, so that the rise is by no means insignificant, and the further we go no rth, the higher they become. An old woman, who was I believe the mayoress of Wang Taphâ, came on board as pilot, and after a three-hours run, during which we passed at least an equal number of considerable villages we got, at two o'clock in the afternoon to Tha-luang Mu'ang Mai. This is the 'port' of the provincial town of Phichit, said to be five miles distant inland to the west. Two very obliging officials came on board here, who gave me as much firewood as the launch and boat could carry, refused payment, and insisted on accompanying me for the rest of the day's journey. They say that the mountains seen this morning are only one day's journey distant, and lie in the province of Phitsanulôk, while those of Lôm lie beyond them, at a distance of three days more (which would make altogether some sixty miles). So that the communicative villagers of Wang Taphâ were wrong, as such people usually are when you ask them about mountains and other topographical details. I shall never forget an answer I once received in Japan to the usual question "how far is it to the next village" - "How should I know, don't you see I'm a woman." That was in 1870, before the schoolmaster began to be abroad in that country.

At five o'clock we landed in front of a large temple named Wat Thalô, the grounds of which were full of magnificent trees. The country immediately behind proved to be covered with fields of rice still in the ear. This must be the variety that is called "dry rice" or "hill rice" from its not requiring to have its roots constantly soaked in water. Bananas and mango trees were plentiful. We are evidently getting into a more cultivated country, which is explained to be due to the comparative freedom from floods. And from here up to Utaradit, where I finally left the river, the same aspect prevails, the banks becoming more and more populous and well planted with fruit-bearing trees of all sorts. A *Khlong* or stream capable of being ascended for two or three days in boats, falls in here on the left bank, taking its name from the *wat*.

At a quarter past six we stopped for the night at Ban Pak-Khwang. In the immediate vicinity lay extensive rice-fields with a few tobacco plantations and some patches of sweet potatoes. Fruit trees, such as mangoes, oranges and pumelo, were plentiful.

I kept the two officials to dinner on board my boat, and they duly appreciated the honour, sitting on the edges of their chairs as if their very presence was an offence only to be explained by incontinently slipping down on to the deck of the cabin. But things never went so far as that, I am happy to say. Their conversation, when not prompted by questions, generally turned upon the oppressive character of the Siamese administration, which they declared must be reformed. That they were speaking the truth I have not the least doubt. They were of too low a rank in the official hierarchy to have much opportunity of plundering on their own account, and their sympathies with the common people were therefore likely to be genuine. Chill penury had not sufficed to depress their noble zeal for the welfare of their country, nor had the excessive qualification of avarice blunted the natural indignation which every decent man feels at the sight of unrestrained despotism.

December 10. A quarter of an hour after starting we found the river widen into a sort of basin, whence a creek seems to branch off to the left leading to Phichit, and if report may be trusted it was, until some fifty years ago, the main channel of the river. We plodded on in the usual way till a quarter past seven, and then tied up for the night.

December 11. After about four hours steaming we arrived at Phitsanulôk towards eleven. As we approached, we passed a large number of boats lying below the town, and finally came to a stop near some huts that had been erected for the accommodation of the troops. These form part of the expedition previously referred to as being sent against the Chinese encroachers on Siamese territory on the eastern side of the Mëkhong (or Cambodia River). There is a famous temple here, named Wat Phra Chinarat, and the first thing we did on landing was to go in search of it. On our way we fell in with a Siamese artillery officer who received his education in England, and is really a good fellow. Of all those who have visited Europe he is by far the most Europeanized. He is second in command of part of the expedition, and is a sort of chief of the staff to the nominal commander-in-chief, who is one of the King's half broth-ers. * There are 250 to 300 drilled soldiers here, and a battery of six mountain guns, waiting for supplies and transport. The men are armed with Snider rifles and wear a neat uniform of strong brown cloth, ap-parently what is called Khakee in India, with white leather helmets. They are stout-looking fellows, and would no doubt fight if well led. There are no Europeans with this section of the force.

We also aroused from an early siesta a pock-marked, heavy-looking official belonging to the Ministry of the North, and carried him along with us to the temple. This is a very ancient foundation, and was I believe dedicated originally to the Brahmin god Vishnu, after whom the town is named. It has recently been repaired, but still exhibits some signs of antiquity in the shape of doors inlaid with mother of pearl, bearing an inscription in some obsolete form of Siamese, and a multi-tude of old and dilapidated images. The main building consists of a nave with two aisles on either side, the roof being supported by cylin-drical pillars of plastered brick, covered with a somewhat dingy gilt pattern. At the further end is a very ancient bronze sitting figure of Buddha, about eight feet high, with statues of the two disciples Mokalé

* [This was Phra Amorawisai Soradet (To Bunnag), the Woolwich-trained grandson of the late ex-Regent, and future Chaophraya Surawong Wattanasak. The royal half-brother referred to is Prince Prachak Sinlapakhom. Ed.]

and Sariphut at the outer corner of the altar, with their faces turned towards their master. Many of the images of Northern Siam have been removed to Bangkok in recent years, but when the attempt was made to lower this one from his pedestal, he refused to budge. It was therefore inferred that the god was unwilling to change his abode and he was left there in peace, to the great joy of the country round, to whose inhabitants he is an object of the devoutest worship. People come here on pilgrimages from many days' distance. In the courtyards are the remains of numerous chapels and *phra-chedi*, one of which is however in a fair state of preservation. In a small building by himself was a merry-faced, fat-looking deity, closely resembling a figure common both in China and Japan. He is a particular object of veneration and propitiation to people who desire to get a family. In Japan he is called Hotei, and is generally represented with a large sack full of children on one shoulder.

The rapid destruction of brick buildings in this country is due to a species of fig, the seeds of which are transported by the wind or by birds, and readily germinate in any convenient cranny. But it is very seldom indeed that they are interfered with, because religious edifices are mostly "works of merit" executed at the cost of individuals, and to lay hands on them, even for the purpose of repair, as it would involve a certain amount of pulling down, would be equivalent to undoing the good works of the founder and thus interfering with his salvation, or progress towards the beatific condition called Nirvâna.

There is a controversy amongst European students of Buddhism as to the signification of this word, and those who have gone into the question guided rather by their heads than by their hearts, maintain that it means extinction or annihilation. But with all due deference to learned scholars I venture to be of the other opinion. Buddhism certainly teaches that existence is misery, but it does not inculcate cutting one's throat in order to put an end to that misery. It traces our wretched condition to our lusts, and aims at their annihilation, at the extinction of desire, and the goal is perfect bliss, such as they believe the founder of the religion to have attained to. Buddhism has however taken many forms in different lands, and it might perhaps be difficult to set forth with certainty the whole of the doctrines held by the immediate followers of Gautama, say, in the first generation after his death. And there is another difficulty and another danger that has to be encountered in attempting a theory of Buddhism, namely that it can only be explained by comparing it with our own religion, as to which, though different men may employ similar language, it is unlikely that they hold precisely identical ideas, any more than when two persons look at a landscape they receive exactly similar impressions. Our minds in reality differ as much as, and perhaps more than, the tone of our voices. But to say that Buddhism is idolatry, or that it teaches the mortality of the soul, is certainly untrue. There were a number of old fragments of bronze lying about, that had belonged to the ancient building, and the artillery officer made me a present of one of these that had already been appropriated by the pock-marked man, who resigned it without a murmur. It was an almost perfect specimen of the five-headed snake which is so important a figure in the sacred architecture of Indo-China and on account of its undoubted antiquity, is of great value.

The same day, about half past two, we left Phitsanulôk. I should have noted that this is the first town where the houses stand in separate enclosures, and it has a wide road running along the bank of the river, showing a marked difference from the arrangements further south, where there are no fences, and privacy is consequently unknown. It is evident that here, at least, the river seldom overflows its banks, and fruit-trees of various sorts are abundant. One tree in particular becomes commoner as one goes northwards, and that is the cocoanut-palm. It does not, however, produce as much fruit as on the sea-shore, which is its natural habitat. The river-banks, where available for cultivation, are planted with beans, sweet potatoes, sesame, and tobacco.

At half- past five we stopped for the night at a place called Bab-Pak-Thok, where a fair-sized tributary stream falls in on the left bank. Here my rest was much disturbed by an abominable odour, which proved to emanate from a preparation of rotten fish that was maturing on a sand bank. It is sold to the Laos, and serves as a relish for their otherwise insipid food, which consists chiefly of glutinous rice. Every nation eats something offensive to the nostrils or palate of its neighbours.

The Japanese have a pickled radish-turnip; the Chinese have salted eggs, water chestnuts, and a variety of other things that no European would look at; Germans have sauerkraut; Frenchmen eat frogs and snails; all Europe has cheese, especially Limburg, some of which I would not sit in the same room with for two minutes for any consideration; the Malays have balachang, the Burmese gnapi, and the Siamese kapi - to say nothing of the offensive durian fruit so common and so highly prized in Indo-China and the Malay Archipelago. So we must not be too hard on the poor Laos for liking *plara*, as their particular form of high food is called.

December 12. Today we had to part with the launch. Almost from the hour of starting she began to stick on sand banks; and though, by dint of casting off our boat and sending out men to wade in search of a navigable channel, we managed to get her past some of the difficult places, we at last came to a bank that stretched right across the river, which she could not "negotiate" by any means. In ordinary years there would have been no difficulty in her going another fifty miles further up; but, owing to the deficient rainfall of last summer, the stream was far below its usual level at this season. So we gave it up as a bad job, and I sent her back to Bangkok.

I landed, and walked part of the way along the right bank. The river had shrunk to one-half of its normal width, leaving a wide patch of sand now on the one side, now on the other, of the channel. The houses here, as at Phitsanulôk, stand each in its own enclosure, formed by a neat bamboo fence, and the country seems thickly populated. But when you diverge from the line of houses, you find nothing but forest, intersected by cart-roads, which, no doubt, lead to the paddy-fields situated further inland. It is difficult to realize that this deep, wide channel should ever become full of water, but such is undoubtedly the case, and then the sight of the massive stream swirling along must be magnificent.

We got into the boat again at half-past ten, and the men took to their poles. It was not a pleasant change from the calm motion resulting from the boat being towed by the launch, and our progress was certainly much slower; but then there was the satisfaction of feeling that it was the normal native method of progression, and in a strange country it is proper to be as native as possible - otherwise you are apt to be out of sympathy with the people. The odd thing about these upper reaches is that they are so much wider than lower down, but this is partly due, I think, to the sandy soil here being more subject to removal by the current. If the river is wider, it is certainly much shallower, so that a lesser quantity of water covers an apparently larger space.

In the afternoon, about four, we landed at a small village named Kaphuang, inhabited solely by Chinese, who carry on the cultivation of cotton. From the branches of a tree some half-mile behind it, we got a glimpse of a long range of hills about ten miles away to the eastward, apparently the same as those which were visible to us from Ban Taphâ. After the boatmen had eaten their evening meal, I made them continue poling till about nine o'clock, to make up for our slow progress during the day, and as they had rested the whole way from Bangkok, it was only reasonable to suppose that there was a reserve of hoarded-up muscular energy in their arms which needed to be expended.

December 13. Started at 6.15. We save a little time in the morning by not having to wait for the launch to get up steam, but, on the other hand, the boatmen seem unwilling to start until they perceive that we are fairly awake, and the bedding put away; so, after all, the gain is not very material. No more mosquitoes now, and the detested curtain can be dispensed with. The mornings are pretty fresh, and a mist covers the water till about seven. On its lifting, we see a mountain ahead of us, about 25°E. of N., which the steersman says is Khao Kong.

We stopped for a while at the village of Nong Khëm, on the right bank. There are extensive plantations of sugar-cane close by, besides groups of sugar-palms and rice-fields stretching away for several miles in the direction of the jungle, which as retired far from the river. To the west lies a range of low hills.

There is an iron industry here, which supplies the neighbourhood with knives and hatchets, the metal being brought up from Bangkok by Chinese traders, who retail it at a little over 2d. a pound, or £21 a ton. The blacksmiths use a double air-pump, consisting of two upright bamboo tubes, having at their base slender pipes converging towards each other and working alternately so as to keep up a continual blast. The charcoal which they use is made from the *mai yang*, or dammar oil-tree. It is a primitive-looking arrangement, but the principle seems to be adopted all over the East, bellows being entirely unknown. They have the air-pump in Japan, but it is differently arranged there, being a wooden box in which the piston is worked horizontally by a boy sitting on the ground.

At three in the afternoon we reached a small town called Sapharom. Behind the houses we found sugar-cane growing in large quantities, the fields extending as far as the eye could reach, while new ground was being broken up for planting. A general air of comfort, such as the Siamese know nothing of, pervades this part of the country. Here I received the visit of a youngish-looking man, the Governor of Nontaburi, near Bangkok, who was travelling up-country with his mother to visit the Phra-then, one of the shrines of Buddha, Utaradit. He had a broad, open forehead, with curly hair - at least what remained of it - for he is one of the few Siamese who show signs of baldness. Having with some trouble obtained a pilot, we started again at 4.15. Soon afterwards we encountered a line of fishing-stakes, consisting of bamboos, planted right across the river, with an opening here and there for boats or for fish-baskets. As the stream rushes through the bamboos, it causes them to vibrate freely, and the fish, being frightened, attempt to get away again with their heads up-river. At last, however, they find themselves in front of one of those passages and, fancying it is all right, rush head-long into the traps that have been awaiting them.

You can well imagine that it is not easy work travelling by night on a river obstructed at every turn by these rows of stakes. But, as there was a moon, I made the men pole till ten o'clock in the evening, when we came to a stop close by a stretch of sandy shore planted with beans and sweet-potatoes. The dew fell heavily, like rain, and converted the light surface of the ground into thick mud.

December 14. The bed of the river seems to have been continually getting wider since the day before yesterday, and the sand banks at the projecting curves are more extensive than lower down. After five hours poling, we reached the town of Phichhai at eleven o'clock, and fastened the boat to a bamboo shanty on the bank, just below the house of the Governor. He had been absent from his post about two years on a military excursion against the Chinese marauders on the north-eastern frontier, so I learned nothing of him except by report; but that was favourable. In these distant provinces, the Governors are almost as independent as the Viceroys in China were said to be before the introduction of the electric telegraph; and, as long as they pay a certain portion of the taxes into the King's treasury, no questions are asked. Phya Phichai, however, possesses the reputation of being a righteous man, and will be much regretted. (I heard of his death on arriving at Chiengmai.) His house is built of brick, with windows, in European style - an imposing edifice for a spot so remote from European influences. Above it, on the left hand, lies a wide open space between the river and the real bank partly swamp, partly cultivated. During the rains, it forms, no doubt, a

portion of the riverbed. Further on is a grassy plain, occupied by the
temporary barracks, with space reserved for a parade-ground.

After landing, without knowing exactly whither I was going, I shortly
found myself in front of the General's quarters. The officer on guard,
imagining that I intended to pay his commander a visit, invited me in,
and, not possessing sufficient Siamese, I did not know how to refuse.
The General (Phra Naiwai, as he is called, for the sake of shortness) is
a heavy-browed, sallow man of some five-and-thirty, with a not altogether prepossessing face. * His physician, a Siamese, acted as interpreter, and we talked about the expedition and its hoped-for results,
and my own journey. The General gave me a couple of photographs of
a famous temple that lay on my intended route, which he pressed me to
visit, and told me of an ancient woman who gives herself out to be a
hundred and I-don't-know-how-many years of age, and who lives on
the other side of the river.

* [This is the future (Chao)phraya Surasak Montri (Choem Seng-Chuto). Ed.]

PART 2

RUINS OF SUKKHOTHAI
AND SAWANKHALOK

The result of my inquiries had been that Phichhai was the most convenient starting-point for a visit to the ancient cities of Sukkhothai and
Sawankhalôk, and at Phitsanulôk I had arranged with an officer whom
I met there to procure eight elephants for the journey. On these were
loaded a portion of our stores, and baggage sufficient for a week's use,
the rest being sent on by the boat up to Utaradit on the same river. It
took a couple of hours to pack the elephants, as the drivers are very
careful not to load their animals, and it is no easy matter to divide a
large number of packages so that each beast gets a weight proportioned
to his strength. Two elephants were specially reserved for Archer and
myself, but I preferred starting on foot. The path lay for some distance
through the jungle, which was still wet with dew, and then came out to
a monastery (Wat Mô) standing amongst shady groves of fruit-trees on
the left bank of the river. But it was already getting too hot to walk, so
we rejoined the main track to wait for the elephants, which soon made
their appearance.

As a rule it may be said that in Siam an elephant carrying what is
considered a full load makes from two to two and a half miles an hour.
It (he or she) appears to move each leg separately, and the rocking
motion thus communicated to the howdah is extremely fatiguing. When
I got off my elephant the first day after about three hours' ride, my loins
ached as if they had been well beaten, and even after becoming more

accustomed to being shaken in this way, I never
cared to ride on the elephant except when fatigued
by walking or by riding on horseback at a foot-pace.

The howdah is a sort of covered tray supported
by a wooden frame-work in the shape of a V turned
upside down, the covering being so constructed that
the rider can see but little of the country through
which he is passing. Underneath the tray there is
sufficient space to hold a few light boxes of no great
size. You spread a small mattress in the howdah,

and wedge yourself in as best you can with pillows and cushions. Perhaps the least uncomfortable way of travelling on an elephant is to sit in front of the howdah with your feet on his neck, and your knees consequently somewhat pushed up towards your face. The mahout rides on the front part of the animal's neck with his legs, which he constantly agitates, dangling behind the huge ears, and it is the pressure on the latter that indicates to the elephant which way to go. A certain number of words are used to direct him to kneel down, lean his body on one side to avoid a projecting branch, or tear off with his trunk a bough that threatens to strike the howdah. When the elephant is disobedient the mahout strikes him on the head with a sharp spike fixed into a wooden

handle, and not seldom makes the blood flow. When the elephant is displeased or frightened he either "trumpets" or omits a harsh snort like the sudden letting-off of steam. As he goes along he is constantly engaged in eating grass, leaves of trees, young twigs and branches, no matter whether thorny or not. Even bamboos covered with prickles are not despised.

When he gets in at night, he is fed with coconut leaves or sliced banana stems. After using his trunk all day in procuring his food, or smelling the ground in order to find where to place his next footsteps, he curls up its end and rests it on the earth. Sometimes you will see him with his trunk hanging over one of his tusks, in an attitude of deep contemplation. He is very fond of squirting dust over his back and under his belly, and of washing himself when he gets a chance. In passing a stream he never loses the opportunity of getting a drink of water, which he sucks up his nostrils as far as the root of his trunk, and then inserting the end into his mouth, he discharges the contents without even as much noise as well-bred people make in eating their soup. He has a tail like a bellpull, fringed at the end with hairs, and a small yellow eye indicative of cunning. The ear is like the door of a small cupboard, constantly flapping backwards and forwards. Looked at from behind he resembles a short-necked old gentleman with a scanty pigtail, whose gouty legs, encased in baggy shapeless trousers, move with the greatest possible deliberation.

From the spot where I mounted my elephant, which I

had to do by climbing up a ruined tree, the mountains were visible far away to the east over a wide plain. Soon we had to leave the open track, and plunge into dense thickets, where the mahouts cut their way with knives through the overhanging branches and matted creepers. These knives, which are made in the country, resemble a midshipman's hanger, and may be used for a variety of purposes, including self-defence. However, you will oftener find a man employing his weapon to divide an areca-nut or to peel a section of sugar cane. About noon we came to the river, and descended the steep bank with perfect ease and safety. I suppose an elephant scarcely ever stumbles in the course of a long life. In going down hill, where he cannot walk, he folds his hind legs under him and slides slowly down, using his forelegs to regulate the rate of descent, while to ascend he adopts the opposite plan of climbing up on his front knees and pushing his huge bulk upwards with his hind legs. We crossed the river at Tha Maphueng, the grown-up elephants wading, while a baby elephant who came along with his mother swam with the tip of his trunk just above water. This little creature, who stood about three feet and a half in his stockings, was inclined to be gamesome, and offered to charge anyone who went near him, but his weight made it advisable not to try a fall. He seemed to be a pet with the other elephants, almost as much as with his own mother.

I did not see any signs of the vindictive character so often ascribed to these animals, and certainly if they were capable of resentment, they would exhibit it towards their mahouts. But on the contrary, they stand in the greatest awe of their drivers, and their personal courage is in the inverse proportion of their size. They displayed the greatest alarm at the sight of a horse, and Archer's little black dog was a terror to them. That old story of the tailor who was deluged with dirty water by an elephant in return for a prick with a needle comes from Siam. It is told by one of the Frenchmen who visited Siam about 200 years ago, but I have never been able to find any confirmation of it, though I have inquired of several Siamese. Probably it was invented by one of the resident European merchants, and swallowed with the same avidity as the modern globe-trotter gulps down the fables he picks up at dinner-parties on his way round the world. The best account of the elephant I have ever seen is to be found in Sir Emerson Tennent's "Ceylon". At first I was rather kept in awe by all I had heard about the animal, but afterwards becoming more familiar, used to offer them bananas, which they took from my hand with the greatest gentleness, using however the mouth instead of the trunk, which they do not like to have touched. You never saw anything more weak-looking than an elephant's mouth, with its long pointed under lip, like that of an old man who has lost all his teeth. An hour after crossing the river we passed a few houses, and arrived at a *sala* or large wooden shed by the side of a pond, where I was glad to get down on to my feet again. Hearing that the next stage would be a long one, I resolved to remain here for the night. The sala was charmingly situated, in the middle of a forest, and surrounded by deep grassy glades, with groups of cocoanut and sugar-palms dotted about here and there. There were no mosquitoes, though the stagnant pond looked well contrived for breeding them in myriads.

December 16. The thermometer at 5.20 this morning stood at 64°. We managed to start at 6.30 after a good deal of trouble in getting the elephants loaded. Every mahout tried to secure for his animal as light a burden as possible, so that no unloaded elephants were left for the servants. At 7.20 we passed a small village called Ban Phakaphi, and had to flounder a considerable distance along the edge of a paddy-field swamp. Long cords of twisted straw were stretched across the swamp to frighten the birds away from the ripening grain, and a young girl was seated on a small raised platform, roughly thatched with grass, whose duty was to agitate the cords now and then as if to warn the winged robbers that their enemy man was on the look out. To the swamp succeeded a long and tedious ride through the dense forest. At one o'clock we issued from the trees and found ourselves at the village of Paknam, where our guide would have had a stop for the night. He managed to waste three quarters of an hour in bringing us to the village *wat* which lay on the opposite side of a deep and muddy creek. Here we tiffined, and at three o'clock made a fresh start, recrossing the creek and making the circuit of the village.

For three hours and a half we journeyed on, through scattered hamlets, a muddy way among long grass that often rose above the top of the howdah and in places was twenty feet high. The sun shone right into my howdah, as our course lay southwest, and the heat was almost insupportable. But that was nothing to the rank smell of decaying vegetation which arose from the muddy pools that lay among the tall reeds. Most of the servants had chosen the better part of riding on an elephant behind the howdah, but the Chinese cook, who was rather in a fright of these monsters, preferred floundering through the sloughs up to his waist. At Ban Krong Talat we found a number of people employed in building temporary huts and cutting down the reeds to plant tobacco. They come here from long distances during the dry season, sow the seed, watch the plants grow to maturity, and then return with the crop to their homes above the level of the annual floods. At 6.30, just as night came on, we reached Ban Koh Më-dëng, where we found a somewhat dilapidated *sala* standing in a banana plantation, where we stopped for the night. My back and loins ached terribly from the motion of the elephant, and I began almost to regret having undertaken this cross-country excursion which seemed to promise so much fatigue, and to present such very uninteresting scenery. But after an hour's rest in my canvas chair and eating a fairly good dinner, I felt my energies revive, enough to allow of my journal being written. During the greater part of my travels I have always managed to be nearly up to date with it.

December 17. At 6 a.m. the thermometer marked 64°. On issuing from the temple grove we found ourselves at the summit of a gently descending slope. And for the first hour or so our path lay in a south-easterly direction, past open fields where men were engaged in breaking up the soil with a primitive-looking plough drawn by a pair of buffaloes. The big mountain which we had seen yesterday afternoon, though I had forgotten to mention it, which the natives call Khao Luang, as they do every high mountain, seemed to bear S.S.W. from the point where it first caught our sight. It looks rocky and precipitous near its double summit, tree-clad for the greater part, and grassy on the top, but at such a distance appearances are deceptive. The guide says that a road from Sukhothai passes by its northern base to Rahëng on the Më-ping, and another along its south side to Kamphëng Phët on the same river. These places I shall see on my return journey from Chiengmai to Bangkok.

At the bottom of the slope we passed through a large village (query Ban Suen) and then through a pleasant open jungle, with light undergrowth, where the elephants had no trouble in passing, and the mahout's hanger was no longer called into requisition; the path was good and descended very gradually. I learnt afterwards that Sukhothai lies in a shallow basin, which must be converted almost into a huge lake during the rainy season. Here, as I was walking along ahead of the caravan, I met a man riding a pony that had a circlet of small jingling bells round its neck. At a word from the guide who was with me he dismounted, took off saddle and bells, and led his animal among the trees. This reminded me of the custom which used to prevail in Japan, where a man of the people when meeting a person of rank used to dismount out of respect, and I asked myself with some surprise whether the Siamese were subject to the same laws of etiquette. Afterwards I learnt that he did so in order that the elephants might not be alarmed, which at first seemed so incredible, that I fancied the story was an imposition on my ignorance.

Shortly afterwards I passed a dammar-oil tree, near whose root gaped a large black cavity. The guide struck a match and gathering some rotten wood, lit a fire in the hole. As the flame increased a sort of black sweat began to exude from the charred surface, and to trickle down into the bottom of the cavity, while the flame grew and flared, threatening to devour the very tree. This is the method of obtaining the wood-oil of these countries, and all over the forests the appearance of the finest trees is marred by these black, scorched holes that look like the results of some violent disease. The remarkable thing about it is that the tree does not suffer from this ill-treatment. But shortly the elephant-bells announced their approach, and the fire had to be hastily extinguished. So I had a second lesson, in the course of that morning on the timidity of the elephant, and afterwards felt somewhat anxious in approaching a patch of burning grass, for the elephant when thoroughly frightened runs pellmell through the forest, all heedless of what may happen to his rider, and the danger of being hurled to the ground or being dashed against an overhanging branch is not agreeable to anticipate. Archer heard some jungle fowl crying among the trees, and went in pursuit with his gun, but could not get a shot. It is a curious fact that our domestic fowls are descended in a direct line from the wild bird that inhabits the jungles of Siam and the Malay peninsula, and it is likewise probable that the peacock and the cat also hail from these countries.

At ten o'clock we got out of the forest into an open space of considerable extent covered with ripening rice, sown not broadcast as for the most part in Southern Siam, but planted in tufts in small fields divided by low ridges of earth as in Japan. A few women were engaged in scaring birds, but as soon as they saw me, it was their turn to be frightened, and they ran away leaving me to repose in solitary gloom on the shady platform which they had been occupying. The big mountain now bears a little more to the West than when we started. I waited till the elephants arrived, and climbed back into my howdah. An hour and a quarter more brought us to a large village, the name of which I did not manage to ascertain, and then we had three quarters of an hour in open forest with an undergrowth of grass till we passed a solitary *sala*. Two species of bauhinia, one of the handsomest flowering trees of these countries, are pretty common in these jungles. They have a curious double leaf, by which they are easily recognised, and a finely scented flower, white or deep mauve. I have seen one in full blossom which from a distance looked like a peach tree in bloom, such as one sees in Japan at Spring-time on certain hill sides.

After passing a thick moist jungle, resembling one of the mangrove swamps that are so common on the seashore in the tropics, succeeded by a long stretch of country covered with tall grass, we reached at two o'clock in the afternoon the town of Sukhothai, built on both banks of the Më-yom, which is here deep though narrow.

The vice-governor of the province, who was at Phitsanulôk when I passed through on the 11th, had been sent across country to make preparations for my reception, and I found he had got quarters ready for me in a large hall belonging to the principal temple of the town. It was what the Siamese call *Kan-burien*, a sort of church, provided with three magnificently carved and gilded pulpits. Round the upper part of the wall ran a painted frieze, representing scenes from the anterior lives of Buddha, but unfortunately there was no one in the place who could explain them. Such knowledge is extremely rare among the Siamese, perhaps rarer than that of the lives of the Catholic saints in England amongst Protestants. The roof was supported by rows of lofty circular pillars of rosewood, nearly two feet in diameter. It is perhaps necessary to observe that this timber takes its name not from the tree whence it is obtained, but from its red colour (couleur rouge). Along the side of the hall ran a raised platform on which we deposited our baggage and had our bedding spread out. The rest of the afternoon was spent in arranging for a visit to the ruins of the ancient town of Sachanalai, in collecting information about the resources of the province, and in exploring the temple grounds. There was nothing particularly remarkable about the principal building containing the image of Buddha (*wihan*), but in a shed close by I found a collection of old bronze figures which had been brought from the ruins, and were now undergoing restoration with the aid of pieces of wood, paint and the replacement of lost arms and legs by modern castings. Archer occupied himself in superintending a tracing of a native map of the province which the Vice-Governor had lent us, and in getting from that worthy various items of information which have appeared in the official report of our journey. Not being able to speak Siamese, I left all such matters entirely in his hands.

December 18. At six o'clock this morning the thermometer stood at 69°, showing that we must have descended considerably since we left Phichhai. At half past seven we started on elephants from the opposite bank of the river for Sachanalai. The road lay at first along the muddy bank of a creek, which it then crossed, and we did not see it again till shortly before we got to the ruins. We passed three small hamlets, and traversed a good deal of rice-land, of which only about one half had been sown this year, owing to the deficient rainfall; for, as you know, the cultivation of rice is almost entirely dependent on an abundant supply of water. Every now and then our followers climbed a fence to rob a sugar-cane field of its luscious produce, which they peeled and devoured greedily, not however without giving the elephants a share. At a quarter past ten we passed a tall *phra-chedi* of comparatively modern date rising among some trees to our left, and entering a wood reached in half an hour more a *wat* standing on the edge of a lotus pond. Here on an island in the middle of the water is a half-ruined *phra-chedi* of stuccoed brick. Halting for a few moments at the *sala*, we proceeded on our elephants for 40 minutes more to the principal ruins, which the Vice-Governor had caused to be cleared in great part of the overgrowth of bushes that would otherwise have rendered them inaccessible.

The first object that attracted my attention was a massive square structure standing on a platform rising by steps from the general level of the soil, and on examining it closer, I found the platform to be constructed entirely of blocks of stone, covered with a coating of very hard chunam. This is a very important fact. All of the buildings in Bangkok are of brick and that material seems to have been universally employed in modern times, so that the mere fact of stone having been used is by itself an indication of great antiquity. The Sachanalai stone is laterite which when dug out of the ground is so soft that it can easily be cut, but it becomes extremely hard after exposure to the air. Being of a deep red colour, it is a very effective material, and in Rangoon, where it abounds, it has been recently utilized for public buildings. In the centre of the eastern side was a narrow and lofty opening, the sides of which approached each other towards the top, forming a truncated acute angle, and across which were laid slabs of what looked like green slate. The outer dimensions were 53 ft. 4 inches on every side, the height being

apparently the same, and the base was nearly eighty feet square. At the top of the wall were remains of an elegantly moulded cornice. All signs of a roof had disappeared, but I incline to a belief that it must have been pyramidal. There were traces of a porch having existed over the doorway. I attempted a rough sketch from the ruined *wihan* on the eastern side, which I here append. It shows the image inside through the doorway with two smaller ones on a heap of rubbish amongst some stone pillars on the outside. I am afraid you will find some want of perspective about it.

Next let me add a ground plan of the building showing the arrangement of the steps which form the platform, and the great thickness of the walls, especially at the corners, with a staircase and concealed passage in the wall itself. And finally here is a sketch of the interior taken from the lap of the rather dilapidated image, which is built up out of large bricks covered with stucco, much of which has fallen down. From the

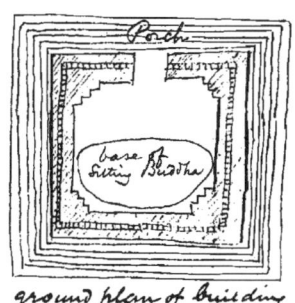

ground plan of building at Wāt Si-chum

measurements I took, the walls appear to be over eight feet thick at the sides, and the inside of the building is therefore only about thirty-seven feet across. At about three quarters of their height from the floor the walls begin to incline inwards, and if continued upwards in the same curve would terminate in a sharp many-sided point. The concealed pas-

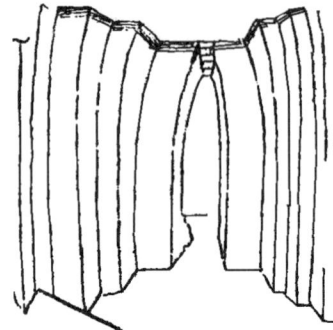

sage starts from one side of the entrance, and winding upwards, seems to pass out on to the top of the wall behind the image. On the South side it opens into the interior by a doorway five feet high and two feet wide. Unluckily we had no candles, and therefore could not explore the passage. These passages have since been examined by Pere Schmitt *, who found them to be covered with sculpture incised on blocks of stone. The walls are of large red bricks, covered with stucco.

East of this building there had been a *wihan*, the outer walls composed of low cylindrical laterite pillars covered with stucco, the space between having been filled up with brick, while two rows of similar columns mark off the aisles. Fragments of a coarse pottery, having a pale stone-coloured glaze, and picked out with designs in light brown, were lying scattered about. They take the form of Buddhist angels, lions and small pagodas, their precise employment being uncertain, but they were probably intended for decorative purposes. There are also numerous small Buddhist images of a fine grained green stone resembling slate, the largest fragment being a head about eight inches high.

From this place I returned with Archer to the *sala* for lunch, and afterwards visited the ruins of a temple mentioned in history as the Wat Na Phra-that. It consists of a much larger group of buildings than the first one. The principal edifice is a *wihan* 136 feet in length, and about 40 feet wide. The roof and walls have long ago disappeared, but many of the four rows of laterite pillars which ran down each side of the building, giving it three aisles with a broad nave between, are still erect. These pillars diminish in height and size from the nave outward, the highest being about twenty-five feet, and are built up with thick circular slabs of stone, covered however with chunam. The outer walls were of brick. At the eastern end we found a block of green stone half sunk in the ground bearing an imperfect inscription. Beyond this is a small shrine raised high above the level of the floor, the roof of which had

* [A German Catholic missionary. Ed.]

been supported on four pillars. The image of Buddha which this shrine once protected from the weather is still in position, though much dilapidated.

At the other end of the building is a large *phra prang*, or group of nine pagodas having a common base built partly of brick and partly of laterite. Much of this is in ruins, but considerable remains of chunam reliefs show that it was once a very fine work of art. One of these reliefs appears to represent the death of Buddha. Behind it are 8 pillars belonging to the *bôt*, a building where the consecration of the priests takes place. On either side of this again rose a sort of cella with thick walls, containing an image of Buddha forty feet high, nicknamed Sao sip-ha pi, "the girl of fifteen years", the tradition being that they are the exclusive handiwork of a damsel of that age. Close by there is a stone called the Khóm dam din or "Cambodian who dived into the ground". It is connected with the legend of the freeing of Siam from the yoke of the Cambodians by the celebrated magic-working King Phra Ruang. He had fled hither from Cambodia, and was pursued by a Cambodian general, who dived through the earth in search of the fugitive, and came out at this spot in the centre of the temple. On his inquiring where Phra Ruang was to be found, the latter replied "Remain where you are till he comes", and the Cambodian thereupon was transformed into stone. It is said that the present stone is only the remains of a pillar, fragments of which have been carried off from time to time to be used as charms, so that very little of it is now left. According to the Siamese official chronology Phra Ruang reigned about 1250 years ago, so that the temple would be even older, but I fear their dates are not to be trusted.

More remains of buildings were to be seen in the jungle, but it was impossible to trace their outline, owing to the thickness of the brushwood that has been allowed to almost cover them from sight.

We took just three hours to get back to Sukkhothai, arriving there after sunset by the light of the full moon.

December 19. I was anxious to see something of the river, and had persuaded the vice-governor to provide me with a boat, in which we embarked with our servants and provisions for a couple of days, sending the rest of the baggage northwards to Sawankhalôk by elephant. We got away at 7.30 in what is called a *rua pet* rowed by six men. This is a very fast sort of boat, but deep in the hull, and it has no keel. As our cargo was extremely light it rolled most uncomfortably, for the men stood up to row like the Venetian gondoliers, and it was difficult to balance our craft properly. She was some thirty feet in length, with a well-built cabin eight feet long. The cook followed us in a smaller boat with two rowers. The river winds very frequently just above Sukkhothai. I tried for some time to trace its course with the aid of the compass, but after a couple of hours work we reached a place so extremely tortuous that it was impossible to keep count of the angles made by the needle, and besides the variations in our speed were so great, according as the stream widened or contracted, that I could not obtain a definite rate of progress. But the general course seemed to be a little East of North. The banks at first were about nine or ten feet high.

A little after 8 o'clock we passed some boats fishing with a scoop-net, of the same pattern that the Chinese and Japanese use. Each boat had two men, one to row the other to manage the net. Shortly afterwards the boatmen stopped to cook their breakfast, and were very impertinent when Archer asked why they had not eaten their meal before starting. It became necessary therefore to rebuke them, which he did very effectually, and they behaved most respectfully during the rest of the journey. Archer thought they were probably the vice-governor's slaves, insolence being a general characteristic of that class, who have nothing to gain by civility, and nothing to lose by rudeness. I measured the breadth of the river here, and found it to be thirty-four yards, though it looked much less. After wasting over an hour, the boatmen addressed themselves again to their business. The current now became stronger, and the height of the banks grew less. I note this because a half day's journey further up they were at least twenty feet above the level of the stream, and the diminution in height at this point showed that we were passing through a depression in the general level of the soil.

About half past ten we noticed a tributary stream on the left (the Khlong Ban-khlong). Here we saw gangs of greenish monkeys playing on the banks, which were overhung with dense foliage, so much so that the boat now and then came in collision with branches of trees. A few white herons also presented themselves on the sand-banks. We saw not a sign of cultivation or habitation till noon, when we reached a hamlet named Ban Tawet, where a small stream falls in on the left bank. The breadth of the river here was not more than twenty yards. We landed at a *sala*, and had our lunch in the shade, with chairs and tables arranged as comfortably as is possible on such a journey. We left again at 1.20. The river here runs constantly through jungle, winding rapidly in tortuous curves, its breadth constantly diminishing. It was the hottest afternoon since we had left Bangkok. About half past three we entered a short cut called Khlong Lat Khanang, very narrow and full of "snags". The water rushed past with such violence that the boatmen had great difficulty in making way against it, and there was scarcely room to force the boat through. The banks seemed not more than two feet out of water. The rapidity of the current at this point is attributed to the outflow from a large swamp (Nong Chông) close by.

At five we reached Ban Wang Thông, a village of some size. Here the jovial but attenuated official who had accompanied me from Sukhothai turned back, and the boatmen had their dinner. Behind the village stretched an extensive rice-field plain. The inhabitants were just returning home from harvesting the ripe grain, which is sown broadcast. They gave a good account of the crop, which was much better than at Sukhothai. Two low ranges of hills were seen on the western and north western horizon.

We left again at 6.20. The river gradually widens, the banks rise and the reaches are longer, facts which indicate that we are getting out of the fertile bottom of the basin of Sukhothai. At 7.20 we passed a considerable village on the left bank called Klong Tan, and at five minutes past eight reached Ban Khlong Kai-chang, at the frontier of the two provinces of Sukhothai and Sawankhalôk. Here the bank is at least twenty feet high. By this time the sun is far below the horizon, but a bright moon shines on palmtree and tamarind, forming the most romantic and beautiful combination imaginable. We took our dinner in a floating *sala* at the water's edge. The evening was cold, and the natives squatted about huddled up in their cotton blankets, looking like frozen-out frogs. Here is a rough sketch of one with the words *nao thi dio* "very cold" written beneath by Archer. A white mist began to rise from the water, and we though it better to sleep in a *wat* on the bank above us, in spite of the low temperature. I was glad to have a thick blanket doubled over me, and a railway-rug and a dressing-gown in addition to that.

December 20. The thermometer stood at 60° at six o'clock this morning. We got off a little after seven. The banks are cultivated in the same way as on the Menam Phô, and thickly planted with tamarind, jack-fruit, mango, orange, pumelo and cocoanut trees. Garlic and onions are planted in small terraces built up with the sandy soil of the sloping banks, and fenced in with planks to retain the water. There are plenty of small hamlets scattered along our course, and we pass large numbers of big heavy boats, shaped like a walnut-shell, which came up when the river was full of water, to buy cotton, dammar oil and resin. They lie here during the dry season, collecting their cargoes, and go southwards when the rains begin in May. Where we stopped last night the water was eight to ten feet deep close to the shore, but before long it becomes shallower. Owing to the great height of the banks, they are seldom flooded for more than one or two days towards the close of the year, but the ground slopes away from the river east and west, so that the water which comes down from the hills and jungles converts the interior of the country into a swamp, suitable for the cultivation of rice.

At 8.30 we passed Ban Tha Kasen, and half an hour later stuck on a sandbank. Some minutes were spent in crossing from side to side of the river in search of a channel, and when it was found the men abandoned their sculls for poles, for the current had suddenly become swifter. The official who accompanied us today was very communicative. He said that last year 500 men were impressed in Sukkhothai for military service against the Chinese on the northeast frontier, of whom 200 deserted and returned to their homes. They were recaptured and sent up again this year in company with 300 more, of whom sixty-five have already found their way back. He added that buffalo theft was very common. Some time ago the Governor issued very stringent proclamations, in consequence of which several of the thieves were arrested, and confined in prison, but after six or seven months detention they were released upon the payment of heavy fines, i.e. bribes to the governor. We are given to understand that this official grievously oppresses the people, but his province lies out of the ordinary trade routes, and his misdeeds are seldom reported to the king.

About half past one on December 20 we reached Ban Wang Mekôn, the seat of government of the province of Sawankhalôk. The court house (*sala Klang*), on the left bank about the middle of the town, had been fitted up for my accommodation by bringing away from the governor's house (he was absent) part of the bamboo and palm-leaf walls and partitions, and supplementing them with curtains. Moreover, there were tables and chairs lent by a rich Chinaman, the local spirit-farmer. Mats and carpets had been laid down, the neighbouring ground had been cleared of weeds, and a kitchen and bathroom had been constructed close by. The elephants arrived by land at the same moment as we came in by water, but as the authorities had taken so much trouble to make things comfortable, I renounced my intention of going on that day. In the absence of the Governor at the seat of war on the north east frontier, I was received by the *palat* or vice-governor, a one-eyed man who seemed to be crammed with want of knowledge about the resources of his province. Sawankhalôk is famous for the ancient china-ware which was made at the old city in prehistoric times, and specimens are now and then available. I asked the vice-governor if he could help me to purchase some, and later on he brought a bowl of earthenware with a pale green glaze, which he pressed me to accept as a present. I declined to deprive him of this valuable curiosity, but regretted afterwards the excess of delicacy that had led me to refuse the offer, when I learnt that he had appropriated it from the original owner without payment.

The river is now very shallow, but it is said that at high water boats can go much farther up, namely to Mu'ang Long on the frontier of Lakhon and Phrë, where there are rapids which prevent any further progress. The bank is about thirty feet above the present level of the river. Along the left bank extend the houses of the principal officials, built of wood, each standing in a separate compound full of fruit-trees, such as have been enumerated above. In this it differs markedly from Sukkhothai, where the houses are built side by side close to the river bank, without any path running along in front, and not a sign of a tree. Here the houses are so surrounded as to be almost invisible from the river. To judge from the mere outward appearance you would fancy yourself in the country of the Laos, instead of in Siam.

We made the acquaintance of the spirit-farmer, who speaks very bad Siamese, though he has lived thirty years in the country and has a houseful of Siamese wives. He is the head of some 300 Chinamen who reside in the province. Amongst these are only four who claim the privileges of British subjects. Parties of Burmese, or more probably Toungthoos, sometimes come here to trade. In the afternoon we walked along the bank under the shade of the fruit-trees to the house of this Chinaman, and were entertained with old musty tea served in dirty European breakfast-cups that looked as if they had not been washed for years; the sides were incrusted with tea that had overflowed many a time when they had been used before, and I did not venture to drink. Thick jungle seemed to lie close behind the houses, but there were paths leading through it to the rice fields beyond.

December 21 The thermometer stood this morning at 62° in my bedroom, and had probably been lower outside during the night. We started at 7.15 after the usual difficulty about loading the elephants, some of the mahouts declaring that Saburo, who had undertaken the office of baggage-master, wanted to make them carry too much. Disputes of this kind occurred every day until the end of the journey. At last he adopted a plan which he fancied would put an end to all wrangling for the future. Every elephant was to have a number, and tickets bearing this number were to be pasted on to each of his packages. We cut up I don't know how many sheets of foolscap paper for this purpose, and the system was inaugurated with every prospect of success. But some of the mahouts managed to evade it by loading a few of their packages, and then, when Saburo's back was turned, moving off into the forest and going on ahead before he knew what had become of them. So that the last two or three would be left with more than their fair share. It was a constant subject of difference between Archer and myself, I maintaining the theoretical beauty of the plan, and he very practically objecting that as Saburo did not know Siamese he could not carry it out.

At the upper end of the town we crossed in a long dug-out canoe that had ferried over an old lady carrying presents of 'made-dishes' to the priests, who in this country have to live on what their charitable neighbours put each morning into their begging bowls. But people say that the rice thus collected is eaten by the novices, and that the better class of monks have their own cooks who provide them with every luxury in season. I walked for about an hour along the path on the right bank, past peasants' houses, each standing in its own separate enclosure, surrounded by mangoes, jack-fruit, oranges and bananas in abundance. Near the bank are sugar-plantations, then a strip of forest, and rice-fields further inland. The banks of the river here are certainly very picturesque. The numerous fruit-trees impart an air of well-being to the homesteads, and it looks as if it would be for ever enjoyable to follow the shady path in front of the houses. There is something like privacy about the dwellings of the people, which is much more to our European taste than the huddling and herding together of the villages lower down in Siam.

At 8.30 we reached a temple, Wat Pa Ma: Mu'ang (the monastery of the mango orchards) where I mounted my elephant, and shortly afterwards we came to a part of the river that seemed quite uninhabited. Jungle thickly overgrown with creepers, chiefly the mauve-tinted Thunbergia, lay to the right and left, and there was an unpleasant closeness about the air. Further on we met a caravan of fifty or sixty of the neatest possible little dun-coloured bullocks carrying empty panniers, under the charge of a number of Laos from Mu'ang Thön (between Rahëng and Lakhon) going south to buy dried fish. At a quarter to ten we passed the village of Tai-chai, extending on both sides of the river. There were a considerable number of trading-boats laid up for the season, and in connection with almost every one there had been built a rough shanty on a raft of teak-logs. A good many Chinese were stopping here, and of course they had established the inevitable gaming house, distinguished by its orange paper placards covered with characters in black ink. About a quarter before eleven, I caught sight of a lofty *phra-chedi* in a conspicuous position on the high river bank, and passing to the right of a considerable hill, covered as usual with trees to its very summit, we arrived by noon at a wood and bamboo building that had been erected some months since for the accommodation of a Siamese prince. * It had been much overgrown with weeds, but these had been cleared away in anticipation of my arrival, and were lying in festering heaps in the hot sun. The bamboos of which the inner rooms were constructed had been gnawed by a disagreeable little insect, and the walls were absolutely covered with a thick deposit of yellow dust. The outer part of the building was a sort of open shed with a raised floor and a verandah running round three sides on a lower level. This was utilized as a dining-room and reception hall for ourselves, while the mahouts and servants lay about on the verandah taking a silent part in the conversation.

It was not long before we were visited by some priests from the ruined temple close by, and I took the opportunity of asking whether any specimens of the old pottery were procurable. To my great joy they produced two fragments, one of which would have been worth, according

* [This was Prince Phichit Prichakon, a royal half-brother and High Commissioner for Chiangmai 1883-84. Ed.]

to their estimate, a couple of ticals if it had been whole. I bought both pieces at that price, and the word was immediately passed round the hamlet to bring more. In the course of the afternoon child after child appeared, each with two or three examples that he had dug out of the ruined kiln where they had been baked centuries ago. I purchased everything. Not one specimen was perfect, and this is the best proof of their genuineness. China and Japan are the only countries where green celadon is produced now, and it would not be worth anyone's while to import from those countries the potters' failures, on the meagre chance of selling them at Sawankhalôk to any collector who might come that way. Their very condition confirms the story that they are found from time to time in the heaps of rubbish surrounding the remains of the kiln. I regret I did not visit the spot, which is said to lie some distance to the north in the jungle beyond the old city walls. Of all the pieces I obtained, only one resembled porcelain. It is a small dumpy jar-shaped bottle, with three figures of Buddhist angels under the white glaze. Another resembled our stoneware, and a few specimens were what is called crackle. But the finest were jars of green pottery much constricted at the neck. Here are drawings of some of the shapes. The small one to the left is almost pure white, while the remaining two are of green celadon. You will notice that all three are more or less damaged, and

that is what has caused their preservation in the heaps of rubbish where they were thrown by the potters. They are drawn here about a quarter of the actual size.

At old Sawankhalôk there are some thirty-five ruined temples of which the foundations can still be traced, mostly overgrown with brushwood and hidden in the jungle. But close by the rest-house rises the lofty pagoda we saw as we approached the place in the morning, and another temple called Wat Na-Phra-that. This consists of a *wihan* thirty-two yards long by ten in width. The nave was originally supported by ten octagonal pillars of laterite, covered with chunam, while the outer walls were built up of brick-shaped laterite blocks between pillars of the same material. These pillars are about three-quarters of a yard in diameter, and about twenty feet high. The sidewalls are pierced with windows in this style. At the west end is a large sitting figure of Buddha built of stone blocks, plastered with chunam, and piled all about the  pedestal are a number of smaller images in bronze, ivory, terracotta and wood, in an advanced state of rust and decay, and mostly wanting arms, legs or head. I persuaded the priest who showed us round to sell three of these for a tical each.

A Siamese official would probably have taken them away without payment. At the eastern end of this *wat* are the ruins of a lofty *pra-chedi* built of the same stone as the *wihan*, but so disfigured that its original outlines are no longer visible. The *wihan* however is in decent repair, having been until lately inhabited by the priests. At the south-east corner, outside the porch, is a cella with thick walls, containing an erect figure of Buddha, as at Sachanalai, and likewise nicknamed the maiden of fifteen. The whole area is surrounded by a solid wall of laterite blocks, on the top of which is a coping of the same stone.

Beyond this, and almost in the centre of an oblong enclosure rises the well-preserved *phra-chedi* already mentioned, forming part of the monastery of Wat Phra-prang. This is the ground plan. The *phra-chedi* must at least be eighty feet high, perhaps a hundred. The inhabitants give it about 134 feet, but that is no doubt an exaggeration. At the outer entrance to the central cell, which is approached from either side by a steep flight of steps, are a pair of wooden doors, carved in high relief,

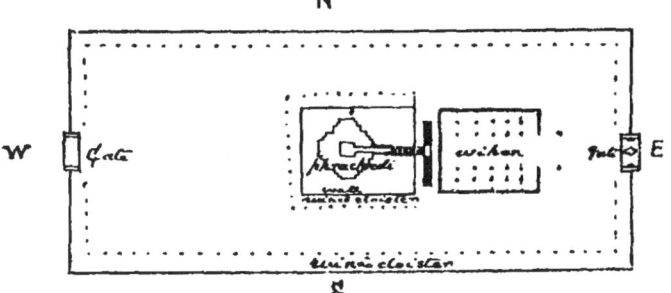

representing two angels. I tried to make a sketch but found it impossible to give the expression of the faces. The drapery is boldly rendered, and recalls to mind the finest specimens of Buddhist sculpture to be seen in Japan, which are, as is well known, at least eight centuries old. In modern times all these countries have fallen far below their ancient artistic standard, which seems to have been affected by Greek influences derived from north western India, or more exactly speaking, the Punjáb. At the end of a narrow passage a massive slab of wood closes the inner entrance to the cell, in which is a sitting figure of Buddha of no particular merit.

Immediately east of the *phra-chedi* is a *wihan* of which most of the pillars and outer wall are still standing. They are octagonal, as in the other temple. At the west end, with its back to the *phra-chedi*, is a sitting figure of Buddha. We can see how these images came to occupy the important place they do in the Buddhist temples. The *phra-chedi* was supposed to contain relics of the cremated body of Gautama, and in front of it the devotees built a shed or hall to protect them from the weather while saying their prayers. Afterwards they placed a representation of Gautama, generally in the act of preaching, before the entrance to the shrine containing his relics, and thus in course of time the ignorant populace addressing their prayers to the image came to be idolaters, though their priests, as long as they continued to be educated in their religion, knew well enough that the image was a mere symbol and aid to devotion.

The enclosure is formed by a wall of massive circular stone columns placed close together and surmounted by a heavy coping. Round the inside there once ran a cloister supported on circular pillars the capitals of which were richly decorated with designs in chunam, and the exterior wall of the *phra-chedi* was similarly surrounded by a cloister. At the east and west ends are gateways each formed of three massive cylindrical pillars, now half buried in the ground. Indeed it is worth noting that the level outside is much higher than that of the enclosure, which is no doubt to be ascribed to the gradual deposit of soil by the annual floods. Here is the gateway on a small scale and an enlarged sketch of a portion of it, with a monster in chunam which formed part of the decoration. These gates go

Part of the gateway enlarged

by the name of *Pratu chang* "Elephant Gate" but it is difficult to see how an elephant can ever have managed to squeeze his body through such a small opening.

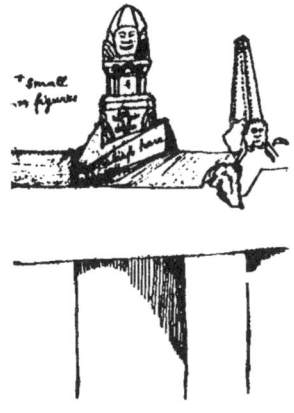

Monster called "Rahu" by the Siamese (enlarged from the last sketch)

Outside the enclosure and still further east is a square building with a pyramidal roof. Here the people still come to present offerings to the Manes of the prehistoric King Phra Ruang, who reigned here as well as at Sukhothai. I found it crowded with a mass of trash such as clay elephants with half-burnt bits of joss-stick inserted in the hole where the head should have been, pieces of dirty rag, etc. etc.. I sent one of our boatmen on to the roof to clear away the growth of weeds and bushes, when it exhibited the form here depicted.

The examination of these buildings in a broiling sun was rather hard work, and we went back to the rest-house for a cup of tea before starting for the outer ruins, which were said to be some distance off. In fact we found it took three quarters of an hour to get there. The path lay along the western bank of the river for a long way, and then plunging into the jungle we reached the ruins of Wat Chan Lom, passing what is said to be the site of the old palace. But of this nothing remained, and no wonder, since until within a few years all Siamese buildings, except temples, were constructed of wood. We found the main portion of the ruins to consist of a stone wall enclosing a ruined *phra-chedi*. This stood on a lofty basement, surrounded by seven life-sized stuccoed elephants on each face, except where there was a staircase giving access to the platform. At each corner stood a still larger elephant. Round the next stage were rows of sitting Buddhas in horseshoe niches, five on a side. The spire was quite plain. The enclosure wall is of cylindrical pillars set close together, with a coping.

One point worth noting is that the stone is never carved, all the sculptural ornament being produced by the aid of very hard chunam, which probably would last for ever, but for the ruinous force of the plants, chiefly a species of ficus, which thrust down their roots wherever they get a chance and thus destroy an uncared for building in an incredibly short space of time.

Portions of the old city wall are still to be discerned, and in fact they lie for some distance along the river bank. The stream makes a very sharp bend just beyond Wat Phra-prang, and the angle thus formed was doubtless entirely occupied by the city, a line being drawn across the base of the angle so as to connect the bank at two points. About two miles above the bend, within a short distance of each other, are two sets of rapids formed by masses of rock lying in the bed of the river. We descended to the upper rapids. Large blocks of laterite half-buried in the bank lay close to the path, and it is evident that the stone used in constructing the temples must have been quarried in this vicinity, although the priests and villagers said, in answer to questions, that they did not know where it was to be found. The fall of the water at this rapid seemed to be about ten feet, and it makes a considerable roar as it rushes down the narrow channel between the rocks. Above it stretches a long placid reach, curving somewhat to the east, between high grassy banks crowned by tall forest trees, while below the river flows away less peacefully to the south east between two low islets. There were three men on the opposite side of the channel engaged in pushing a long narrow canoe upwards over the rapid, selecting the points where the current was least strong, and projecting rocks gave them additional "purchase". It is as much as they can do to hold their own, and at last they call to their aid one of a crew who have already safely passed, and are reloading their boat. A woman belonging to this party, dressed in a black jacket and the Lao petticoat, passes lightly from rock to rock throwing a bait to the numerous fish which enliven the river with their sudden springs into the air, and seems to take no more interest in the labours of her fellow-voyagers than if they were inhabitants of another world. This was a spot where one could have lingered for ever: there is perhaps nothing so fascinating as the perpetually varying yet monotonous flow of water over rocks or down a precipice. You cannot find any reason why you should go away as long as there is any water left, until at last sunset arrives and warns you that it is time to return to the serious business of life, of which the first instalment will be the despatch of dinner. Our evening was spent in bargaining for bits of broken pottery, the price of which seemed to rise with each purchase.

December 22. The thermometer stood at 60° when I got up about six o'clock. We started on our elephants at a quarter past seven, and after following the right bank for about a mile, crossed over to the other side of the river. Plunging at once into the forest, we travelled in a north easterly direction all day. At eight o'clock we passed an open swamp devoted to rice-cultivation and then entered a forest where the undergrowth was chiefly of grass about three feet high. A lofty tree with convoluted pink flowers was very common here, and I afterwards met with it frequently on the way to Chiengmai. At half-past eight we passed a *sala*, and soon got into jungle thickly matted with creepers. This and the more open kind of forest alternated during the whole day's journey, but the latter predominated. There are no signs of cultivation except at the swamp just mentioned, and not a single inhabited house. At 9.30 we passed a small creek, and an hour further came to another *sala*, but it was as yet too early to stop for lunch. At 10.40 we crossed a second creek, reaching at one o'clock a third *sala* close to a swamp or pond entirely covered with the cup-shaped green weed that during the latter end of the rainy season appears in the river at Bangkok, having floated all the way down from the interior of the country. This *sala*, which is raised on piles about ten feet from the ground, so as to be well out of the reach of the floods, is used as a frontier station between two provinces, but there was no one in charge. The country round is covered with forest, and during the rains must be one huge lake.

In three quarters of an hour we had despatched our lunch and got away again, still on our elephants. At 2.10 we crossed a sluggish stream and twenty minutes later saw over the tops of the trees to our left the mountains of Laplë, a little settlement of the Laos in Siamese territory, which we afterwards visited. At three o'clock we came to a stream flowing to the south, from which it was clear that we had now crossed the watershed between the Më Yom and the Nam Phô, though without noticing it. I found growing here pretty abundantly a plant resembling the Cycas so common in Japan; the Siamese call it *maphrao tao* or "tortoise cocoanut", perhaps on account of its dwarf size and its fronds closely resembling those of the cocoanut palm. I had a couple dug up, which were afterwards sent to Bangkok and planted in my garden, but owing no doubt to want of care during the transit they withered away. Attempts at transplanting from one soil to another require both care and good luck to render them successful.

At a quarter to five we issued from the jungle, and following the muddy track by the side of a little trestle bridge, crossed a rice-field swamp to the low hills on the opposite side. This year owing to the deficient supply of water, only one half had been under cultivation. Soon afterwards we turned up to the left through a wood, and after ascending gently for ten minutes passed down an avenue of old Plumieria trees to the courtyard of the temple known as Phra Thën (*t h* pronounced separately). This tree, which originally came from South America, is now extremely common in Siam, and chiefly in the neighbourhood of

Buddhist temples. It has a white flower with orange centre which gives forth a delicious scent. In the dry season it loses all its leaves, and the fat podgy branches and twigs then look very ugly. But in April, when it is covered with white blossom, it looks extremely beautiful in masses.

This photograph [on the preceding page], taken by a Siamese operator, was given to me by the general whom I met at Phichhai, and on [this] page you will see the carved door of the temple obtained from the same source. The building is probably modern, but it stands on a foundation of laterite blocks.In fact the whole hill is composed of that stone, and its neglect as building material is not a little remarkable. The Siamese evidently do not understand the secret of its use, which is simply to remove the outer portion which has hardened through exposure to the atmosphere and cut out the soft stone underneath. In fact it is difficult not to avoid the conjecture that these stone buildings were erected by a race who preceded the Siamese in Indo-China. In the porch on either side of the curved door the walls are covered with drawings of hunting scenes which are evidently the work of a Chinese artist.

The interior is decorated with brightly coloured frescoes, while the beams of the roof are red picked out with gold. A dim religious light penetrates it from two small doors behind the altar, which is a large stone slab enclosed in a carved and gilded casing, and covered with a yellow brocade cloth. The stone, on which the Buddha is said to have sat while he consumed a frugal lunch, is not shown to strangers. The elephants had preceded us, and on leaving we walked for ten minutes along an avenue of lofty sugar-cane to another temple, the Wat Phra Yuen.

This is a square building with a pyramidal roof covered with tiles. It is the depository of a *phra bat* or foot print of the Buddha, carved on the surface of a circular stone shaped like the conventional lotus flower. It is completely covered by a thick coating of gold leaf, the footprints being thirty and a half inches long by fifteen inches in width. Round it are banners hung up as ex-votos, one of which represents four  Siamese armed with various weapons, vigorously attacking a gigantic centipede, in black on a white ground. It is very roughly done, for I had to stand up to draw and neither paper nor pencil were suited to the purpose.

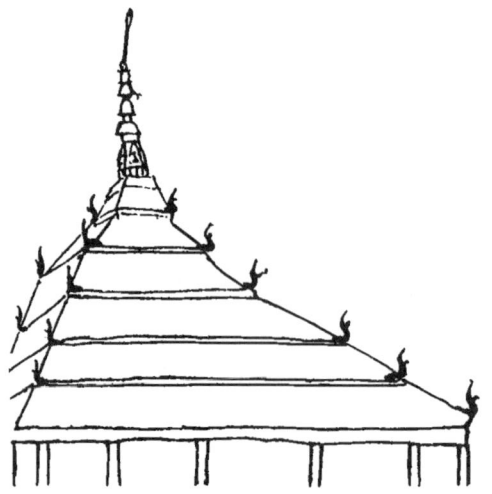

The pointed projections at the corner of each tier are gargoyles (animals above, human faces below) which remind one strongly of grotesque ornaments of old Gothic buildings, and it is surmounted by an elegant stucco spire, on the lower section of which are four gro-tesque faces. Behind the temple are three small *phra-chedi* of laterite stone, of various geometrical forms combined in tiers.

It was now getting dark, and we had to hurry on down the hill to the village of Thung-yâng, where we found everything had been made com-fortable for us in the large *sala*. The governor, an old man of eighty, came to call before dinner. His sons fill all the subordinate official appointments, and it would seem as if the district (which is under the jurisdiction of Phichhai) were a private estate, out of whose revenues provision had to be made for all the younger members of the family. On our way from Wat Phra Yu'en we had been attacked by myriads of mosquitoes, but they seemed to have gone home to bed, for at Thung-yâng there were none, and we were able to sleep without curtains.

December 23. Thermometer 63° this morning. Before starting we went to see the temple. There is little about it worth noting, except the pierced wood carvings on the outside of the porch, and some rude wall paint-ings representing the governor's house as it existed some years ago. These would be worth copying, as they present a curious picture of the details of Siamese domestic life. The *phra-chedi* in the rear of the *wihan* had partly tumbled over, and the central wooden pillar round which it is built, so as to ensure the straightness of the spire, was exposed. Fragments of laterite scattered about led to the conclusion that the build-ings were originally constructed of that stone, and have been restored in brick in more modern times. As yet I have not been able to discover in architectural forms any criterion of the relative age of temple build-ings, and all that can be safely asserted is that the laterite structures are of earlier date than those in brick.

We walked along a broad road, which had recently been cleared of weeds, to Utaradit on the Mënam Phô, a distance of about three miles. Here we found the boat which we had quitted at Phichhai, lying in front of a couple of bamboo huts erected on the bank of the river. In the best of these had ensconced himself the official who had been sent ahead from Bangkok to make preparation for the overland portion of my jour-ney. His name was Luang Thoranen, which his character led me to infer was connected in some way with the familiar word "taradiddle", and he was very soon rechristened "the Father of Lies". At first he affected to take no notice of Archer and myself, but after a while apparently recollected who we were, and descending from the mattress on which he was taking his morning rest, crossed over to the other hut, where we had by this time taken up our quarters. He said he had been waiting twenty-nine days for me, but in spite of this fact he had not yet made any inquiries about the road to Phrë, what points in the jungle were most convenient for the nightly encampments, nor the distances from place to place, and he had not even written to the chiefs of Phrë and Lakhon to announce my coming. I felt very much disposed to send him back to Bangkok, as it was quite evident that he would be of no use on the journey, but softheartedness won the day, and upon his expressing great contrition and finally descending from the high horse he had attempted to ride, I said I would still take him with me.

There is no town, properly speaking of Utaradit. That is the name of a district forming part of the province of Phichhai. But on the higher bank a hundred yards behind our two huts there is a row of cottages, while north and south of us, separated about a mile from each other, are the two riverine hamlets of Tha-it and Bang-pho where a considerable number of trading boats are tied to stakes close in shore. Tha-it is a trading station for the Chinese who come down from Yunnan with opium, silk and beeswax, but principally the first, for the Shans (called Ngio by the Siamese) who trade all over the Lao states, and for the Chinese dealers in European piece-goods from Bangkok.

Having heard that a caravan of Chinese had arrived at Tha-it, we procured ponies and rode thither, but found only two of the head men, the rest of the men being encamped further up the river. One of them spoke Pekingese: and I had some trouble to recall my small knowledge of that dialect, in order to converse with him. He said they had brought down opium for sale, but could not come to an agreement with the man who exercises the local monopoly of the drug. This man was a great traveller, and had been as far as Rangoon. He wanted a letter from me to the Bangkok authorities, and expressed his readiness to become a British subject in order to obtain it. But that of course was out of the question. These Chinese had come from Tali-fu in western Yunnan by way of Pu-erh, Szu-mao, Chienghung (where they cross to the right bank of the Më-Khong), Mu'ang Lim, Chiengsen (where they enter the Siamese Lao provinces), Chienghai, Prayao, and Phrë, and had been three months on the way. They were mussulmen, and wore turbans.

December 24, 7 a.m. - Thermometer 64° (This, you must remember, was in a bamboo hut, with nothing to keep out the night air.) It was so warm that I slept with a single blanket.

At 8 o'clock Archer and I started out on ponies, guided by an unfortunate Siamese who had evidently never bestridden any animal in his life. Luckily, in such cases, there is not far to fall, the ponies being of rather a diminutive breed. For the first hour we were riding in jungle in a north-westerly direction, till we came to a delicious gurgling stream - almost the first I had seen in Siam, for at Bangkok the water runs in ditches and creeks, muddy and offensive to the eye and nose.

A little further on, we passed through the grounds of a large monastery, and found ourselves on the edge of a wide rice-field plain, surrounded entirely with trees, either primeval forest or areca-palm. Here the people were busy gathering in the rice crop. Skirting the western end, we crossed a low ridge and entered a second basin secluded from the world by wooded hills on every side. To the west rise the mountains of Laplë, 1500 feet to 2000 feet high. Crossing the plain, we reached the village at 9.40. The elephants carrying the luncheon-basket, a table, and two folding chairs, which left at the same time as we did, arrived at eleven. It is pretended that the elephant will not go anywhere by himself - he must have a companion of his species - so a couple of them were needed to carry this little bundle, which the smallest pony would have made light of.

The inhabitants of Laplë are Laos; and here for the first time I saw the peculiar dress of the women. It consists of a petticoat fastened under the armpits, and is almost straight up and down. Imagine a long strip of white calico, a piece of striped cotton cloth, and lastly a very coarse piece of black native material; stitch or run them together lengthwise, join the ends, and you have a wide skirt with the stripes running horizontally. Draw this over your head and shoulders, with the white strip under your arms and the black strip reaching to your ankles, bring the surplus width of the material to the front, and, folding it to fit round the body, tuck in the ends to hold it in position and you will be dressed in Laos fashion. The peasant women usually wear a black petticoat with a broad red horizontal stripe above and below where the three pieces are joined together, and it looks both effective and serviceable.

Then these women do their hair up in a decent bunch, instead of cutting it into the shape of a blacking-brush, as their Siamese sisters do, and so are more acceptable to a European eye. The children are not dressed so fully as the grown-up men and women. I saw one whose entire costume consisted of a bunch of yellow flowers stuck behind the ear. Some are even more naked.

There were a considerable number of buffaloes lazily enjoying their mud baths in the corners of the fields; they would scarcely turn their heads to look as we passed. The whole district contains about 480 houses, but you can scarcely see them for the trees. Water is abundant, and is found eight or ten feet below the surface. The people therefore draw their supply from wells, which are also used to some extent for purposes of irrigation. They are very wide in proportion to their depth, and are lined with bricks moulded in segments of a circle, which shows some ingenuity in these otherwise quite ignorant people; this practice prevails throughout the Lao states that I have visited, but I could never manage to see the moulds.

We went for a walk through the village, which is nothing but a huge orchard of palms with a house here and there. You cannot conceive a place more deliciously cool and shady. The areca palm is as straight as an arrow, and almost as slender. Its green stem shoots up to a height of forty or fifty feet, and is crowned by a thick umbrella of large fronds, under which hang bunches of the precious nut. They are planted as close together as hop-poles, entirely shutting out the sun, so that the ground underneath is quite damp even after three months of continuous drought.

The cottages are built on lofty wooden piles, and their walls of mat-work lean outward. Of dirt there is no lack. We came across some women drying betel leaves in an iron pan, over a hole in the ground. They did not seem in the least shy, and we took care to behave so that their free-and-easy manners should receive no shock. I do not know of any country where the female sex enjoys so much independence as in the Laos, and their morals are certainly no worse than those of Asiatic women who are confined in Zenanas. We stayed here so late that it was dark long before we got back to our huts on the banks of the river below Tha-it. During the night, mists were floating in long horizontal wreaths along the low ground opposite, and dripping along the surface of the river.

I noticed the song of a bird which I heard singing in the woods as we rode out this morning, repeated over again. Asiatic nations have no idea of triple time, and their music is not complicated in melody, nor is it, as a rule, harmonized. Do you think that it is because they have not been able to improve upon their feathered instructors? I have an idea that the songs of most birds could be written down, and that they would be found to be based on the diatonic scale in use among modern nations.

PART 3

UTARADIT TO PHRË

December 25. During the two days I had spent at Utaradit, the "Father of Lies" had been making what his lazy temperament led him to believe, or at least to say, were adequate preparations for ensuring my finding suitable quarters on the way to Chiengmai. He had sent a courier (which in this country means a man who walks about two miles an hour) with a circular despatch announcing my speedy approach to the chiefs of Phrë, Lakhon and Lamphunchhai, besides a party of labourers to construct huts on the spots that had been selected for camping-places.

In Siam the length of a journey by land is reckoned not by days but by the number of nights you have to spend on the road; so that six days are always spoken of as "five nights". For the transport of my own party the Siamese Government had provided eight elephants and two ponies, besides which I had the six belonging to the Chiengmai Vice-Consulate. Luang Thoranen, whose private intention was to travel in state, in order to give the Laos an idea that I was under his charge and not he at my orders, had requisitioned and procured eight elephants for himself, which he was keeping carefully hidden away. As he had very little baggage, and I had a great deal, I tried to make him give up some of these animals - which he had, in fact, procured by making use of my name - but on this he denied having a single one, and declared that he had been obliged to put his packages on the elephants of a rich Chinaman who happened to be travelling the same way as ourselves.

I must tell you that I had at this time a weak habit of believing almost everything that was told me, unless it was a patent untruth; but experience has since taught me that in the case of a Siamese, with but few exceptions, the rule should be quite the other way. You must always suppose him to be lying, unless you know the facts to be in accordance with what he says. But in the present instance I did not see any ground for doubting his statement; and my numerous heavy boxes of stores, the bedding, and the portable furniture had therefore to be divided among the fourteen elephants as carefully as possible, in order to prevent inequality of loads; space being left, however, in the howdahs for a servant or two. I consoled myself also with the reflection that the loads would get lighter the further we went.

Archer had brought English saddles and bridles from Bangkok, and we were to ride the two ponies. A great deal of time was wasted in sorting the loads, and in other preparations for departure, so that it was nine o'clock in the morning before we started from the huts at Utaradit on the journey which was to conduct us into the Laos country by the shortest route, which only one European had ever traversed before.

The road lay at first along the bank of the river, sometimes over-hanging its very brink, and now diving down under thick thorny underbrush, where you had to bend low on the pony's neck in order to save your head, or at least your hat, from being carried away by the overhanging branches as the animal cantered through. On the opposite bank were plantations of broad-leaved bananas and tall, feathery palms in the foreground of the primeval jungle; while straight ahead of us rose some considerable ranges of mountains to the north-west, amongst which the Khae Phung (Honey Mount) is the most conspicuous. Our course lay almost due north.

We passed on our right the floating village of Tha-it, and in half an hour reached Wat-Tha-sao, where the Chinese opium traders from Yunnan were still encamped. We alighted for a few moments to look at a well from which the water is drawn by a windlass carrying a couple of basket-ware buckets bedaubed with resin. This was the only place dur-ing the journey where I noticed this contrivance in use.

Here I met the rich Chinaman already spoken of, riding on one of his elephants, and followed by the remainder, carrying his baggage. I now saw the deceit that had been practised. Luang Thoranen had care-fully concealed his own elephants as long as I was present, while the Chinaman's had been brought up to corroborate the story that he had borrowed them; but they were left unloaded. Then, as soon as my back had disappeared along the road to Phrë, the Chinaman started, and Luang Thoranen began lazily to prepare for his own departure, intending to take it easy the whole day. The two confederates did not calculate on my stopping anywhere on the road, and hoped their trick would remain undiscovered, as they would try to reach the camp late in the afternoon.

I also acquired another and more valuable piece of information, namely: that when travelling with elephants, it is advisable to have your baggage made up into small parcels, sufficiently light to be handed into the howdah without any fuss or trouble. I had brought from Bangkok a couple of strong teak-wood boxes, full of stores, and weighing at least a hundredweight each, which gave no end of trouble, until at last we substituted clothing for their heavy contents, and divided the preserved meat and biscuits into handy quantities which could easily be moved.

From the temple, after a pleasant ride over some dry grassy fields, we struck into a good broad path leading through the forest. But we had not gone far before we came to a parting of the roads, where the guide declared that he could not tell which to take. In fact, he said, he had never been to Phrë in his life. Here was another instance of how Luang Thoranen performed his duty. Instead of carefully selecting a man thoroughly acquainted with the route and its byepaths, he picked up the first he could find, had him put on the back of a pony, careless whether he could ride or not, and dubbed him guide. I must further tell you that there are usually two roads to any place in Northern Siam, one for the dry season, which passes straight across the paddy fields, and another, considerably longer, for the wet season, which tries to keep to the higher ground in order to avoid the floods. Besides these, there are a number of short cuts which serve as compromises between the long and the short routes during the intermediate period when the rice fields are neither all dry nor all wet. So that you want as guide a man who not only is familiar with the country, but who knows its actual condition at any given moment. I was naturally very angry at finding that the man knew nothing of the road, and sitting down on a log to smoke a cigar, despatched him back to tell Luang Thoranen to come quickly, and send me some one who could show the way. I intended to wait until he appeared, but a log without a back to it is not a comfortable seat, and I was glad therefore to be overtaken a little later by the Chinaman, who having come from Phrë a few days before, had men with him who fulfilled the required conditions. So on we went again.

The road soon became very bad, owing to the continual pounding it had undergone at the feet of elephants and baggage cattle. Wherever one of these animals passes, he leaves a footprint in which the next one takes great care to step, and the rain fills up the deep holes thus formed, to the level of the ground. Then the beasts become suspicious. They do not like holes full of water; so they begin a new series, and the process goes on until the road is converted into a quagmire, with concealed inequalities at its bottom, which the elephants find it necessary to investigate with the greatest care before proceeding to deal with them. In

the bad portions of the road your rate of progress is consequently reduced to something less than a mile an hour. At the time of my journey,
however, the quagmires had for the most part dried up, and the ponies
had great difficulty in keeping their footing on the hard, uneven ridges
left by the subsidence of the waters. At half past eleven we climbed
round the base of a wooded hill to our right, and descended into a broad
valley, watered by a wandering stream which had to be frequently forded.
At every crossing there were abundant traces of the caravans, which
always encamp close to water, on a convenient open space where they
can find grass for their cattle. In this country road-mending is unknown. It is chiefly the elephant that makes and unmakes the tracks.
So the descent of the bank to a ford is perfectly easy and comfortable for
him, but for a pony rather perilous, you would say. But our little animals
had learnt to slide down steep places and climb up over projecting roots
of trees with the activity of goats, and the only occasion on which I
came to grief was when the girths of my saddle had been left so loose
that it slipped right over my pony's head, as we were going down a hill,
before I had time to guess what was going to happen.

The route lay through forest for the rest of the day's ride. Sometimes it consisted of lofty trees, running up seventy or eighty feet without
a branch, and having at their base huge buttresses which appear to be
an outgrowth of the trunk. I was much struck with the abundance and
variety of the butterflies which frequented the fords, where a combination
of cattle-droppings and moisture appear to afford them the intensest
enjoyment. I note the fact because I have heard so many foreigners in
Bangkok, of the class of people who habitually go about "with their
eyes in their pockets" and limit the area of their travels to a daily walk
of two miles outside the city, maintain that there are no butterflies in
Siam. As they haven't seen any, that is sufficient for them. What does
not appear, does not exist. After all, it matters very little. They are
there, not to learn anything about the country, but to make their for-
tunes and go away; and it is wisdom on their part not to lumber themselves with useless knowledge. However, as all men must inevitably
form some mental picture of their surroundings they create, partly by
guesswork and partly by tradition handed down from older residents,
an artificial Siam, or China, or Japan, as the case may be, and there
they abide contentedly. Most of the accounts given to the world by
globetrotters are based upon information obtained after dinner from

people who have learnt to "know all about the country" by this labour-saving process.

About two o'clock, as I was beginning to feel rather tired of going at a snail's pace over rough places on the back of a short-legged pony, we came to a clearing known as Dan Laplë, which means the "frontier station" of the district so called. Here were a tumble-down *sala* and some newly constructed huts built of poles and palm branches. We had taken the precaution of sending on a couple of elephants with chairs, table and luncheon basket, so that everything was ready for our arrival. The first elephants came in at a quarter past three, and the rest soon after. Luang Thoranen was had up, and Archer gave him a gentle scolding for his negligence not without a light reference to his lies about the elephants. He at first defended himself, then apologized penitently, and finally said his life was in my hands. If I reported him, the King would have him flogged and then decapitated. So I made him promise to accommodate some of my stores on his elephants, and peace was made - until next time.

As the evening came on fires were lighted here and there in front of the huts which the mahouts had hastily constructed for themselves with the branches of trees. The elephants, some of them hobbled, were led away into the forest to browse on the succulent palm leaves, and the tinkling of their bells re-echoed on every side. A heavy dew fell like rain-drops through the leafy thatch of our hut, and we had to throw the Union Jack over all as a protection. A platform of split green bamboos afforded me a bedplace, while Archer slept in a hammock. There was a complete absence of mosquitoes and of all other insects, and we fell asleep at peace with the world and with its inhabitants.

December 26. The thermometer at half past six stood at 59°. Whilst our baggage was being packed into the howdahs, the mahouts tore down the palm-leaf thatch and walls of the hut, and cut them up for the elephants' breakfast, so that very speedily nothing was left but the bare poles. The next travellers passing that way would make use of them to light their fires, and the accommodation at the Dan Laplë in a day or two would be reduced again to the ruined *sala*. We got away at eight o' clock, and pursued the track which continued to ascend the valley. At a quarter to ten the bed of the stream, which we had been crossing repeatedly, became rocky and narrow between steep banks covered with dense forest. I got off my pony and throwing the bridle to a servant, pursued my way on foot along the rocks, jumping from stone to stone, and getting my feet thoroughly wet. How deliciously cool and shady it was. In stagnant pools formed here and there by a barrier of rock grew thick beds of a species of Colocasia, whose root, stem and leaves are eaten by the Siamese in famine time. An hour further we met a party of thirty Shans from Chiengtung accompanied by their pack-cattle, going towards Utaradit, where they intended to lay in a stock of English piece goods to hawk about the country, through Phrë, Nan and other Lao states. Here we rested half an hour, and then crossing the stream as it flowed away to the left, began to ascend a steep hill, where it was necessary to dismount from our ponies. In twelve minutes we were at the top, and then winding a short distance round the side of a hill to our left, reached a spot which the guide said was the boundary between Laplë and Phrë. We then coasted round a hill to the right for a few minutes, and descended to a stream flowing in the opposite direction to that which we had just quitted; it falls eventually into the Më Phuek which we shall cross further on. This bit crossing the hill was the worst part of the road, which otherwise lay almost entirely at the bottom of two streams. Yet the Shan traders said that they were in the habit of passing along it during the rainy season when they have to wade for miles through water up to their waists.

Wandering on down the valley, we crossed the stream every few minutes, and reached our encampment at Panyao at half past twelve. The time actually occupied in travelling had been only a few minutes over four hours, and the elephants that carried the luncheon basket and chairs entered the clearing along with us. The huts had been only just begun, although if Luang Thoranen had taken proper precautions, they would have been completed a couple of days earlier. But as there was a prospect of reaching a habitable *sala* on the morrow we found less reason to growl at his negligence. The baggage arrived by degrees, but we heard with concern that one of our Chiengmai elephants was missing, as well as two belonging to the rich Chinaman. The first story told was that they had been stolen, and we at once recollected that on the previous evening there had been an alarm of thieves which no one at the time would believe to be genuine. Then the Chinese cook arrived on foot, with the dismal news that his pots and pans had been left behind for want of an elephant to carry them. The prospects of dinner were immediately relegated to the dim and distant courses of the future. Saburo my Japanese servant was indignant with the cook; it was every man's duty, he thought, to stick to his weapons, and carry them himself if no one else would. However, the missing beasts eventually turned up during the course of the afternoon. We had stimulated the energies of the men who were employed in constructing the huts, and made ours bigger and more comfortable than the one we occupied the previous night. The *yokrabat* or vice-governor of Utaradit, who had turned up in Luang Thoranen's train, lent us some curtains to throw on the roof as a protection against the dew. Then a solid sleeping-place was constructed, more than six feet square, of bamboos cut in the jungle. At night the scene was very picturesque. Trees rose all round like a lofty black wall of varying height whose top stood out clearly against a bright starry sky. Our huts were situated on the higher ground, while the Chinaman had pitched his tent below. Here and there hung a lamp, and the dull flicker of the fires died slowly away. At one in the morning came a couple of elephants to receive the furniture and luncheon-basket which had to go on ahead, their bells calling up reminiscences of Switzerland as they issued from the jungle where they had been feeding for the last eight or ten hours.

December 27. We got away at eight, and proceeded onwards, now riding and now on foot. At a quarter to ten we reached a *sala*, but found no water there, and after resting a few minutes, rode on to the Më Phuek, which we reached at half past ten. The path had been on the whole much better than that of the day before, and the latter part under the shade of the trees was very pleasant. It turned out that Luang Thoranen in concert with the mahouts had fixed on this place for our final stage to-day, but I resolved to go on, in spite of the protestations of an old official from Phrë who assured us that we should not reach the next resting place till the evening. He added that there were nineteen ranges of mountains to be crossed on the way. I waited until the Father of Lies came up in order to give him a piece of my mind, and after lunching went on again at a quarter past twelve in spite of the warning. As the elephants came up one after the other they were sent on ahead, without the slightest remonstrance on the part of the drivers, who must have had bad consciences after the discovery of the trick they had attempted to play. Not even our own man, the head mahout from

Chiengmai, had given us the slightest hint of what was in preparation. These people are never in a hurry to arrive. They would rather travel one hour a day than six.

After a short ride over undulating ground through a teak forest we reached the Më Chua, on the right bank of which was a good grassy camping ground occupied by a caravan of cattle carrying panniers; like many others we had met, they were going to join the army at Phichhai. I should explain that a teak-forest does not mean one that includes no other kind of timber. The teak, which are easily distinguished by their broad flat leaves, are found scattered about among other trees of many different species, such as rosewood, *mai-inge* (which produces rosin), *mai-yang* (the dammar oil tree) and the curious *mai phuei*, which is easily distinguished by the shape assumed by its trunk after a certain age, when it resembles a cluster of slender columns such as you see in Gothic cathedrals. The best teak timber is found on the slopes of the hills. A considerable number of logs were lying about, some in the Më Phuek, others in the forest, having been dragged to the side of the path along which we were passing.

Beyond the Më Chua the way led across a sandy plateau, entirely covered with trees, but with very little underwood. The leaves had fallen, and the rays of the sun striking upon the glaring gray sand produced an intense degree of heat. The ponies seemed to feel it as much as we did, and could scarcely be induced to go at more than a footpace. To walk was less exhausting than to remain in the saddle. About three o'clock we came upon signs of cultivation in the shape of deserted paddy fields. It was noticeable that these were all divided by "bunds" or "balks" into small enclosures, unlike the widespreading rice fields of the south. The soil was parched and dusty, and evidently the want of rain had been felt here as well as in other parts of the country, for the fields through which we passed bore no vestiges of a crop. Our road lay to the north, while ranges of mountains were visible to the east and west at a distance of a few miles. In fact we had entered the plain of Phrë, one of those extensive basins formed along the course of the Laos rivers by successive contractions and expansions of the valleys through which they run. In twenty minutes after issuing from the forest we reached Ban Ton-phüng, a village of some size, owning plantations of bananas and cocoanut trees. The time actually occupied in travelling to-day was four hours fifty minutes, and of this our slothful guides had wished to make a two days' journey!

The elephants had arrived in advance of us, and we found everything comfortably arranged in a solidly built *sala*, much superior to the majority of buildings of that class in southern Siam. No sooner were we installed than I received a visit from a merry-faced old Lao, the owner of a pretty loud voice, who introduced himself as Phya Chai Raccha. He said he was on duty here collecting elephants to send to the army at Phichhai, and as the chief of Phrë had only twenty of his own, he had to hire the others from the teak-foresters, many of whom are, or pretend to be, British subjects. His age was sixty-nine, but he looked less. After he had gone, we walked out into the fields to look at the surrounding prospect, and came accidentally on the old fellow's encampment. It consisted of a simple tent eight or nine feet square, and not high enough to stand upright in, erected on the half swampy soil of a rice-field, straw being liberally strewn on the ground to make a floor. His numerous retainers bivouacked in the open air. We sat down and renewed our conversation. From this spot we enjoyed an extensive view of the mountains to the West, South and North. The river, he told us, forced its way through the mountain barrier almost due south, where there are a number of rapids, impassable except by small boats. Due East rose a lofty triple-headed peak named Doi Pachang (Doi being the Lao word for mountain), the summit of which appeared to be bare rock. The rice crop, which the peasants had just finished harvesting, had been only one fourth of the annual average. The people had consequently been forced to go elsewhere to buy grain, and in some places had to content themselves with wild potatoes. For the same reason that had prevented the paddy-fields being cultivated this year, the take of fish in the river and its tributary streams had been small. At all times, however, dried fish has to be imported from Utaradit. The province produces cotton and tobacco of good quality, but no silk. Other products are areca nut, betel-pepper and chillies. The population is not known with exactness, but the number of inhabited houses is estimated at 4,000, and there are about 2,000 able-bodied men on the muster-rolls.

We could see that the fields are very carefully irrigated by damming up the streams at intervals and cutting small canals to distribute the water over the plain. This system is universal over the four states which I visited on this journey, and is no doubt of ancient origin. It is, however, capable of improvement, but as the people are completely at the

mercy of their chiefs both as regards life and property, there is no inducement to grow more food-stuffs than will keep body and soul together,
and consequently no attempts are made to extend the area of cultivation.

After dinner Phya Chai Raccha and his brother paid us another visit,
bringing a present of fresh beef, which was very acceptable. There are
large numbers of cattle in the provinces, which are sometimes used for
food, as the Laos are not by any means strict Buddhists and disregard
without hesitation the prohibition against taking life. I gave our callers
some tea, but they refused both claret and whisky. At last I persuaded
the elder brother to try a small glass of maraschino. He emptied the
glass, and seemed to be holding the liqueur in his mouth to enjoy the
flavour, when suddenly his face assumed the most horrible of grimaces,
and rushing to the edge of the verandah, he spat the whole out on the
ground. Afterwards I was told that the results of the experiment had
made him ill during the whole night. The Laos are not averse to spirits
as a general rule, and as those who are settled in Siam have the reputation of being great drinkers, our friend was perhaps exceptionally weak-
headed. We parted on the best of terms, and he promised to accompany
us to the town next day, to see that proper arrangements were made
for my entry in state.

December 28. Phya Chai Raccha failed to make his appearance
this morning, on the pretence that he had not terminated his business
that had brought him to Ban Ton-phüng, but he deputed some of
his subordinates to act as guides, sending on a messenger in advance
to give the Phrë authorities due notice of my approach. It was
suggested that I ought to put on full uniform, but not having
anticipated such a request, I had left it behind at Bangkok. I had not
even a dress suit, and so was compelled to fall back on a suit of
dittoes, a white flannel shirt and a billycock.

The servants were despatched ahead on the ponies by a different
path, while we mounted our elephants almost for the first time since
leaving Utaradit. It was a part of the duties imposed by our official
position. We started at half-past eight, and marched across the stubble
plain for miles. At eleven we crossed a stream called the Më Chai
where the elephants had to exert all their address to get safely down the
one bank and up the other. We were shortly afterwards met by a body of
twenty men, armed, some with muskets, some with silver shafted spears;

others carrying a drum, and a gong, and a huge gilt umbrella. These were followed by two elephants with gorgeously gilded black howdahs on their backs. It was proposed that we should change over to them, as they had been sent out by the chief as a mark of respect, but the operation is a difficult one to execute with dignity, and it was therefore decided that we should remain as we were, the state elephants taking the first place in front. The procession was then formed. One man went ahead, carrying a large silver vase of repoussé work containing a few flowers and slender wax tapers; then came the drum, gong and umbrella, then the army, and finally our long string of twenty-two elephants. About a mile outside the town of Phrë we fell in with the Chao Uparat, eldest son of the chief, and the second man in the state, who had come out on foot with a few followers. It was thought sufficient for me to bow to him without alighting - a fact which shows that it will not do to blindly follow European ideas of courtesy in an Eastern Country.

At one o'clock we turned into a broad street, lined with cottages, standing each in its own compound, and five minutes later reached the entrance of the town. This so-called "Gate of Victory" is a mere opening between two portions of ruined wall. Above and to the left stood a couple of priests, who sprinkled on us water from their bowls as we passed - a ceremony which was explained to have the effect of purifying us from any contagion we might have caught in journeying through the "spirit"-haunted jungle. From the gate we proceeded down the main street of the town, passing a couple of Buddhist temples on our left and a ruinous red brick battlemented wall to the right, formerly containing the residence of the present chief's father. Next we came to the chief's residence and that of the Chao Uparat on opposite sides of the street. All the population seemed to have turned out to enjoy the unusual sight, and I noticed several pleasant faces among the women, who seem to be entirely free from the scowl that disfigures their sex in Siam. Ten minutes brought us to the gate on the other side of the town, where we turned off to the right and crossed a piece of waste ground to a large wooden building not far from the left bank of the river. Here we took up our quarters, and shortly afterwards received a formal visit from the Chao Uparat. This man has a somewhat forbidding countenance, which is entirely in harmony with what I afterwards learnt of his character as exhibited in his actions; but, to hear him talk, you would have thought butter would not melt in his mouth.

I sent a messenger to the chief to say that I wished to pay him a visit, but a reply came back to the effect that he would prefer to call on me himself in the course of the afternoon. Accordingly, about half-past four he arrived on a litter carried by four men; and, having first called at the quarters of Luang Thoranen, which were close by, he came over to me. I went to the head of the steps to receive him, and found a skinny old man, who could not walk without assistance, and had one hand partially paralyzed. He told me that it was the custom of the country for the chief to pay the first visit to a stranger of distinction; but I did not find the same anxiety to make my acquaintance on the part of the chiefs of Lakhon and other states, and can therefore only suppose that he was for some reason or other especially desirous of showing courtesy to the first representative of a European sovereign who had travelled through his country. His age is seventy-four and, though his sight has somewhat faded, his hearing is remarkably good.

He complained bitterly of the heavy burden that had been put upon the resources of his little state by the general at Phichhai, who had requisitioned a large number of men, elephants, and cattle, while next to nothing had been demanded from Nan, a much larger and richer Lao state to the north east, but wound up by declaring himself the servant of the King of Siam, to whom he said the state of Phrë really belonged. As a matter of fact he practically enjoys complete independence as regards the internal administration of his dominions, and the only mark of his subjection to Bangkok is a visit now and then to capital, in order to present the gold and silver trees which are the tokens of his subordination to the King. His visit was succeeded by that of a rich Shan from Moné, one of the states dependent on Upper Burmah, accompanied by a British subject from Maulmein, who spoke very fair English. The Shan had been resident in Phrë eight years, and was engaged in working timber forests. He stated that he had 12,000 logs lying ready to be floated away as soon as the waters should rise high enough. This man was as fat as every millionaire ought to be, and wore a very handsome silk gown.

In the evening I sent Saburo along with a Siamese servant to carry the chief a small present consisting of a carpet, a majolica jar and some tinned fruits; to the Uparat I sent a walking-stick with a hollow in the handle for scent, and a handsome mirror. My messengers had no difficulty in obtaining access for both of them, and reported that they appeared to be much pleased with these trifles.

On the following morning I went into the town to return the chief's call. His reception-room is a sort of shed, open on two sides, just within a gate on the further side of a courtyard opening into the street. The background was occupied by a number of dusty howdahs and a rice-vat or two. These vats are a sort of large beehive of woven bamboo, besmeared with resin, in which the domestic store of paddy is kept. A few very common kerosene lamps with reflectors decorated the posts that supported the roof. There was no ceiling. Carpets were spread on the floors, on which were laid small velvet mattresses with wedge-shaped pillows for the chief and his son, while cane-bottomed chairs were set for Archer and myself. It did not appear to them in the slightest degree undignified to lie on the floor while we occupied chairs. These were merely the modes of repose prescribed by our respective national customs. The conversation was confined to generalities, and everyone present took a share in it as he pleased. Among these intruders were the rich Chinaman who had travelled with us from Utaradit, and a Burmese British subject of rather shady reputation, who, I found, had contrived to become the right-hand man of the Chao Uparat. The chief introduced one of his grandsons, a remarkably fat boy of fifteen or sixteen. Bad cigars and inferior tea formed the staple of the entertainment. No allusion was made by the chief to the gifts I had sent on the previous evening.

After my return to the *sala*, presents arrived from the chief and his son consisting of cut tobacco, cigarettes rolled up in banana leaf, waxtapers, and oranges. They were carried in large vases of silver repoussé work, which are made in the country. These things are very difficult to buy, and, in fact, the only way of obtaining them is to give a sufficient number of rupees to a silver-smith, and await his convenience.

My friend the fat Shan of Moné came to call, accompanied by his interpreter and another Shan whom he must have selected as a foil to his own obese beauty, for it would have been difficult to find a more dried-up, wizened old creature anywhere. They brought some specimens of Lao woven goods which I had asked them to procure for me, and I selected a woman's petticoat, two other pieces of striped cotton cloth, and a Lao's cotton travelling bag. Then the question of payment was discussed. The fat man wished to make me a present of these articles, but I told him it was contrary to our rules to accept anything

from a British subject, and eventually the price was fixed at seven rupees.
It is a remarkable fact that the rupee has quite superseded the native
silver coin among the Laos, as far as commercial purposes are concerned, and that the Siamese tical is not, and apparently never has been,
current in the dependent states. The native coin which is still used in
paying fines is a round "blob" of metal, flat on one side, and raised on
the other, and hollow, like a flattened bubble. I frequently inquired
how it was made, and though the accounts differed somewhat, came to
the conclusion that the molten metal having been poured from a ladle
on to a flat surface (probably a stone or a brick), the
end of a slender bamboo tube is inserted into the silver before it has time to harden, and the surface raised
by blowing through the tube. Finally a small stamp
is impressed near the edge of the blackened and corrugated surface. The skin of the bubble is so thin
that it easily yields to pressure. On the lower surface, which is much thicker, irregular, a hole is usu-
ally broken inwards. There is another silver coin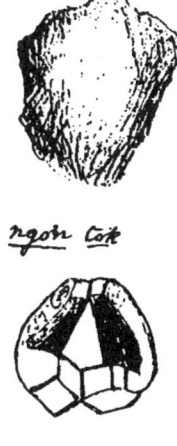
made out of a small bar of silver, which is split up
for the greater part of its length, the two ends being
then bent round into a circular form. These are rough
attempts to represent the two coins. In the Eastern
Lao States there is another ancient silver coin, in the
shape of a rough spindle or pencil sharpened at both
ends, which is sometimes procurable in Chiengmai.

ngon cot

I had made inquiries of the chief about the method of tattooing used
by the Laos, and in the afternoon he came to call accompanied by his
own man, who brought his tools with him. It is a simple process. The
tattooing instrument I saw was seventeen inches in length, consisting
of three parts. At one end were three thick strips of brass, each having
six points, held together by a ring. This bundle is fixed into a brass
tube, and the other end is weighted with lead. The colouring matter is
said to be the gall of the wild bull or of the bear. The pattern is pricked
out according to fancy, and the gall rubbed over the places, which is left
to heal as best it may. The tattooing in most cases extends from the
waist to below the knees, but is apparently seldom completed as on one
occasion I saw a large proportion of the young fellows going about their
work incompletely decorated. What Carl Bock says in his book about

the use of opium to deaden the pain and occasional deaths resulting from finishing the operation at one sitting was confirmed to me by various persons, and I am glad to be able to give this testimony to the occasional correctness of this otherwise extremely inexact writer.

The town certainly does not look picturesque from the outside. It is surrounded by a high mound of earth and a moat, its greatest length being from north to south. Formerly there was a continuous brick wall all round, but more than half of it has disappeared; towards the south west it abuts on the river, where it flows under a steep bank. The chief says it was constructed about a hundred years ago, but as he did not seem to have any precise notion of chronology, I take this to mean merely what appears to a Lao the general term for high antiquity. Near the Northeast corner of the city there is a very old tamarind tree on the mound, so that the latter at least must date from more than a century back. In spite of the town lying high above the usual level of the river, floods sometimes cross the sill of the west gate and deluge the houses. This happened a few years ago, and many of the inhabitants were drowned. There are four gates, one in each side of the wall. On the east the moat is broad and full of water with water lilies and other aquatic plants floating on its surface, but on the river face it is quite dry. As in all the Lao towns there are hardly any shops, and each house stands in a garden by itself. Probably the whole population inside the walls does not exceed three thousand, to which should be added the dwellers in the suburb lying to the east of the "gate of victory". In 1884 a fire destroyed one of the temples and a large number of houses in the south-west quarter of the town, and our old friend Phya Chai Raccha was one of the sufferers. The houses are constructed entirely of wood, raised on low piles and thinly thatched, as in Upper Siam. The architecture of the temple resembles in the main the Siamese style, with the exception of the front gable which is usually decorated with glazed leaden leaf, and the sides are open, instead of being walled up. The pagodas on the whole are constructed on the same plan as in Siam, but in Lamphun and Chiengmai traces of Burmese influence are discernible. I shall only add that standing on the wall, you can hardly see the houses for the trees with which the gardens are thickly planted, while all round you extends a vast densely-wooded plain bounded by lofty mountains except towards the north, where the range appears lower, owing to its much greater distance. The sources of the Më Yom however do not lie in Phrë territory, the Nan people on the east and those of Lakhon on the west having encroached upon the upper part of the valley. Mount Doi Pachang is a conspicuous object on the eastern horizon, bearing about 112° from the gate. It has three conspicuous peaks, and the upper part seems free from trees, a fact which in the tropics implies great altitude. Unfortunately we had no time to make the ascent.

Later in the afternoon the second chief's little daughter, a child of five years came to pay me a visit, accompanied by her nurses. She was at first rather shy, but thawed after a while. Her hair was drawn off her plump round face, and done up in a knot behind, which was tied with a gold chain, a tiara-headed pin being thrust through it. On her ankles and wrists she wore gold bangles. Her petticoat was of Chinese gold brocade, and a yellow gauze scarf was tied across her breast and under the arms. She was not pretty but pleasing. I gave her a pair of old-fashioned enamelled studs to wear in her ears, with which she seemed much pleased.

A little before sunset I went out for a walk, and on returning through the town met a number of women coming back from their labour in the fields. As the men are obliged to work for the chief, they are in a great measure prevented from looking after their crops, and the proportion of men to women as agricultural labourers is as one to two, according to what Phya Chai Raccha told us.

The tax on rice is two and a half per cent of the crop, which is certainly not heavy, and the royalty on teak is four rupees a log. The officials said there were no other taxes, and if they told the truth the people of Phrë must be living under a most mild despotism. But from other sources I heard that they are sorely oppressed, and that the second chief in particular is a great brute. The gambling farm is leased to a Chinaman for 5,000 rupees a year, but the production of spirits is untaxed.

After dinner the Chief came again, accompanied by three flageolet players and some singers, chiefly women. They wore no special costume. The music was somewhat monotonous. In fact the Laos seem to be very deficient in musical invention. There is one tune called Chiengsen, another is Chiengrai, a third Lakhon; apparently each state possesses a national air peculiar to itself and borrows from the others, so that the total number is but five or six. These pieces are played in unison, as far as I could make out, on three flutes, which differ in pitch.

Only one singer performed at a time, taking a lighted wax-taper in each hand, and putting on long recurved silver finger-tips. She waved about a pair of well-shaped arms as she chanted her improvisations in a not unmelodious voice. A rather odd effect is produced every now and then by shutting the mouth and humming the note in the throat.

The subject seemed generally to be of a congratulatory character in honour of the distinguished visitors from the far West, the good fortune of the people of Phrë in having an opportunity of seeing men of a race that had never before come there, and thanks for a promise (which I gave at the repeated and urgent request of the Chief) that we would stay another day or two, with a great deal of repetition. Last of all a rather sour-visaged middle-aged woman chanted without accompaniment what was interpreted to us as a lament over the hard treatment which the Laos of Phrë received from the Siamese, how every advantage was taken of the state being smaller than the other four to impose upon it excessive burdens, and how their hands and feet were shortened so that they were helpless against the oppressor. Luang Thoranen, who understands the Lao dialect, hung his head and looked very uncomfortable. The old chief lay on a velvet mattress, resting one arm on a wedge-shaped pillow. He refused everything I offered him but a cup of tea and a cigar, which when half-smoked he gave to Luang Thoranen to finish. But that is nothing in a country where a slave always takes two or three initial whiffs of the cigarette before handing it to his master to smoke. The second chief, the two 'ministers' and a fat grandson of the chief's, who seemed to be a great favourite, were the only persons inside the room; outside squatted a crowd of men and women slaves, huddled up in cotton blankets and evidently feeling the cold acutely, as I did too, the temperature being as low as 67°.

December 30. At the special request of the second chief I went to pay him a visit at his own house, which is much bigger and better than his father's place. It consists of three large buildings, united by a planked courtyard, the whole being raised about six feet above the ground, in fact nothing more than the usual Lao habitation on a grand scale. The posts which supported the roof were decorated with a miscellaneous collection of guns, binocular glasses, baskets, bird-cages and all sorts of odds and ends. The floor was spread with carpets, and all about were scattered hard square or wedge-shaped pillows. We reclined on the

floor in Lao fashion, and talked for an hour on indifferent subjects.
Among his servants was one who imitated a dog's bark and the cries of
various birds in a very natural manner. The little girl was there too,
much less shy than on the previous day. Her name is Yuong-Kam, and
her father gave me to understand that she is his only child. But that I
take to be meant in the sense that the law of England would give to the
term. His reputation as an admirer of the sex on a considerable scale by
no means accords with the account he gave us of his domestic condition. The little girl talked quite freely to Archer, and among other
things said that her chief desire was to go to Bangkok in order to see the
King. In the afternoon she came to present us each with a pillow,
supposed officially to be worked by herself, and a black Yunnanese dog
to me from her father. I gave her in return a red and yellow silk umbrella, which was carried off in great triumph by one of her nurses.

The Phrë people seemed to have completely thawed towards us, and
I had willingly accepted their invitation to stop another day. In the
evening the two chiefs and their 'ministers' came to perform a ceremony called *rie kwan*, the object of which was to preserve us from
harm whilst traversing the jungle on our way to Lakhon. Before each
of us was placed a pyramidal arrangement of silver vases and small
circular tables such as the Lao people eat off, decorated with banana
leaves, purple immortelles, pink oleander flowers and yellow chrysan-
themums. The topmost bowl contained cakes, bananas, betel, hard-boiled
eggs, rice and a wax candle and from each hung a couple of skeins of
white cotton yarn. On the floor again in front of each pyramid was
another bowl containing amaranths and wax tapers. When everyone
had taken his place in solemn silence, the 'doctor' or exorcist as he ought
more properly to be called, repeated a short prefatory prayer, and then
lighting the tapers, fixed them on the side of the bowl. Next he peeled
the bananas, broke the eggs and crumbled the rice, probably by way of
propitiatory offering to the 'spirits'. To each of us was given a skein of
yarn to hold.

His preparations being now completed, he began to chant long lita-
nies, composed in great part of Pali phrases, interspersed with mutterings
in a low voice, all with great rapidity of utterance. These over, he broke
off a small piece of yarn, with which he stroked my hands in turn,
repeating exorcisms all the while, and finally tied a bit of yarn round
each of my wrists. Then the chief took his place, and tied pieces of yarn

in the same manner, blowing upon the knot while fastening it. He was followed by the second chief and Phya Chai Raccha. The same ceremony was gone through with Archer. We were told that the yarn must be worn until it broke of its own accord. The custom of giving a money fee to the 'Doctor' was duly observed in conclusion. We then drank some champagne together, and as the old chief seemed to think that it did him good, I presented him with a few bottles. He insisted on giving to each of us a pony, as part of the ceremony, and there was no way of refusing the present. When he went away, I thanked him warmly for the kind reception he had given me, said I should never forget my stay in Phrë, and expressed the hope of seeing him some day in Bangkok. So we parted the best of friends. He referred again this evening to his dispute with the chief of Nan about a valuable tract of forest, and begged me to assist him in regaining his rights. From what the second chief told Archer this morning, it appears that about two years ago Luang Thoranen helped them to administer bribes to certain of the Bangkok authorities in order to secure a judgment in their favour, but he had deceived them to his own advantage, and filled his pockets with the money intended for the payment of advocates.

The chief seems to rule in a patriarchial fashion, but is not proud of his despotic authority over the people, and has the air rather of a gentleman of ancient estate than of a sovereign. It is said that he has not legally the power of life and death, but he certainly exercises it. His people, even the 'ministers', pay him the most profound respect. The second chief is his only surviving son, and the latter has five daughters, but no sons. The present man succeeded his uncle, and will in all probability be succeeded by his son. But just as in Siam, there is no law of primogeniture. The Phrë chiefs can only count six or seven generations back, and have no knowledge of their earlier history, nor any written annals. The only books we saw were some bundles of palm leaves at the second chief's, which he says were used for fortune-telling: what laws they have probably reside in the chief's breast. The references in the recitation of last evening, which had been at first interpreted to be directed against Siamese tyranny were now re-explained, to refer to the bullying which the little state of Phrë undergoes at the hands of its more powerful neighbour of Nan, but it is likely that Luang Thoranen advised them to give this assurance, lest worse trouble should come upon them. I was afterwards told by one who is no friend of the chiefs of Phrë that they were not really discontented with the excessive requisitions for elephant and cattle made on them in connection with the expedition against the Chinese marauders, because, although they were obliged to expend money for the hire of the animals, the fact of their having done so furnished a pretext for levying an extra tax upon the people, which would enable them to put a few thousand rupees into their own pockets. It may be true, but I give it only as a hearsay.

PART 4

PHRË TO LAKHON

December 31. Early this morning the Peguan wife of Mong Guna, the British subject of doubtful reputation (already mentioned as at present sojourning in Phrë), and the Lao wives of several other British subjects brought me a few *pha hom*, or native cotton blankets, which the Laos wear in the morning and evening as a protection against the cold, and which serve also as bed-covering at night. Wrapped up in this cloth, a Lao tumbles down anywhere, and takes comfortable repose. These they offered as a present, which I refused to accept, but with much difficulty they were persuaded to sell me one. Its price was three rupees, about a fair value for a piece of coarse thick material four yards long and as many feet wide, unadorned by any pattern. The stuff is only half that width, and two lengths are sewn together to make the blanket.

The thermometer at eight in the morning stood at 57°. Shortly af terwards we started on horseback, preceded by a man who was reputed to know the way. We forded the river close to the *sala*, the water not coming up to our stirrups, and followed the right bank for half a mile, through low jungle of thorny shrubs. To this succeeded a belt of bamboo clumps through which we came out to a patch of upland rice-field. Our guide here displayed complete ignorance of the road, and we had to appeal to a peasant for help. This man had come out to labour on his land, and carried a day's full allowance of cigarettes thrust through the lobes of his ears. The use of cigarettes is not so universal here as in Lower Siam; some of the people smoke cut tobacco out of rude pipes carved from a bamboo root. The peasant directed us wrongly, as we discovered at the end of the day. Crossing the paddy-fields we passed a hamlet called Ban Tung Kamot, and thirty-five minutes later (one hour and twenty-five minutes from Phrë) reached Ban Ai. Here we entered the hills by a dry stony water course, which further up ran between steep rocky banks, thickly covered with forest. The path or track grew worse and worse till we had to dismount and walk, in spite of the frequent pools of water.

Then suddenly we ascended a hill, which led us to a hut in the middle of a deserted cotton field. It was now nearly noon, and as we had overtaken the luncheon elephants, I resolved to halt at the first convenient spot. This soon presented itself in the shape of an open grassy glade, where we passed an hour pleasantly enough under the trees. The watershed was only a quarter of an hour further, some 500 feet above Phrë (which I calculated to lie about 1000 feet above the sea level), and in ten minutes we had reached the stream on the other side, which flows westward. Thus there was a distance of but twenty minutes walking between the two streams. The path now lay through a level forest for an hour, where I noticed a considerable number of teak logs lying in the bed of the stream, waiting to be floated out by the floods of next summer. On issuing from the jungle we passed close by a picturesque rocky summit rising immediately on our right, which is probably part of the mountain afterwards pointed out to us a Pha Lai. Here tobacco cultivation is carried on to a considerable extent by the villagers of Ban Phaimok, but there was only a single cottage inhabited by Shans or Ngio, as they are called in Siamese. For the next three quarters of an hour we descended the bed of the stream, the water ever increasing in depth until it threatened to become impassable. On the left hand rose a precipitous rocky bank covered with lofty trees much overgrown with creepers, while to the right a high level platform seemed to stretch away towards Mount Pha Lai. The rock here is hard, black and stratified, while the water-shed passed just after noon was chiefly of red clay.

At last we quitted the stream, and ascended a steep path on the right, to a teak forest, always in doubt about the road, especially as we seemed to have found our way into a lumber slide which at first had simulated the appearance of a mountain path. From the top we wound through a disjointed mass of well-clad hills, often along a narrow path overhanging the rapidly falling side of some deep shady glen. But for the uncertainty about the road this would have been the most enjoyable bit of woodland scenery we had met with on the journey. Towards half past four we began to descend again, and soon reached a patch of rice cultivation, where a caravan of cattle was already bivouacked. Close by were a few unoccupied huts inhabited by the peasants during the seasons of planting out and harvest. Half an hour's ride at a foot pace through a teak forest on level ground brought us to Ban Phaimok, a village of some twenty to thirty houses, situated on the left bank of the Më Ta, where after some aimless wandering in search of shelter for the night, we got hold of the mayor (*Kamnan*) who installed us in the church of the local Buddhist temple. It was a small and shabby building with a clay floor, on which was spread some coarse bamboo matting. A couple of mattresses and dirty pillows having been brought, I presently took a nap, feeling rather feverish from fatigue.

On waking about sunset, I found there were no signs of our elephants, except the two which had brought our lunch and camp-chairs, and judging from the time occupied by ourselves in getting to this place, it was evident that the main body could not come up before nine or ten o'clock. The immediate question that presented itself was how to dine, and how to see our dinner when we had got it. Luckily there was a case of tinned provisions in one of the howdahs, which proved to include a tongue and some preserved plums. A couple of small biscuits, a few slices of cold beef and some pickles in a 'Liebig' pot still remained over from tiffin, and thus with a bottle of Bangkok rain-water we contrived to furnish forth the materials of a decent repast. Some slender wax-tapers supplied by the mayor just lasted till dinner was over. Then came the question of bedding. As it was already getting cold, we transferred to the floor of the *wihan* the embers of a fire that had been kindled outside for the followers to warm themselves at, and a couple of extremely dirty *pha hom* were obtained for my covering, while Archer wrapped himself in the Union Jack. He certainly had the best of it as far as appearances went, and bunting, though loose of texture, is almost as warm as a blanket.

Of course the non-appearance of our baggage animals and servants had become an increasingly persistent topic of discussion, and we now learnt for the first time that there are two routes from Phrë into the district named Muang Ta, after the river whose banks we had reached. The native map by whose guidance we were travelling erroneously represents Muang Ta as a town, whereas it is as large as a good-sized county, and the guide after all was not to blame, as he had no directions from Luang Thoranen to take either road in preference to the other. He was told to bring us to Muang Ta, and he had done it. The second road which crosses the hills further north was said to be shorter than the one we had come by, and we came to the conclusion that the servants and baggage must have followed it, probably as far as a certain village called Ban Wieng. So, hopeless as it appeared at this late hour that they would be able to rejoin us, we sent off messengers thither, not forgetting at the same time to despatch a couple of men back to the tobacco fields we had passed early in the afternoon, in case they should after all have taken the same road as ourselves. Luang Thoranen's ears must have tingled, if a Siamese is capable of such a sensation, at our remarks on the gross carelessness which had led us into this quandary, and condemned us to huddle round a wood fire, in order to get light enough to smoke our cigars before going to sleep on the mud floor of a wretched temple, with greasy native pillows and all-too-short-and-narrow Siamese mattresses for bedding. From the very first the qualities he had displayed were laziness and stupidity; thinking only of diminishing his own discomforts and utterly careless of the object for which he had been attached to me by the Siamese Government. The ground of his being specially selected for this service was his reputed knowledge of the Lao country, but of that he seemed to be as ignorant as ourselves. Our messengers to Ban Wieng came back in the small hours of the night, with a message from the main body to say they would not budge, but expected to meet us next day somewhere on *their* road.

January 1. 1886. I rose this morning utterly unconscious that a New Year had dawned, but with a bad head-ache, which went on increasing all the forenoon. We started a little before nine, after a mild breakfast of bananas and slices of tongue. For the first forty minutes we ascended the course of the Më Ta, crossing it from side to side in order to keep on the sand-banks, and then turned into the jungle on the right bank. It began to get very hot, and in places where the track passed through tall grass the atmosphere was almost stifling. At ten minutes to ten we reached the bed of the Më Phông, having crossed a low hill between the two streams, and then wandered up its broad bed, strewn with teak logs awaiting transport, till a quarter to eleven. We had now reached a clearing in the forest known as Phông Sa-Këng, which is much used as a camping place. A man who had accompanied us from Ban Phaimok said that this was the meeting-place of the two paths. We had been led to expect that the other party would wait for us here, and as they were not in sight, the first idea was that we had anticipated their arrival notwithstanding the lateness of our start. But as it was safer not to trust to their promises, we cast about backwards and forwards till fresh footprints of elephants and other traces were discovered, which made it almost certain that they had already passed. Before this, I had despatched my pious Siamese servant Plien on the back of a pony to follow the track westwards, and to bring back the other party from wherever he managed to overtake them, and we now started again, after having lost three quarters of an hour in finding the trail. We had not gone far before we met the messenger returning with the elephants close behind him.

After some deliberation, though I felt very unwell, I decided to push on to an open space which Noi Sinkâ, our Chiengmai chief of the mahouts, described as being at no great distance, and in every way well suited for encampment. It turned out however that he had taken to himself credit for a knowledge of the country which he did not possess, for we went on up the stream for a couple of miles more, and ultimately were obliged to stop for the day close by its dry bed at a spot where the underwood had first to be cut down and the ground hastily cleared before a level space sufficient for even a chair could be found. I was on horseback in the rear of the train, and had to stop at least a dozen times in order not to approach too near to the elephants, who would not for anything in the world have got out of a walking pace; and indeed the frequent logs which obstructed the continually narrowing bed of the stream would not have permitted them to proceed much faster. Deducting the time occupied by various halts we had been only three hours coming from Ban Phaimok - rather a short day's journey. I was however only too glad of any excuse to get into a chair and comfort myself with a cup of tea. In the meantime the guides who had come with us from Ban Phaimok set to work to build a hut, assisted by some of the followers of Luang Thoranen, who arrived shortly after the delivery of a letter to Archer, in which the old humbug explained the cause of his not having rejoined me on the previous evening. Some distance on the other side of Ban Wieng he had hurt his elbow in getting into or out of his howdah, and an attack of *lom* or 'wind' had supervened, which necessitated his stopping to take medicine. 'Wind' is the Siamese term for all affections which originate in the nerves. Presently the old fellow presented himself, looking very woe-begone and penitent, for he was by this time aware of the trouble which his stupid negligence had caused. I said little, having arrived at the conclusion that he was incorrigible.

This route between Lakhon and Phrë is apparently not much used, for we passed only a couple of camping places. Both of these states possess other outlets for their produce, Lakhon by the Më Wang down to Rahëng, and Phrë by land to Utaradit. And whilst they recognise

themselves as belonging to the group of Five States which are bound
to give help to each other in war-time, there is no love lost between
them. Phrë being small and weak is subject to oppression at the hands
of both its neighbours.

There were some fine-looking orchids growing on the trees near the
encampment, and I offered a rupee to any of the men who might be
willing to climb up and procure me a few specimens. But the money
seemed hardly to be a sufficient inducement, and it was with difficulty
that one of the Laos was at last persuaded to gratify my wish. Probably
there would have been less unwillingness if he had been simply ordered
to get the plants, without any promise of a reward. The surrounding
forest was too dense for walking and I felt no inclination to explore the
sandy bed of the stream in anticipation of the morrow's journey. One
learns by experience to understand the lethargy that seems to weigh
down the inhabitants of Indo-China. Nature is so all-powerful that
contention against her is useless, and even the inborn energy of the
European at last succumbs under the influence of such obstacles as
climate and vegetation opposed to his action. Mere existence here
becomes at last almost too troublesome, only less so than the resolution to end it. Eat, sleep, smoke tobacco and chew betel - that is
all a man is fit for here.

January 2. The thermometer at 7 a.m. stood at 57°. We started at
eight o'clock on foot, and after some minutes walk left the stream, near
an open space called Phë Ta-dan, well suited for camping. This is the
place we should have come to last night, had our guide known anything
of the country. From here we ascended over granite blocks in an advanced state of disintegration, through an open wood devoid of undergrowth, to the top of the pass, in a quarter of an hour more. To the
north rises a pointed hill 510 feet above the pass (measured with an
aneroid), while close by on the south side is a smaller one. Either
affords a good view looking towards Phrë, of ranges of mountains rising
beyond the dense forest which stretches away at our feet. South-east
again of the smaller hill stand a pair of peaks whose height I estimate to
be about 400 feet above the pass; they are distinguished by masses of
precipitous rock at their summits. We climbed first the lesser hill in
five minutes. The wood is sparse and there are no creepers, for the
granite soil is incapable by itself of nourishing a luxuriant vegetation,

such as that which characterizes the lower jungles, besides being too porous to retain sufficient moisture. At the present season it is of course perfectly dry. But the prospect from this point was not satisfying, and we therefore betook ourselves to the other hill, whose summit it took us only twenty-five minutes to attain. Our native followers evidently thought us mad, and only two of them were willing to accompany us to the top. Perhaps their reluctance arose from the belief that the hill was infested by malignant spirits, whose presence can always be invoked as an excuse for declining to undertake any exertion not properly included in the day's work.

It was necessary to cut down some bamboos in order to obtain a good view, and we then found it possible to take bearings of the more prominent points on the road from Phrë. Doi Pachang assumes quite a different shape from that which it presents when seen from Phrë, but as there was no other conspicuously lofty summit along the eastern horizon, it was not possible to be mistaken about the identity of this mountain. On the near side of Phrë extended another long range, in which the two passes already spoken of were distinctly visible, while in front of this stretched a long-cockscomb-shaped ridge, the hither flank of which, being thrown into a deep shade by the morning sun, looked almost perpendicular. The name of this is Doi Phalai, and the path we had taken to Ban Phaimok must lie across its southern end. Beyond a gap to our north ran a remarkable group of rocks resembling a distant "city set upon a hill." To the west a large mountain pass was discernible through the foliage, apparently close at hand, while to the south-west we saw the tops of several mountains, whose lower slopes were cut off by the intervening trees. The Cycad which I had met with on the road from Old Sawankhalôk to Thung-yang was common on this mountain; it bears a fruit (or flower) remarkably like a ripe fir-cone. We found another Cycad-like plant, having longer and more flexible fronds and a stem in some cases as much as two feet in height.

We got down again to the top of the pass by eleven o'clock, not without some difficulty, as there was no path and the grass was exceedingly slippery. Eight minutes brought us down to the Më Lan, a small tributary of the Më Ta. Here a caravan of cattle occupied the grassy camping ground on the other side of the ford. Shortly afterwards we got into the bed of another rivulet called Më Song (or Som), and followed one of its minor tributaries through dense jungle, rising continually till one o'clock, when we reached the watershed situated among thickly wooded hills; height, say 1,000 feet above the sea. Here we overtook the elephants, and passing them descended in 20 minutes to the bank of a stream. It was a convenient place for lunch; the elephants were halted, and we rested for about an hour. Feeling fatigued from the climbing and also somewhat upset in consequence of a fall from my pony due to loose girths, I here took to my elephant, while Archer and the servants rode ahead on horseback.

The track was shut in on every side by the dreary thick jungle. At 3.30 I passed a good sized hut on piles, standing well to one side of an extensive camping ground, and a quarter of an hour afterwards fell in with a party of Siamese engaged in measuring the road with a long cord composed of rattan links, in anticipation of the erection of a line of telegraph from Lakhon to Phrë. The chief surveyor cheered me greatly with the information that I had only 2,000 *wa* or 14,000 feet more to accomplish before reaching the banks of the Më Chang, where we were to pass the night. About this time I entered a forest composed entirely of tall, slender, straight bamboos, disposed in small scattered groups, quite unlike the thick and thorny masses which occur in the vicinity of rivers or swamps. Here the bamboo clumps as they bent towards each other assumed the appearance of an endless assemblage of Gothic arches almost obscuring the sky, and carpeted with short, spare grass. This makes the fifth variety as yet observed; we have passed short bamboos resembling the Japanese *sasa*, others tall and leafy, with slender stems spreading outwards on all sides as they spring from the ground, others again fine and leafy like the densely growing *ma-dake* in the neighbourhood of Hakoné in Japan. To this succeeded forest of *mai nge*, on rocky soil, well-suited to such coarse-barked lanky trees and the half-starved long grass which grows under their incomplete shade.

Towards five o'clock I passed a few deserted rice-fields and ten minutes later dropped into the bed of the Më Tun flowing north west, then turning a corner struck the Më Chang flowing north to south. My elephant had been going at a steady pace, and had accomplished the distance of two and two-thirds miles in an hour and a half. It thus becomes easy to understand how fifteen miles comes to be reckoned a good day's work with these animals. Of the Më Chang it should be said that the river consisted at this period of a series of disconnected stagnant pools.

Archer was waiting for me on a cleared space above the right bank, which I feared at first represented the village where we were to pass the night; but he speedily led the way to a deserted cottage at no great distance, which had been secured for us by his 'boatman'! This man deserves mention as a brilliant exception to the general rule of lazy, almost useless Siamese servants. He was born in the Consulate at Bangkok, where his father had been boatman before him, and for the past twenty-five years, or at least from the time when he was old enough to make himself useful, has always been in the employ of one or other of the Consular staff. Profiting by his opportunities he has become an industrious and faithful servant, intelligent and indefatigable, as some few chosen Orientals are, whom Providence has destined to be the comfort of exiled Englishmen in the far East. My Japanese servant Saburo is one of the same kind. When you once are fortunate enough to light upon such a man, treasure him like gold and precious stones. Archer's man had gone from Ban Phaimok on the last night but one to Ban Wieng, whence he returned with provisions intended for our yesterday morning's breakfast. But arriving after our departure, he had immediately started again without a guide, and taking a different path, had reached the Më Chang the same night in a manner partaking almost of instinct; he had now been waiting twenty-four hours for us.

The cottage, which contained but two rooms, stood in a small clearing in the middle of the jungle. It was erected on wooden piles, the superstructure being chiefly of bamboo. The floor consisted of bamboo flattened out like thin planks, laid on bamboo joists, the walls being woven sheets of flattened bamboos tied on to the uprights, and inclining outwards from their lower edges. The inner room had no opening besides the doorway, but there was abundance of natural ventilation through floor, roof and walls; in one corner was the clay hearth, without chimney, and the roof (for there is hardly ever a ceiling in a native house) was black with soot. The outer room was open on two sides, and beyond it extended an unroofed platform. The thatch was of thin grass 'ataps', a word which may perhaps be best explained by calling it a large vegetable tile. Here are a plan and a sketch of the house. This may be taken as a fair example of the ordinary peasant's hut in the outlying Lao districts. The previous occupiers had moved elsewhere, probably driven away from their home by the imputation of witchcraft, and it

ladder

had no longer an owner. So we had not even to pay for our night's lodging. This was an exceptional piece of good luck, for the traveller in the Lao States has seldom any other choice than between sleeping in the open air and putting up in a dark and dirty *sala*.

Close by, in the angle formed by the Më Tun and the Më Chang, rises a noble rocky hill, covered with trees, to a height of 1,000 or 1,500 feet, the top of which must command an extensive prospect. Unluckily my exertions on the previous day had brought on an attack of diarrhoea, which though yielding to medicine, forbade any more climbing for the present, and we therefore left this mountain to the enterprise of some succeeding explorer. It would probably be a fair day's work, owing to the density of the underwood, and the necessity for cutting a path the whole way from the stream up to the summit. Among the people who had accompanied us from Ban Phaimok were three squat, broad-shouldered, thick-legged, brown-skinned square-faced figures, with strongly marked features and beadlike black eyes, whose bodies were entirely free from tattoo marks, and who wore a mixed costume, partly Lao and partly belonging to some other race, perhaps their own native habit. These were Khamu, whose home is among the mountains to the north of Luang Phrabang, a sturdy hardworking race, who enjoy immunity from jungle fever and are therefore much in request in the teak-forests. It is they who perform most of the labour of felling teak throughout the five Lao States, and even in northern Siam. They hire themselves out in gangs to the lessees of the forests for their food and a moderate wage, the accumulation of which they are said to convert into gongs, which they carry home with them. Their language has not yet been investigated.

January 3. The thermometer stood at 64° this morning. Height above sea level 630 feet. I was not well enough to travel on horseback, and therefore had recourse to an elephant, while Archer went on ahead with his pony. We started at 8.30 and after passing a few rice-fields, entered a jungle composed of slender bamboos like those described in yesterday's record. To these succeeded an open forest of scraggy trees called *mai pao*. Looking backwards we enjoyed a fine view of the mountain at whose foot we slept last night. At 11.30 we crossed the Më Mo, and then rose on to an undulating country which terminated in a stony plateau averaging 900 feet above sea level. It was covered with large fragments of what looked like lava, and the Cycad already mentioned was abundant. The trees were lank *mai pao*, with a thin undergrowth of emaciated grass; scarcely any other kind of vegetation was to be seen. One might fairly call it a desert, but for the prevalent notion that the desert is bare unmitigated sand; for here no cultivation would be possible, and at this season not a drop of water is to be found for miles.

At 2.45 I reached a ruinous *sala* close to the foot of the mountains to the north-west of which lies the town of Lakhon, and found Archer there, who having decided for himself that it was better to push on, had already despatched the greater portion of the baggage elephants. As the distance still to be traversed before reaching the town was represented as being quite short, there seemed every reason for ratifying his decision. I stopped however to lunch, while Archer rode on, and I did not resume my march until 3.15. Just beyond the *sala* we crossed a small stream, almost dry, and immediately after crossing this began to ascend. At 4.20 we reached the highest point, 1,020 feet above sea-level. There was no view either backwards or forwards. We began to descend at once, and after traversing a continuous forest, passed at ten minutes past six some rice-fields lying to the right of the road in a picturesque little dell. These had been cultivated and the people were now busy gathering in the crop, as was the case with some more fields on the left hand just beyond. Then succeeded another stretch of forest. At half past six we passed a Burmese temple standing at the foot of a hill to the right, and the night began to close in rapidly. The smoke of burning grass shrouded the stone dry rice-fields across which our track wound.

Owing to lack of water not a grain of rice had been raised from them during the season that was just over. A number of elephants were wandering about, browsing on the scanty herbage which they managed to pick up.

At last we came to a *sala* standing at the head of a broad muddy road leading to the city gate; on the right hand side a trestle-bridge for foot passengers extends for a quarter of a mile in the same direction. In front of the gate is a demi-lune, with its entrance exactly opposite, rather an unusual arrangement in Lao towns. My mahout did not know the place, and instead of following the direct road across the town to the Vice-Consulate, which stands on the other side of the river, took me past the Chief's residence, then turned to the right and going out at the north gate, doubled back along a path outside the palisade which here does duty for a wall, until we reached the ford. In passing through the main street, I caught glimpses of interiors lighted up - cosy houses on piles, standing each in its own garden, in the midst of thickly-growing fruit trees, with an open room in front, and a mosquito curtain hanging up behind thick enough to exclude air as well as insects. There seemed to be a complete absence of tables and chairs. On arriving at the gate in the palisade directly opposite to that by which we had entered the town, my mahout drove the elephant in the darkness down a steep bank into the shallow river. Here we got by mistake on to a little island, lost our way among teak-logs and small enclosures, crossed another arm of the river, ascended the bank and so northwards again past a row of houses to the Vice-Consulate by half past seven.

I was scarcely seated in the room which serves both as drawing room, office and public reception room, when an American gentleman, who unites in himself the qualification of missionary and doctor, came in accompanied by a young Siamese named Luang Suriya, a half-brother of the Siamese Chief Commissioner at Chiengmai. The latter was the bearer of a very civil letter from his brother, and told me he was to place himself at my disposal until the end of my journey. Of this I was extremely glad, as he spoke English fluently, and seemed to be what we call a nice boy. They went away at half past nine, and we at last got to dinner.

LAKHON

January 4. It has already been explained that in 1883 the British Government concluded a treaty with Siam by which the jurisdiction over British subjects in the Northern Lao States was handed over to the Siamese, with certain exceptions, and that a Vice-Consul has been appointed to watch over its execution. His headquarters are at Chiengmai, where most of the said British subjects, almost without exception natives of Burmah, reside, but as there are also a considerable number of them in the province of Lakhon, he is obliged to travel thither from time to time, and a residence had therefore to be built. The chief obligingly gave a piece of ground on the right bank of the river in a good situation commanding a view of the mountains, the only drawback being that as there is no bridge, the river has to be forded whenever the Vice-Consul has business with the officials, who live on the other side. During the winter you can ride over on horseback on most days without wetting your feet, if you draw them well up behind you, but during the rains you must cross on an elephant. No one seems ever to have thought of establishing a ferry, and the natives wade across as long as the water is not too deep. The house is entirely built of wood, and cost only 2,000 rupees, which is less than £150 at the present low rate of silver, and probably there is no consular building of this size adequate to its purpose, in any part of the world, that has been constructed at less expense.

After breakfast we went for a walk with our visitors of last night, who had offered to show us the ancient walls on this side of the Më Wang. The outline is very irregular, and there seem to be two enclosures belonging to different periods. One of these is of brick, with a core of earth, and is in a fair state of repair, but the other is reduced to a mere embankment crowned by a palisade of split logs, now much decayed. In one place is a small opening, which at first sight you might take for a postern, but I believe it to have been an embrasure for cannon. Probably the river at some earlier period flowed outside the town of Lakhon, but afterwards altering its course, broke down the wall at the northern end, and so made a new channel for itself. This habit the Më Wang has not yet lost, and you can see that while constantly engaged in undermining the bank on its right, it is depositing soil on the opposite hand, where new houses and kitchen gardens are springing into existence. Unless the current changes its present direction, the whole of the suburb on the western bank will be entirely swept away in the course of time.

There are several temples on this side of the river, of which the most interesting is Wat Sanuk, where they point out a mound surrounded by a *phra-chedi*. Here the Laos are said to have successfully resisted an assault in force by the Burmese during the invasion that took place at the end of last century. Otherwise there was nothing worthy of special note about this temple, nor at any of the others.

In the afternoon I proceeded across the river to pay a visit to the chief, having previously given him notice of my intention. He lives in a much better house than either of the Phrë chiefs. It stands in an enclosure surrounded by a red brick wall with an embattled top, and is raised some six or eight feet from the ground. He came out to the top of the steps, and conducted me into a large reception room panelled with teak, but open on two sides. Ricketty chairs covered with reps were placed round a table, but for him an armchair was reserved in which cushions had been piled so thickly that when he sat down his feet dangled helplessly in the air. It was a sacrifice of comfort to dignity. The chief judge and the minister for war sat on chairs, as did also Luang Suriya and Luang Thoranen, but the minister of finance squatted on the floor. Besides these high functionaries the state of Lakhon boasts a minister of agriculture, whose duties, as in Siam proper, are confined to collecting the land tax, a minister of the interior (*Mahatthai*) and a minister of the household. All of them are *chao*, that is to say they are more or less distant relations of the chief. To my congratulations on his hale appearance, the old man replied with much satisfaction that his hearing and sight were good, but his head sometimes troubled him. He can walk well and dislikes riding on elephants as the motion hurts his back. He is seventy-four years old, and was appointed chief ten years ago, receiving the insignia of office from the King of Siam on the same day as the chief of Chiengmai. He is descended from a chief of Lakhon who had seven sons. Some went to re-colonize Chiengmai after its delivery from the Burmese yoke about the beginning of this century, one received Lamphun as his portion, and the rest remained here. He therefore considers himself the senior of all the chiefs in these three provinces. It is six years since he was last in Bangkok to do homage, and he is now excused from further attendance on account of his advanced age. But the Uparat or second chief is down there at present on business.

I thanked him for having given such a good site for the Vice-Consulate, but he pretended not to understand what I meant, although the two
Siamese Luangs and the chief judge did their best to explain what the
word "thanks" signifies. At last he gave way, so far as to say that "there
would have been trouble if the site had not given satisfaction," which
enigmatical way of putting it was interpreted to mean that if he had not
pleased the vice-consul in the matter there would have been a row between Lakhon and Great Britain. But after all, I believe his apparent
obtuseness was our fault, and that we ought to have said that it had
caused me "pleasure", instead of saying I wished to "thank" him. He
stuck chiefly to his own dialect, though he talks Siamese well enough.
I think I have said before that Lao is to Siamese as Lowland Scotch is to
English. Archer attempted to engage him in conversation about the
productive capacity of his dominions, but at once becoming suspicious
he replied that there was but little teak, a small extent of rice-fields
here and there, and nothing else. Somebody however mentioned iron,
which is worked in the southern corner of the State. An inquiry about
raw silk induced him to show me some pieces of silk cloth dyed and
woven in Lakhon. The blue colour seems to be indigo, the red saf-
flower, while the yellow is obtained from the prickly pods (?Arnatto)
of a large shrub which is also common in Bangkok. The silk thread
seems to be imported from China. He confessed also to the existence
of the paper-plant (Trophis aspera).

After bidding him goodbye in his lofty chair, from which his dignity
did not allow him to descend, we crossed the platform to an old building called the "Golden Hall", which was formerly the Audience Chamber of the Chiefs of Lakhon. It is in somewhat a dilapidated state, but
was originally a solid structure raised on piles, having massive cylindrical columns decorated with a gold pattern on a red or black ground.
At the further end is some curious panel-work, now much disjointed, in
front of which stands a chair or throne, that must once have been a
gorgeous object, raised a couple of steps above the floor. It was occupied by a photographic portrait of the King of Siam. In one corner was
a red-painted wooden bedstead of the four-post kind, also reached by a
flight of two or three steps, and heavily gilded. In another corner stood
an old bronze *hansa*, which had apparently once decorated the courtyard of a temple; this bird though called the "sacred goose" by foreigners, from the apparent Sanskrit origin of it native name, appeared to me

to bear a much closer resemblance to the fabulous phoenix (*fung hwang*) of the Chinese. The Siamese equivalent *hong*, which might be thought to corroborate this view, is however spelt *hongsa*. Perhaps the form came from China and the name from India.

From the chief's residence we crossed the road to the Wat Luang (chief temple), which Mr Bock in his "Temples and Elephants" describes as being situated outside the town at a distance of half an hour's walk. His account of the building itself is correct enough, but the illustration he gives is far from accurate. It omits the fourth compartment at the rear, and makes the structure too low in proportion to its length, while the drawing of the three headed *nagas* (which he miscalls *rachasi*) forming the balustrade of the front steps is extremely faulty. Further, it appears in the woodcut to be standing in an open space, whereas there is a loggia on the side of the enclosure from which he apparently has sketched it, as far as one can judge from the drawing. In fact the temple is scarcely visible from the point of view that he has chosen, as the intervening loggia allows only the roof to be seen. Another slight inaccuracy appears to be the statement that the door of the library is bolted, nor could the boxes in which the Mss. Scriptures are kept ever have been locked, as he says they were. Here, as at other temples, are to be seen a number of the palm (Borassus flabelli-formis), the leaves of which are commonly used as writing-materials for nearly all purposes by the Laos. In Siam it is chiefly utilized for copies of the sacred Buddhist books.

From the temple we walked out to the Phrabat, about half an hour's distance from the town on the road to Phrë, to which we had to pass through the gate through which we had entered on the evening of the 2nd January. On this side of the river lies the main portion of the town, bounded to the east by a long straight wall of red-brick, and north and south by a much shorter piece at right angles to it. As I said before, it is enclosed towards the river by a palisade of teak-logs split into four, so that the portion on the right bank where the vice-consulate stands must be regarded as a suburb, though probably at one time actually within the walls.

The building which encloses the phrabat is in the form of a Maltese cross, and was undergoing repairs when we saw it. The door-sill is formed of a slab of laterite, but the walls are of brick. This fact leads to the inference that the present temple stands on the foundations of a much earlier structure, dating possibly from the time when the ancestors of the modern Siamese still occupied this part of the country. On each side of the entrance steps is a balustrade formed by a Naga, either devouring or emitting from its mouth another, all modelled in chunam, with the exception of the glass eyes. Something in this style:

You see these creatures everywhere at the entrances of temples in Siam and Laos. The naga who is being swallowed has three heads, which fact explains the eye just below the creature's mouth.

I have not been able to draw this secondary head distinctly. The phrabat is a single foot-print about six feet long, incised in a block of stone standing four or five feet above the ground. At the heel end of the pedestal is a well-conceived bronze figure of a woman squeezing dry her long damp hair. Tradition says that a serpent having attacked the Buddha, in order to make a meal of him, a faithful female disciple wrung out of her thick tresses a flood of water which forced him to beat a retreat. At two annual festivals it is the custom to pour water into the footprint, which through an aperture in the heel flows over the woman's hair and so finds its way into the earth. The statue is admirably moulded, and one is inclined therefore to pronounce it old, on the ground that in the extreme east all modern works of art are inferior in style to the productions of the ancient artificers.

We rode hence on the excellent little ponies of the country to a Burmese temple at the base of a low hill not far off. It has a tin tea-caddy-like exterior, and resembles a copy on a small scale of a certain modern Burmese temple at Maulmein, whose roofs are covered with corrugated iron. On the top of a hill behind stands a *phra-chedi* commanding a fine view of the plain of Lakhon with the mountains which bound it to the south, west and north. Of the town nothing is visible but the wall, all else being hidden by trees, and interminable forests appeared to stretch in every direction, entirely concealing the rice fields that extended along the river banks, excepting those which lay just at our feet. Cultivation is dependent to a very great extent upon the irrigation canals and trenches which have been cut in former times, often of considerable length, and which, when in good order, distribute the waters of the Më Wang and other streams over a large surface. But the present chief does nothing for the people. They are there for his benefit, not he for theirs. To this view of a ruler's duties is mainly attributable the serious drought from which the country suffered in the rainy season in 1885. Thousands of the people were deprived of their sustenance, and not a few emigrated elsewhere in search of food, while of those who remained many had to support life on the bitter tubers of a species of Colocasia that grows wild in the recesses of the mountains.

This evening I sent to the Chief by the hands of a servant a trifling present, consisting of a carpet, a mirror and a box of English scents from Piesse and Lubin. No message of any kind came back in return. The Chief had stared at them, appearing to wonder what in the world they meant, reported the servant. In the matter of good manners the Laos are no better than savages.

5 January. In the neighbourhood of Lakhon are two celebrated sacred fanes, Thât Sadet and Thât Lampang, neither of which have yet been examined by foreigners. As I had only time for one excursion, I chose the latter. It was a cold morning, the thermometer at seven o'clock standing at 51°. We left on horseback at half past eight by the south gate, and rode for some distance along the left bank of the river, sometimes in the shade of the lofty forest, now close to the stream over ground that had once been rice-fields, but is now abandoned owing to the encroachments of the current in flood-time. The route we followed is the main road to Rahëng, broad and one would say well kept, were it not well known that no trouble whatever is expended on the lines of communication in this country. Nature and the ordinary traffic are left to themselves, and the result of their joint action is a good or bad road according to the character of the soil.

After cutting off a large bend, we came back to the river about eleven o'clock, and having forded it, struck across the blazing white surface of dry rice-fields to Lampang, which we reached at twenty minutes to twelve. The temple stands on a slight eminence, and occupies a large area surrounded on all sides by a closed loggia. In the centre of the front is a highly decorated gateway of brick and chunam surmounted by a blunt pyramidal roof in five stages, which reminds one of the style represented in the engravings and photographs of the famous Angkor Wat. A pair of gigantic *rachasi*, which represent the Siamese idea of a lion, guarded the approach to the entrance, and the balustrade on each side of the steps was adorned by a pair of *nagas*, one having its head at the bottom, and its body lying along the top of the wall, while the head of the other was halfway down, with its body forming the base of the balustrade. Brick and chunam were the only materials used in their construction. The main building consists of a nave and side aisles, the pillars of the former being of stone with a covering of lacquer, and octagonal in shape, while those of the aisles are quadrangular. There are no walls, but the end gables are filled in with highly ornamented wooden panelling. At the further end of the nave rises a lofty and well-designed shrine of brick and stucco, containing a gilded Buddha in a sitting posture. The altar was covered with multitudinous smaller images, a few of which were of ivory in an advanced stage of decay, others of reddish slate, but most of them were of gilded wood. Behind the shrine stand four or five erect tablets of a dark slaty stone, about two and a half feet high, inscribed with characters not easily decipherable to persons who are acquainted only with the ordinary Siamese script. Opinion seems to be divided on the question whether they are merely a form of the Lao alphabet or ancient Siamese, but perhaps the latter view is the safer.

In the rear of the main building rises a lofty *phra-chedi*, consisting of a series of varying geometrical forms - square, circular, octagonal - built entirely of brick and covered with gilt plates of copper, some quite plain, others embossed with a design resembling the Japanese 'wheel' of the law, called chakra in Sanskrit. Underneath this *phra-chedi* is said to be buried a hair of the Buddha contained in a golden reliquary, shaped like a fir-cone, a copy of which, deposited in a hollow on the back of a wooden *rachasi*, is to be seen behind the large shrine in the principal building. A good bronze railing surrounds the base, bearing pear-shaped finials, and outside this again comes a row of standard lanterns in stuccoed brick, placed at regular intervals. Right and left of the *phra-chedi* are two smaller chapels, each with its principal image of the Buddha, and countless smaller ones in wood, bronze, stone and ivory. On an elevated platform behind stands a cubical building, crowned with a double pyramidal roof, which forms the shrine of a 'foot-print of the Buddha', but this relic is not visible to the eye. A somewhat ludicrous object was a statuette of Phra Sakachai, fat-bellied and ugly, who reminds one of the Japanese god Hotei. The legend goes that he was originally a man of great personal beauty, who being consequently often mistaken for the Buddha, changed his form to what we now see in order to avoid the guilt of sacrilege. He is to be found in nearly every temple, but I recollect that the first image of him that I met with was at Phitsanulôk.

In an outer courtyard to which access is gained by a doorway on the western side of the loggia stands a gigantic *bo* tree (Ficus religiosa), which is said to have been brought from Ceylon when still a mere sapling. Its widespreading branches are supported by a large number of poles bearing a two pronged fork at the end, many of which are so highly decorated with gilding and colour that they have evidently been placed where they are as ex-votos. We walked round to the cells at the back, where we found a fat head-priest enjoying his dinner. At his right hand stood a long cylindrical basket full of glutinous rice, of which he took a lump from time to time, and having kneaded it with his fingers into a convenient form, dipped it into one of the numerous bowls of curry that stood before him on a low circular table. Archer put some questions to him about the temple and the mysterious tablets, which he was unable to answer, and we came to the conclusion that he found gluttony and ignorance to be the chief elements of happiness for a man of his order.

From the wall of this garden we had a fine view of the mountains to the south and west. To the extreme left rose a mass of mountains crowned by a lofty pinnacle, and then came the depression through which the river makes its exit from the plain of Lakhon. Further to the right stretched high ridges, in front of which stood two sharply pointed conical hills that might be taken for volcanoes were not the general geological characteristics of the country utterly adverse to such an assumption. The whole plain in front of the temple was covered with dense forest, presenting for the most part a brownish appearance, for even in the tropics the deciduous trees are in the majority, and this colour extended up to the tops of the surrounding ranges, though tempered by a bluish haze which increased with the distance. Here and there a clump of dammar oil trees reared its crest above the general level of the forest. Not a cloud was visible in the burning sky, and no water varied the parched aspect of the vast plain. This long dry winter is the perpetual obstacle which nature has opposed to the peopling of the north of Siam on a large scale, for even with the aid of a well conceived system of irrigation it is doubtful whether the cultivable area could be increased to any important extent. During the summer on the other hand the heavy rains and consequent floods interpose equally insurmountable difficulties in the way of agriculture.

On returning home our ponies were more willing than we had found them in the morning, and we got back to the Vice-Consulate in two hours and a half.

In the evening I received the return visit of the Chief. He was escorted by a band of drummers and fiddlers, who made themselves heard in the distance at least ten minutes before they entered our gate. He brought presents of velvet mattresses, square pillows adorned with strips of Chinese brocade, cotton blankets such as these people wear during the cold of morning and evening, silk *pha-nung* (petticoats), together with a pig's head and feet. I received him in the open-air room which has been already mentioned, and gave him Chinese tea to drink. The same ceremony which we had undergone at Phrë by way of protection against the perils of jungle travelling was then performed, but much more expeditiously than on the former occasion. The chief tied the cotton thread round my left wrist only instead of on both, while muttering the exorcism, and the 'Doctor's' part was much abbreviated. The vases of flowers and a part of the presents were lifted up, in order that I might touch them in token of acceptance, which was a slight departure from the form observed at Phrë. I think pressure had been put on him by Luang Suriya, and that otherwise he would never have come near me. But he brought me a lump of iron, from the mines at either Mu'ang Ta or Mu'ang Long in the southeast portion of his territory, and I gave him in return a majolica flowerpot to use as a spittoon, with which he seemed much pleased. He did not remain more than an hour, and was evidently glad to get away.

6 January. The thermometer this morning at 7 o'clock again marked 51°. It was intensely cold, and the bath was a fearful pleasure. But as soon as the sun had dispersed the mists which hung over the river, the air became warm; a pith helmet and an umbrella seemed necessary means of protection against a 'coup de soleil'. After breakfast I got myself ferried across the river with Luang Suriya, and we went for a walk through the bazaar, where there are a few shops kept by Chinamen and by Lao women. Petticoat stuffs, cotton yarns, lucifer matches and scents were the chief foreign goods exposed for sale. Turning a corner we found ourselves at the southern end of the main street, which we traversed as far as the *sala klang*, where my friend Luang Thoranen has taken up his quarters. This is the building where Mr Bock installed himself, as he relates in the book I have referred to more than once, against the wishes of the local authorities. His imprudence in striking a Lao Phya was probably the cause of his subsequent difficulties with the people of Chiengmai and Muang Fang. How far the objections made to his carrying off Buddhist idols from the latter place were due to the word having been passed on from Lakhon, or to genuine religious objections on the part of the inhabitants, it might be difficult to say. The Siamese have no scruples about appropriating broken images from a ruined temple, but they dislike such articles passing into the possession of a foreigner, who owing to the difference of religion would be unlikely to treat them with due respect. Most of us would object to an engraving of, say the Sistine Madonna, being hung up as an ornament in the house of a Siamese 'globe-trotter', or his using an old silver chalice as a tea-pot. The Siamese it is said do not approve of Buddhist images being sold to the foreigners resident in Bangkok, even when they have never been dedicated by being enshrined in some temple. If an European, consequently, happens to acquire any article of this sort he should keep the fact to himself, out of mere tenderness to the scruples of the natives, even when he does not respect such a weakness.

But to return to the *Sala Klang* of Lakhon. I was extremely glad to find that Mr Bock's account of the contrivance for measuring time by means of a brass cup floating in a basin of water turned out to be correct, for I had already detected so many small inaccuracies in his book that I had begun to think that he was incapable of describing anything with exactness. But after some reflection I am inclined to believe that he must have trusted too much to his memory, and too little to his notebook. At the back of the *Sala Klang*, by the horologe in question, were kept the records of the court, consisting of a number of dusty old strips of palm-leaf, tied up in coils by twos and threes. It is to be hoped that the clerks are never called upon to refer to these documents, as they do not seem to be kept in any order, and are exposed to being carried off by any one who might wish to destroy the proof of a transaction passed before the judges.

Resisting Luang Thoranen's bland invitation to come in and have a talk, I finished my peregrination through the town, and came to the conclusion that its population must be small. As at Phrë, each house stands in its own garden, embowered among trees, and there are no rows of shops, except in the bazaar. A country village surrounded by walls, and containing within its limits a disproportionate number of temples, is the impression it leaves on one's mind. Now and then you meet a few elephants stalking along in massive grandeur. I was much struck with a baby elephant with very thin legs and a shambling gait, which I was informed had come into the world on the previous evening. It seemed a great deal too big for the facts, but these were no doubt correctly represented.

Another pleasing sight was afforded by the kitchen-gardens which occupy part of the river bed. As soon as the water begins to fall towards the beginning of winter and sand-banks appear above the surface, the latter are divided off and carefully fenced with bamboo sticks, interlaced with thorn-bushes as a protection against the noses of too inquisitive cattle, who might take a fancy to the garlic, beans and mustard which are the principal vegetables cultivated. The women have exclusive charge of these little patches of garden; it was a curious sight to see them watering their young crops by pouring water from a bucket over a long openwork basket held in the left hand, the object of which is to distribute the stream. Such an idea as that of a watering-pot provided with a rose seems not to have made its way here as yet, but one need not wonder at that in a country where almost the only known mechanical contrivance is a loom of the very simplest construction. The women struck one as being very free in their manners, for they chaffed our elephant drivers, who were mostly complete strangers, as if they had been intimate acquaintances since their childhood. One hears an indifferent account of their morals, which is perhaps not to be wondered at in a country where the female sex apparently is allowed equal rights with the other portion of mankind. They simply claim and exercise the privileges which in most other countries are confined to the men, with a result that may be recommended to the attention of some of our more advanced social reformers.

There is a local coinage of the same kind as at Phrë, having a mark stamped on the upper edge which is supposed to represent an elephant, but the outlines are so indistinct that it might be anything else. The medium of commercial transactions, as elsewhere in the Lao States, is nevertheless the Indian rupee. In the afternoon we all went to the pagoda on the hill above the Burmese village of Ban Pakham to drink tea and take bearings of the mountains round the border of the plain. Unluckily the man who came with us to give the names of the various peaks turned out to know only one, namely Doi Luang on the east of the town, and that we had already learnt. The only resource in such matters, as I have found elsewhere, is to climb each mountain separately in the company of some one who lives at its foot. Then you learn its name and position, and can recognize it afterwards from other points. To many of the peaks in the Lao States a surveyor would nevertheless be obliged to give names of his own invention, as to the natives nearly every mountain is a Doi Luang (Big Hill), or else is called after the nearest village.

Dr and Mrs Peoples who reside here deserve grateful mention. They are missionaries belonging to the American Board of Commissioners of Foreign Missions, or as it is more shortly known in Siam, the A.B.C.F.M. Young and energetic, they have taken up their abode in Lakhon, three days distance from their colleagues in Chiengmai, and on the average two months from Bangkok. The chief is friendly, and has given them a plot of ground some quarter of a mile below the Vice-Consulate where they are about to build a comfortable house. In addition to his spiritual office, Dr Peoples exercises the profession of a physician, and it may safely be prophesied that for the present he will have more calls for the cure of bodies than of souls. He has only three Christian converts to look after, and these are not of his own making. Consequently he has to occupy his spare time as best he can with cycling on very bad roads, riding and shooting. He is superior to most of his class, and very much of a gentleman. As a rule Christianity does not make much progress either in Siam or among the Laos, but to the American missionaries is due the spread of the English language and what few elementary notions of European civilisation have as yet found their way into the minds of the natives. They war constantly against ignorance, superstition and oppression, and for their efforts in these directions they deserve the respect of every candid man. Of course they are not liked, for the reason that they have not been able to lower their standard of conduct to the local level.

PART 5

LAKHON TO LAMPHUN AND CHIENGMAI

January 7. Lakhon is so picturesque, and the mountains invite one so vociferously to go and ascend them, that I would willingly have given some more time to exploring the neighbourhood, but nearly six weeks had already passed since we left Bangkok, and the journey, which according to the original estimate was to have been accomplished in three, remained still uncompleted. So I resolved with regret to quit this abode of primitive society, and make my way to Chiengmai without more delay.

The chief, it is pretty certain, was not sorry to get rid of me, for besides having to furnish me with riding ponies during my stay, he had to comply with all sorts of requisitions made in my name, but on their own behalf, by the two Luangs. That is one of the unpleasant facts in connection with travelling in Siam of which a foreigner must not lose sight. He may resolve to hire elephants, boats and horses with his own money, and to pay for the poultry and vegetables required by his cook. But he will be very sharp indeed if he ensures that the money gets into the right hands. If he entrusts it to one of his native followers to pay out, or to an official attached to him by the Siamese government, he may be certain it will go no further, and the unfortunate peasant whose animals or labour have been taken will get nothing. The chief of course loses little, for the supplies he sends are seized from the people without payment, but he hates having to fetch his elephants in from the jungle, or to divert them from more profitable employment for the benefit of the foreigner. Having found that the Luangs had ordered half a dozen elephants for themselves, saying that I wanted them, I promptly sent to tell the chief that I already had all I required, but as the message was carried by Noi Sinkâ, our head mahout from Chiengmai, in all probability it never reached him. Of Luang Thoranen I saw no more until a few days after I got to Chiengmai, as he carefully remained far behind, and he no doubt travelled with as many elephants as he considered consonant with the dignity of a Special Commissioner of the King of Siam. I could tell a good deal more about the exactions of these gentry, but will refrain, as after all it would be merely hearsay, and all is not true which is repeated from mouth to mouth.

The thermometer's record was the same as yesterday, namely 51° at seven o'clock. We got away at a quarter past eight, calling at Dr. Peoples' as we went past, to see a curious creature called a loris (*ling lom*); this is a slothful gray animal rather bigger than a cat, having large prominent eyes placed very close together, and a dark streak down its back; it prefers to live in almost complete darkness, and is said to be very tame.

Our road followed the right bank of the river for a short distance, and then turned westward. It was much intersected by small irrigation canals, which at this season were completely dry. Passing by a shallow lake in the midst of the woods, we came after an hour's ride to the Më Tui, which had dwindled to a slender thread of water amongst extensive sand-banks. From here to Hangsat, which we reached at half past eleven, paddy-fields extended on both sides of the road. During the wet season, when they are more or less under water, the route followed by travellers from Lakhon to Lamphun makes a wide detour through the woods, as I learnt from Dr. Peoples. On the way we crossed a tiny stream flowing away to our left called the Më Hao, which apparently is entirely absorbed by irrigation, instead of falling into the Më Wang, as it ought to do. At Hangsat there is the Më Tan, a tributary of the Më Yao, which falls into the Më Wang, south of Lampang. Its source is near that of the Më San, which we shall come to later on today, and to that of the Më Ta, which we shall reach tomorrow after crossing the watershed. The Hangsat *sala* was built about ten or twelve years ago, entirely of wood, and without a single nail. There is not a trace of either saw or plane having been employed in its construction, the planks in the floor and the very shingles with which it is roofed having been smoothed with the adze. It seems scarcely credible that the use of civilised tools which have long been known to the Chinese, and for many years now to the Siamese, should not have found its way up to the Lao states, and this strange fact may be taken as typical of the utter indifference of the natives to anything in the way of material progress. Perhaps we ought to envy such a state of mind rather than to wonder at it, for some of the latest of modern philosophers seem to say that Europe is on the wrong road to the ultimate end of existence. A condition of entire satisfaction with things as they are, it appears, would, if we could attain to it, make us truly happy. I hope for my part that they are labouring under an error, and that we have not so totally mistaken the problem before us.

A Lao *sala* is generally a solidly constructed building, superior in that respect at least to what the traveller has to put up with in Siam, but it has two grave defects, namely that it is walled in on two sides, and the eaves project so far that you cannot see out, even when you squat on the floor. Add to this that the droppings of elephants and cattle are left to accumulate at will in the immediate vicinity, and you can understand that as a rule European travellers prefer to use tents in spite of the additional weight which the elephants have to carry and the trouble of pitching them at night and shifting them in the morning, to say nothing of the discomfort of having to do this in pouring rain if your business makes you take to the road in summer.

The elephants took a considerable time to overtake us, and the great heat of the midday sun was provocative of a nap after lunch, so that we did not leave this unattractive resting-place until half past two. Passing over some rice fields and across a long stretch of scrubby forest, a little after three o'clock we forded a dribbling streamlet, and rose on to the undulating sandy soil of an open forest of lofty trees. Here the road had been widened by cutting down the trees close to the ground for the passage of a brother of the King, who had travelled from Chiengmai to Lakhon the previous year. * The trunks were still lying rotting by the wayside. Many of them were of the species known as *mai tung* by the Laos, and *teng-rang* by the Siamese, from which a kind of resin is obtained in great abundance, to be used for rendering baskets watertight and so converting them into buckets. At a quarter to four we left this tract of woodland, and descended into the bed of the Më San, at a spot called Pak-Kong Nai (mouth of the creek). For more than an hour we followed its course, crossing it frequently from side to side and cutting off the sharpest bends. Here and there it flowed along in a slender rivulet, losing itself under the sand in the intervals, but good clear water can always be obtained by digging a small hole in the riverbed. Signs of cultivation were few, and of habitation none. At last we reached the *sala* of Pak-Kong, situated on a knoll to the left of the stream, but the elephants had to go back some distance for water and fodder. This place is the frontier station between the States of Lakhon and Lamphun,

* [See above, p. 69. Ed.]

and boasts of a small stockade, where a rabble of frontier guards were stationed to collect the dues said to be levied on the Shan traders. A few orchids were found growing on the trees round the *sala*, but they were mostly out of reach and our people did not care to climb for them. Chiengmai being famous for the number and beauty of the species to be found in the neighbouring woods, it seemed scarcely necessary to begin collecting at present.

January 8. Thermometer 51°. Height above the sea about 850 feet. We started at twenty minutes to eight, and descending the hill, soon came to a long grassy stretch by the side of the stream, intended by nature for a camping ground. On both sides rose steep hills covered with thick forest of no great height. After following the stream for about an hour, we ascended a steep hill which we at first took to be the watershed, the barometer showing a height of 1440 feet, but to the right there was a wide opening through which the Më San descends from its source, and we had still another streamlet to cross. Just here we met a caravan of Shan traders with a number of pack-cattle. They were one and all armed with flint-lock muskets and long knives. Archer asked them some questions in good Siamese, but they laughed derisively, and pretended not to understand. It is rather a curious fact that the commerce of these parts should be carried on by Shans, but the probability is that the Laos are too much in the position of slaves to be able to move about at liberty from province to province, and would not be able to keep their profits to themselves. The Shans, as far as one can judge from their appearance and what is reported of them, are by far the most energetic section of the Thai race.

The prevailing formation of these hills appears to be granite. After crossing the streamlet, we ascended once more for about a quarter of an hour to a deep trench cut through the top of the hill, where the actual boundary between Lakhon and Lamphun is marked by a stake driven into the ground. Phi-pan-nam or 'spirit divide water' which is the name of this spot, corresponds very closely with the German term *Wasserscheide*. The height is about 1560 feet above the sea, and the thermometer marked 61° on the grass. We got there at ten minutes to ten, and rested for half an hour. The name is exactly descriptive of the spot, for the streamlet just spoken of terminated close to its eastern side, and on passing through the trench we found another trickling down through the brushwood on the right of the path. The descent was at first very rapid, over hard rock, and then, as the valley widened out, became more gradual. The forest was sparser, and most of the trees had shed their leaves, so that the hillside presented a wintry aspect. After crossing the stream a few times, we left it as it flowed away on our right, and soon found ourselves in a teak forest occupying a wide level tract of black soil. Here we met some Laos gathering the bark of a tree called *mëkok*, * which they mix with their rice, probably from motives of economy. They told us the distance to the Më Ta was about as far as a musket-shot could be heard, and as we walked for fully three quarters of an hour before reaching the stream, it was a natural conclusion that the ear of a Lao is more sensitive to sound than that of a European. Our way here seemed to lie due north by the compass. Just at noon we found ourselves on the left bank of the Më Ta, now dwindled to a rivulet scarcely four yards broad in the midst of a sandy bed a dozen times as wide. On the opposite side stand a few peasants' huts and two *salas*. Height above the sea about 950 feet.

Luang Suriya and Archer rode on ahead, the former intending to gain Lamphun the same evening, and the latter to please himself. Being rather fatigued by the morning's walk, I waited till a quarter to four for my elephant, whose motion though by no means comfortable is sometimes preferable to jogging along on a pony at a foot pace. I passed by some rice-fields into a wood, and being absorbed in a book, did not notice what was going on until I found myself near to the top of a very steep and stony hill. It was half past five when I reached the bottom on the other side, where I had hoped to find a *sala*, but we had still a long and wearisome tramp to perform along a straight path through the forest, past low hills on the left and then through a village before reaching the halting-place for the night. The grass was burning here and there on both sides of the way, and I expected every moment that my elephant would take to her heels. I may note here that Mr. Carl Bock is entirely wrong in stating that it is considered *infra dig.* to ride a female elephant. It is true that the males are used on state occasions, because they are as a rule taller and more imposing, but the chief of Chiengmai himself, a very proud and haughty man, prefers a female for comfort, and I may also add that his description of the pass between Lakhon and

* [*mai-kok*? Ed.]

Lamphun is ridiculously exaggerated, where he says (p. 192) that his road lay along the edge of a precipice, "some two hundred feet deep, down which a single false step of our trusty elephants would have pre-cipitated us into a tangled mass of trees, creepers, and great boulders." All this sounds very alarming, but the fact is that the elephant is fa-mous for its cautious surefootedness, and there are no precipices at the spot referred to, so that if Mr. Bock had managed to tumble out of his howdah, he could not have fallen anywhere over a bank more than twenty feet high.

I found myself at a quarter past seven at the *sala* of Ban Kohkrë, having been in total darkness for the past hour and a half. Some of the baggage elephants had already arrived, but of the rest there were as yet no signs. I made an unsuccessful attempt to induce some of our follow-ers to go out with torches to meet them, but such an article was no-where to be procured. At last my pious Siamese boatman started off with a lighted wax-taper, but the others were not to be moved. Amongst both Siamese and Laos the idea of helping others is entirely non-exist-ent. Whatever happens to your neighbour is the result of his conduct in a previous state of existence, and it would be impiety to interfere with the operation of the law of retribution; a most comfortable doctrine for a naturally selfish and indolent man.

January 9. Thermometer 50° this morning at 7 a.m. We got away at a later hour than usual, and turning a corner, reached in ten minutes the temple of Wat Kohkhrë, situated on a small isolated hill, and com-manding a fine view over the plain in which lie the towns of Lamphun and Chiengmai, surrounded on all sides by ranges of mountains. Far away N.W. by N. and almost hidden by the haze rose the massive Doi Su-thëp, at the foot of which Chiengmai is situated; a white *phra-chedi* was a conspicuous object halfway up its side. N.W. by W. glittered the golden pagoda of Lamphun, while on the opposite horizon about E.N.E. the conical summit of Doi Khamô attracted special attention. We sub-sequently ascended the latter, in the expectation of discovering it to be an extinct volcano. At Lakhon I was told that there was a lake at the summit, but already at Wat Kohkrë the lake had decreased, in the mouths of the inhabitants, to a pond. The mountain too had come nearer to Lamphun than at first reported, but was still declared to be a whole day's journey distant from the town. When we eventually came to visit it, both facts diminished still further, as you will read later on. The pass from Lakhon was not visible, but was supposed by the local people to lie S.E. by E. Doi Padang, the steep rocky mountain on the further side of which runs the Më Ta, lay S. by E.

The temple is of no great size, but having been recently repaired, impresses the spectators rather favourably. The eastern gable is richly adorned with the tinsel of glazed lead so common in these parts, which produces a splendid effect of colour when lit up by the morning sun. Outside runs a frieze decorated with figures of Buddhist monks walking in procession, drawn in the true mediaeval style, with the feet represented thus while the body and face front the spectator; costume a red cloak and black cap, the begging-bowl in  the right hand and in the left a round fan of palm-leaf. A loggia opening inwards surrounds the courtyard. This temple is evidently an old building reconstructed from its foundations. Fragments of laterite lie scattered about, and the flight of steps leading up to the main entrance is of the same stone. A long unfinished double wall extends from the base of the hill to the bottom of the steps, the copings of which are formed of a succession of Nagas, each with his tail in the mouth of the succeeding one.

Leaving Wat Khokhrë at a quarter to ten, we regained our saddles, and trotted along a straight causeway raised above the rice-fields, until we met the Phya Ammat and some other officials who had come halfway from the town to welcome me. This road, the first of its kind we had met with in the Lao states, runs right across the plain as if intending to strike the southern end of the town, but on nearing it makes a sudden bend to the right, and enters the eastern gate by a wooden bridge over the Më Kwang. This also is the first structure of its kind, other than the foreign-built bridges of Bangkok, that I have encountered in Siam. We now reduced our pace to a walk, and preceded by the officials just mentioned, arrived about half past ten o'clock at a house on the hither side of the bridge, which had formerly been the residence of the chief of Chiengrai. The prospect which presented itself as we came up nearer the bridge was extremely fine. Among a number of tall cocoanut palms, with the blue sky for a background, appeared the tall tinselled gable of the Wat Luang or Royal Temple, and the gilded pinnacle of the great *phra-chedi*. At their feet stood a lofty pyramidal gateway of slender outline, covered with fantastic ornaments moulded in white chunam, which blazed dazzlingly in the glaring sunshine, and a little to one side rose the brilliantly white roof of another sacred building. The regularly embattled red brick city wall, the city gate, the almost dry bed of the river, and the somewhat ricketty bridge formed the foreground to this truly oriental picture, which recalled to mind the scenes on the southern and eastern shores of the Mediterranean by which many an artist has made his reputation. Nothing I have seen in Siam is better worth remembering.

Shortly after my arrival I received a visit from the Chao Buriratana and two sons of the chief, Chao Racchaput and Phya Chai-Songkram. The first named is either a cousin or an uncle of the chief, who is his junior by three years. He told us the following story of the foundation of the pagoda. A certain hermit having begun to dig a hole in the ground for a domestic purpose that need not be mentioned, was suddenly attacked by a flock of crows and forced to desist from his purpose. Unable to conjecture the cause of their unprovoked attack, he consulted a learned monk, who advised him to bring up a child and a young crow together. In a few years they were able to converse, and the crow then revealed to the child the existence of some relics of the Buddha at the spot where the hermit had originally dug. Search was consequently made, and the relics were discovered in a small golden *phra-chedi*, over which the present pagoda was subsequently erected. The walls of the city, he said, were already in existence when the founder of the existing line of Chiefs of Lamphun migrated hither from Lakhon about a century ago, and are supposed to have been built by the Burmese invaders. It is the custom to repair them on the accession of a new chief.

In the afternoon I visited the Wat Luang, or Wat Phra-thât, as it is also called. The gateway of brick and chunam turns out to be less interesting than it looks when seen from a distance. Outside stand two huge *rachasi* of stuccoed brick painted a bright red. The *wihan* is a large building entirely restored within the last four years, and is consequently very spick and span. Unlike most other Lao temples, it has only a single long roof running from west to east, instead of the usual four roofs of different altitudes. The roof is supported by tall cylindrical columns with a stencilled pattern in gold upon a red ground, the beams and rafters of both aisles and nave being decorated in the same manner, which produces a gorgeous effect. Of the Buddha's image there is little to be said; it struck me as perfectly commonplace. Outside on the north side of the *wihan*, hangs in a sort of gallows a massive circular flat gong seven feet in diameter, bearing an incised inscription in what appears to be old Siamese writing. It is probably antique, as portions of the inscription are worn away or otherwise damaged so as to be illegible.

Mr. Bock's description of the *phra-chedi* or pagoda is so far accurate that there is little to be added. But it should be noted that its base at least is evidently constructed of laterite supposed to have been procured from the neighbourhood of Doi Khamô, and that the whole structure is covered with copper plates gilded with leaf-gold. These are in a bad state of repair, and many of them seem ready to peel off under the influence of wind and rain. The number of shrines in the shape of an ancient junk, with high prow and stern, covered with gilt embossed plates, is two, not one, as he reports. They are said to be models of the reliquary buried underneath the *phra-chedi*. On the south side, outside the bronze paling, stands an ancient drum-shaped bronze lantern of pierced work, about eleven inches high and a foot in diameter, the central portion being filled with figures of *Thepha-phanom* (angels) and tracery, between two rows of small figures representing elephants. It stands on a stuccoed pillar, the core of which is probably laterite. Further off, on the south of the *wihan*, rises a circular pedestal bearing a bronze model of Mount Meru, about six feet in diameter and four feet high. In addition to these, mention should be made of the *Hô-tam* or Library of sacred books, also on the south of the *wihan*, of stuccoed brick, and of a square building on its north side having a pyramidal roof in five sections similar to that of Wat Phra Yuen at Thung-yâng, of which a sketch has already been given, but of smaller dimensions. It contains a sitting Buddha. A loggia surrounds the enclosure with the remains of towers at each corner. To the north of Wat Phra-thât are some ruined temples of brick and chunam, which present no points of interest. We passed through the bazaar and out by the north gate of the city, which is faced waith slabs of laterite, and walked round the moat to the west gate, in front of which is a fort or demi-lune closely resembling those which defend the gates of Peking. The rice-fields extend close up to the city on this side, and are irrigated by canals communicating with the Më Ping, several miles away. The territory of Lamphun extends north wards about half-way to Chiengmai, and on the west as far as the left bank of the Më Ping. Longstanding disputes exist between the two states as to the ownership of certain portions of territory further down this river.

A very striking characteristic of the landscape is a large tree with papilionaceous flowers of a brilliant red, which in some lights looks almost vermilion. Its name is *mai kwao*, probably the Butea frondosa of botanists. The Siamese call it *ton thong*. It is common throughout the western Lao states and in the upper part of the Më Ping valley, and at this season was in full blossom.

As at Phrë and Lakhon a certain quantity of rice, both ordinary and glutinous, was sent to me as a present from the chief, the latter of which was at once made over to the Lao elephant-drivers, who prefer it to the other kind. Poultry and pork were also presented by various people. There is no means of rejecting these gifts, objectionable as they are, without offending the givers.

January 10. Shortly after breakfast I went into the town to pay a visit of ceremony to the chief. He is a hale and hearty old man of sixty, abounding in talk and bonhomie, which doubtless serves to cover a wily character. I was accompanied by Gould, our Vice-Consul at Chiengmai (now promoted to be Consul at Bangkok). There are very few British subjects in the state of Lamphun, and there was only one complaint pending about a piece of land that a son or other relative of the chief's seemed to have wrongfully taken away from one of our people. The conversation was as usual on these occasions limited to generalities. Carving wooden hilts for knives seems to be the favourite occupation of the old man. He has recently built himself a new house of teak, and the room in which he received us was as much superior to the audience hall of the Lakhon chief, as that in its turn was superior to the den in which the chief of Phrë is accustomed to welcome his visitors. He returned my call about an hour later, arriving with a very small retinue, and riding on a square wooden seat supported on a couple of poles carried by four men. An enormous red umbrella was borne behind him. My Japanese servant, who was dressed in his national costume, greatly excited his interest, and he was much perplexed on learning that Gould, Archer, and myself were all unmarried. My stock of presents having been almost exhausted by gifts at Phrë and Lakhon, all I could offer him was a satin parasol, with which he nevertheless seemed to be much pleased.

After an early lunch we started on horseback for Doi Khamô, accompanied by Luang Suriya, the baggage having been despatched ahead on elephants. The information we had obtained about the road was so very contradictory, that I had come to the conclusion to allow a day and a half for the excursion, and after passing the night as near as possible to the base of the mountain, to ascend it on the following morning and return afterwards to Lamphun. But on arriving at a village situated about half-way, we saw that it would probably be feasible to make the ascent that afternoon. It took us ten minutes less than two hours to reach Wat Ban Salëng, a temple at the nearest village, whence we rode on over open grassy glades and through woods to the foot of the mountain. Here we found huge masses of laterite *in situ*, but saw no signs of the stone having been worked in recent times. It took me thirty-five minutes to reach the top, and I estimated the result of the barometrical readings to give a difference of 1100 feet between the base and the summit. The guide who was with me evidently was much impressed by reverence for the spirit of the mountain, who was not accustomed to be visited except at one or two fixed dates during the season. He had been with great difficulty persuaded to accompany us, and now, on our arriving at a small cairn about half-way up, he presented some flowers to the invisible deity, devoutly muttering what sounded like an exorcism in Pali, before he ventured to proceed further.

Doi Khamô is certainly not volcanic, although its outline is that of a cone with extremely steep sides, but it possesses at the top an irregularly circular cavity about twenty feet deep, which is half full of water. This is supposed to have been created by the mere pressure of the Buddha's thumb. All the sacred foot-marks one meets with show that he is supposed to have been of from six to eight times the stature of an ordinary man, but this estimate would not allow him quite so large a thumb as this story requires. There are traces of a temple having once existed here. The view extends over the whole of the vast plain away north of Chiengmai and south of Lamphun, but the atmosphere was so much obscured by the smoke of burning rice straw, that even the gilded pagoda of Lamphun was invisible, though probably not more than ten or twelve miles distant in a direct line. Nor could anything be seen of the city of Chiengmai. In a westerly direction rose chain after chain of mountains, beyond the furthest of which lay the valley of Mu'ang Yuom, famous for its teak-forests, which are worked chiefly by Burmese British subjects, who have transmuted the native name into Mainloongyee. Doi Su-thëp loomed out almost due north-west by the compass, while further again north rose the jagged mass which takes the name of Doi Chiengdao from the village nearest to its foot. Mr. Hallett, * who passed close to it estimated its height at 7000 feet, and if this be correct, Doi Chiengdao is probably the highest mountain in Siamese territory. Behind, on the east, a deep valley separates Doi Khamô from an irregular assemblage of wooded mountains not much superior in height.

We descended in five and twenty minutes, and rode back to the temple at Ban Salëng, arriving there a little after dark. The baggage elephants were there already and our goods and chattels had been installed in the *wihan*. Where there is no decent *sala* it seems to be considered a matter of course that the traveller should sleep in front of the Buddha's altar. Luang Suriya, who was rather fatigued with this, doubtless his first experience in mountain climbing, nevertheless returned at once to Lamphun, to make the necessary arrangements for our continuing the journey to Chiengmai on the morrow. We got some bundles of straw that were lying in a shed to spread on the floor under our mattresses, and went to bed with the calm consciousness of having shown the Laos that we could, compared with them, practically annihilate time.

January 11. At 6 a.m. the thermometer marked 56°. We packed up and started on our way back to Lamphun at a quarter past seven. Just

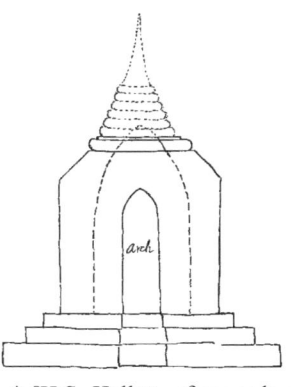

before reaching the town we turned aside to visit Wat Phra-yuen, remarkable for a half ruined quadrangular building behind the *wihan*. It stands on a platform raised several steps above the ground, and has massive brick walls, pierced with lofty arches. The eastern arch had been bricked up at some period subsequent to the first erection of the building, and an erect figure of the Buddha built against the wall. The upper portion of the outer wall was bevelled off, so as to form the

* [H.S. Hallett, afterwards author of *A Thousand Miles on an Elephant* (Edinburgh, 1890). Ed.]

lower portion of a pyramid, and above that a series of concentric circles had probably been raised one above the other, terminating in a pinnacle. In the accompanying attempt at an elevation of one side the dotted lines represent what is imaginary, and the broken lines the curvature of the interior of the walls. The whole is built of brick, and consequently it does not belong to the earliest period of Thai architecture. We got back to Lamphun from Wat Ban Salëng in an hour and three-quarters, having walked our ponies the whole way: so much for the statement of the inhabitants that it would take a whole day to reach Doi Khamô.

We quitted Lamphun about two o'clock the same afternoon, taking a road to the left on leaving the north gate of the town. The distance to Chiengmai by the shortest way is said to be thirteen miles, more or less, but in the wet season, when the rice-fields become a huge swamp, travellers are forced to make a considerable circuit. The road is broad and fairly well-kept as far as the boundary of the two states. About an hour from Lamphun we alighted to seek refuge from the scorching heat under the spreading branches of a *bo* tree in front of a temple. The gable end of this building was effectively decorated with the usual tinsel disposed in a variety of patterns, but it was not otherwise remarkable. The taste of the Laos in such matters is extremely good, and a collection of coloured drawings of their gable decorations would be highly valuable. Inside the enclosure a number of small straw huts had been erected for the accommodation of bonzes from other monasteries who had assembled here for the performance of certain religious services. Some half hour's distance beyond this we got into what looked like the bed of an old river, partly occupied by a magnificent grove of tall dammar oil trees (*mai yang*, Dipterocarpus), the largest of which may be four feet in diameter or even more. Here is the boundary between the two states. Along a portion of this old bed an irrigation canal had been cut, but it was now completely dry. Arriving at a small hamlet some way further on, we found two young elephants undergoing a rather cruel kind of training. They had been tied fast with ropes to a strong framework of posts and beams, and were being prodded with a nail at the end of a stout stick to make them lift up their fore-feet in succession, a treatment which caused them to utter loud cries of pain and anger. This trick they are taught to perform in order to assist their rider in mounting and dismounting.

Our road, which had hitherto been straight, now began to bend gradually round to the left, and we found ourselves rapidly approaching Doi Su-thëp, which now appeared directly in our front. We then traversed an expanse of rice-field, where the trace utterly disappeared, and passing through a belt of woodland came out on to the left bank of the Më Ping not far below the Chiengmai Vice-Consulate, which stands on the opposite side of the river. But the water being too deep for our ponies to ford, we trotted up the path along the bank, past some comfortable-looking bungalows inhabited by American missionaries, crossed a rickety bridge into the eastern suburb, and rode down the other side over some disused rice-fields, reaching the house in about three hours riding from Lamphun. If we had pressed our animals we should have done it in a much shorter time. Poor Gould, who had contracted malaria and gets an attack of fever whenever he exposes himself to the sun, had dropped behind, refusing to have us stay by him till the fit should have spent its force. He came in about two hours later, having waited until he was overtaken by the elephants, when he found rest and quiet in a howdah. Such attacks are not dangerous, but they incapacitate a man for work while they last, and leave him in a rather 'washed-out' condition afterwards. In bad cases they may continue for two or three days, and travellers overtaken by the disease in the jungle during the wet season now and then die of it, as poor Mouhot did, but such instances are comparatively rare. * Quinine affords temporary relief, but a complete cure is unattainable except by change of climate. It is probably the same fever that people suffer in India, and, I am told, in parts of the United States. I contracted it somewhere on the journey, but it did not break out until the day I got back to Bangkok.

* [Henri Mouhot, *Travels in Siam, Cambodia and Laos 1858-1860*, (London, 1864). Ed.]

PART 6

CHIENGMAI

Within a few hours after my arrival I received a visit from the King's Chief Commissioner, Phya Montri by name, * a man of about forty, strongly built and with a pleasing countenance. During my stay, which lasted a whole month, I had occasion frequently to see him on business, but of that I shall say nothing in this journal. He good-naturedly offered to do anything in his power to render my sojourn agreeable, and afterwards fulfilled his promise in a way that proved his words to be more than a mere compliment. Of this official I shall always retain a most agreeable memory.

On the following morning a son of the chief and one of his nephews, the latter an extremely intelligent young fellow named Chao Landokmai, came to call, and after they were gone I went to return the Chief Commissioner's visit at his official residence, a large native building not far from the vice-consulate. Here I made the acquaintance of Phra Uphai, the principal judge of the Court established by the Treaty of 1883 for trying cases between British subjects and those of the King of Siam, among whom the Laos are naturally included. He turned out afterwards to be a very amusing fellow, full of legal stories, and I regretted very much to be unable to converse with him in his own language. In the afternoon I called on Dr. McGilvary and Mr. Martin, two American missionaries, the former of whom has been established here a long time, and on Dr. Cheek, who originally a medical missionary has now gone into the timber business. He speaks Lao like a native, and is a very cultivated man into the bargain. I took a great liking to him, which was increased by a four day tour we took together among the mountains, and we ultimately made the journey down the Më Ping to Bangkok in company.

I had now only to make the chief's acquaintance, which I did on the

* [Satow appears here, and in his original diary, to mis-spell this official's title consistently, and therefore deliberately, as Phya Monkri. His full title was Phya Montri Suriyawong (Cheun Bunnag), and in 1887 he was to transfer to London as Siamese Minister, with his brother, Luang Suriya (Koet Bunnag), as his assistant. Ed.]

following afternoon. He lives in a fine house built in semi-European style, and is a jolly-looking old fellow of sixty-seven, not without a certain measure of native cunning, but intensely ignorant. The furniture was European, and on the floor were spread a number of gaudy Brussels carpets. The conversation turned upon the obstruction to navigation caused by the rapids in the river on the southern boundary of his territory. He wculd not believe that dynamite could be used to destroy rocks. Small boulders could be removed, but the bigger ones-never. There is no doubt that he looks upon the rapids as a heaven-bestowed barrier against aggression from the south, and there can be little doubt that but for their existence the independence of the three Lao States would long ago have become a mere tradition. But someday a railway may be constructed up the Mënam valley, and then we shall witness the complete incorporation of Chiengmai with Siam.

On the next day he returned my call at the Vice-Consulate, arriving there in a sort of shabby victoria drawn by one pony. This is one of the two carriages that Chiengmai boasts of, and it is in constant use for official visits. On this occasion I puzzled the chief very much by asking the name of a tree we have in the Legation grounds at Bangkok, which tradition says was brought from Chiengmai by Sir Robert Schomburgk about twenty-five years ago. I described through the interpreter the flower and leaf, but he would not recognize it, and at last became quite angry at being asked what he evidently thought was a most foolish question. "Why" said he, "all trees have flowers, how should I know?" Then we got upon the subject of orchids, which seemed to interest him very much more. There are perhaps a hundred and fifty species found in the Chiengmai woods, and the women are very fond of wearing them as ornaments for their hair; the same practice is common in Burmah. Many of the better known species have their distinctive native names. There is one which is brought every year from Muang Yuom by the Lawas who inhabit the mountains, and presented to the chief as tribute. It has an insignificant greenish white flower, but is much esteemed for its fine odour, which the chief asserted could be recognized in the city while the tribute-bearers were still several miles off. But the specimens I saw had a very faint scent. I asked him what there was in his dominions particularly worth visiting. Well, there was an ancient temple at a place called Chorm-tong, distant about two days journey on elephants, that I ought certainly to see. I could take it on my way down to Bangkok.

Then there were some hot springs at the village of Ban Punkum, near
Doi Saket, some distance to the northeast. Until within a few years ago
the water used to leap into the air with a loud noise. Then I ought to
visit the pagoda halfway up Doi Su-thëp. I asked him about Doi Chiengdao. Well, the people used formerly to ascend it, but it is now
inaccessible. Did not know why, but the Laos could not go up any
longer. The *Phi* (Spirits) would prevent them.

Of all places in the world where an evening suit was unlikely to be
needed I thought Chiengmai was one of the most improbable. Great
was my horror then when I received a formal invitation to dine with
Phya Montri, and learnt that as the chief would be there, a tail-coat was
expected of me. Luckily I had a black morning coat amongst my baggage, and my host was induced to accept it as a substitute for the gar-
ment prescribed by our etiquette. He has a pleasant private residence in
the city, built of teak, and surrounded by a pretty garden. The drawing-
room and dining-room were completely furnished in simple European
style, and the dinner was provided by a Chinese cook. One of the best
dishes was Siamese curry, which I prefer to all others that I have tasted.
The predominant flavour is derived from lime peel, and it is very
pungent, owing to the free use of chilies, but there is nothing in the
world that comes up to it, not even the prawn curry of Ceylon. Phya
Montri is a man of taste, and his verandah was hung round with ferns
and orchids. He is fond of bric-a-brac, and had already collected some
fine Buddhist bronze statuettes, several of which were extremely ancient. His spittoons of silver repoussé work eighteen or twenty inches
in height were magnificent, and cigars were brought round in a gold
box such as the Chinese workmen of Canton are famous for.

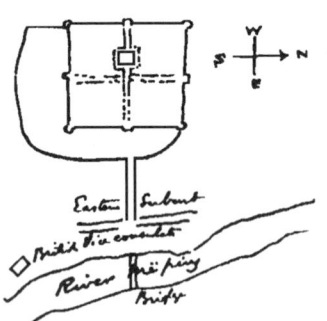

The city of Chiengmai covers a considerable area, and consists of two portions, the original city being square, enclosed by a high wall and a moat, round
two sides of which a more modern addition has been made. Being pretty busy
every day, I never could find time to ride
round it.

By far the most remarkable sight
which Chiengmai affords is the early
morning market. To this between two

and three thousand women flock in every day from the surrounding country, each bringing her small supply of goods for sale, and coming in some cases from long distances, even as far as from Lamphun itself. They line both sides of the road leading up to the outer western gate, the first part of the main street to the second gate and from the cross-roads in the centre of the city they spread right and left for a long distance. Their wares are laid out on mats spread on the ground, behind which they squat in little groups of twos and threes. No shouting or loud-voiced chaffering over sales, as is the case with the Siamese market-women in Bangkok. I have already described their dress and the manner of doing up their hair peculiar to the Lao women. Many of them wear a bunch of flowers at the back of the head. The stock-in-trade of a group seems to be of no great value; a few half dried chillies, some bundles of cut tobacco, three or four pieces of petticoat cloth, a pile of buffalo-hide wafers sprinkled with sesame seed, or a few pounds of pork would furnish out half a dozen of them. It is seldom that you see either fish or rice exposed for sale, and I have no idea where the people who deal in these principal articles of food are to be found. The only shops in the town are small booths which line the street between the first and second gates, and here you may buy English cotton goods, yarns, and lacquered boxes from Burmah. In the cross street outside, which runs northwards and parallel to the river, you can procure a few vegetables and miscellaneous European goods from Chinamen or their native wives. The shops inside the walls seem to be mostly in the hands of the Burmese men and women. There are two European stores outside the town, one kept by an Italian, the other by a German, the latter having his place of business on the left bank of the river. Rupees are the universal currency.

The city is laid out on the same principle as Phrë, Lakhon and Lamphun. You can hardly see the houses for the trees. Each dwelling stands in its own garden of fruit trees, including a fair proportion of areca palms. A Lao city is like an assemblage of rural suburbs turned outside-in and intersected by green lanes. The best theory is that the walls are intended solely as a refuge for the population of the province in time of war, and not as its usual place of habitation. The chief's palace is naturally inside, as are also the houses of his numerous relatives, many, if not most, of whom occupy official posts. Artizans of merit have no freedom. As soon as a man becomes noted for skill in silver repoussé work or the manufacture of lacquered boxes, he is over-whelmed with commands from the chief and his relations, who pay little or nothing for the labour they thus monopolize. Consequently anything like a healthy development of the natural artistic capacity of the people is not to be expected, and there are no shops where you can buy their productions. You must supply a silversmith with rupees, and wait your turn until he can find time to work it up into the cup or basin you require.

One morning I went out riding with Phya Montri, to visit an old temple in the centre of the town, and to inspect the process of lacquering. The Wat Phra Sing stands almost in the centre of the town, in a line with the eastern and western gates. The story goes that the principal image here enshrined was being carried, soon after its completion, across the town to be deposited in a temple that had been built to receive it on the opposite side, but on reaching this spot, apparently declined to proceed any further. No efforts of the porters were sufficient to move it a single inch beyond. They left it for the night, and next morning it was found with its face towards the street by which it had come. This was looked upon as an interposition of the Buddha himself, and no further attempt was made to resist his will. A temple was consequently built over the image, and the main street was deflected so as to pass round it. There are signs that laterite was largely employed in the original construction.

On entering the enclosure, the gateway of which is obstructed as is usual in the Lao states, by a solid log supported on two posts (some-thing like the wooden horse of a gymnasium), you see before you a low wooden building, the gable of which, fronting towards the entrance, is decorated with tinsel. Its uprights and cross beams are much out of line. It has the usual arrangement of several graduated roofs succeed-ing each other along its length, but the sides are enclosed by walls pierced for windows, which is not general. The doorway is guarded by two five-headed nagas in chunam. The pillars which support the roof are decorated with tinsel and stucco mouldings. This building is said to have been at one period the audience-hall of a chief; if so, it would seem to be a reasonable supposition that in earlier times the architec-ture of temples was the same as that of palaces. I was told that formerly it was the custom, on the death of a chief, to present his house to a temple. No doubt it had to be removed and re-erected in the temple grounds, otherwise the priests would in the course of ages have come to possess all the land in the city. Under the eaves were some excellent carved triangular wooden brackets, the upper part of which was occupied by one, two or three nagas, the involution of the serpents being cleverly managed, while the lower part was filled in with open work carving having a conventional design. This building is the *wihan*. Behind and at right angles to it stands a chapel containing an elaborately modelled brick and chunam shrine open on its four sides, having a sitting Buddha in the centre. The interior walls are decorated with paintings in monochrome depicting scenes in heaven and hell.

The third chapel, in which is enshrined the Phra Sing, has been but recently restored. Its exterior is decorated with heavily gilded carvings, while the interior walls are covered with paintings on plaster representing a variety of lively scenes both architectural and landscape. The precious image whose obstinacy led to the foundation of this temple is contained in a solid *dagoba*-like vaulted brick building in close connection with the chapel. This is entered from what is usually the seat of the Buddha's effigy in other sacred buildings, and is closed by an iron door. The walls and ceilings are thickly covered with gold leaf, as is also the image itself, which represents the Founder, sitting cross-legged with the left arm folded across the lap, while the right hand hangs over the knee. The countenance is more characteristic and individual than is usually the case with Buddhist images in Siam. On the base is an inscription in incised characters of the early type already mentioned as occurring at several temples, rendered almost indecipherable by the excess of gilding. The image, which is between three and four feet in height, reposes on a square pedestal of stuccoed brick, painted black. Its age was said to be about three centuries, but, in the absence of any trustworthy chronology amongst these people, it might be of any period previous to the resettlement of Chiengmai by the Lakhon princes. The superior type of face however is in itself an argument in favour of a considerable antiquity. Close by this chapel stands a ruined *phra-chedi* the base of which is surrounded by figures of elephants presenting the front towards the spectator, in style similar to one which exists at Sawankhalôk. To the right of the *wihan* just described is the *hô-tam*, or library of sacred books, a small but comparatively lofty building to which access is obtained by two flights of steps. Its lower story is adorned with life-size chunam figures of

Thepha-phanom or angels.

We also visited the residence of the late Uparat or heir-apparent. Part of the buildings have been pulled down since his death, but the principal one still remains. It is the largest house in Chiengmai, probably not even excepting the palace of the chief. Bands of carving in geometrical patterns run round both exterior and interior. The beams and side-brackets are all carved. Gigantic pillars of teak wood, smoothed with the native knife-sword, support the roof of the audience hall, and here, as elsewhere, the use of saw and plane seems to have been unknown at the date of its erection. At the further end of the hall, on feet modelled as elephants and tigers, stands a handsome wooden screen; its front has a peacock in low relief facing towards us with its tail spread, while other animals such as dogs and tigers, very small in proportion, play about its feet. Behind the screen is a doorway affording access to the other portion of the building, which is entirely without windows. At the near end of it stands a huge wooden cupboard several feet higher

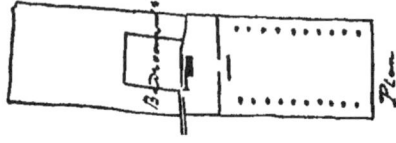

than the floor, which formed the state bedroom of the Uparat; being entirely covered in with planks, there was no provision for the admission of air or light. Its occupant must have felt it possible to sleep securely and soundly. This is said to be a normal style of construction for Lao bedrooms. The eaves of the roof, which come down very low and render the interior extremely obscure, are supported by wooden brackets carved in the form of the fabulous bird *Krut*, the Indian Garuda.

We rode along the southern street through the market, where women were engaged in cutting up and selling the carcases of pigs, and out by the Chiengmai gate to a village occupied by Chieng-tung Shans engaged in the lacquer manufacture. These people or their forefathers were taken prisoners in war, and in accordance with the custom of Indo-China were forced to migrate into the dominions of their conquerors. Men, not territory, are the prize of successful warfare in these countries. In appearance, costume and language they do not differ from the Laos, but their accent is said to be unlike that of the Lao inhabitants of Chiengmai.

The form of the lacquered articles produced by these people is ex-

clusively cylindrical or cup-shaped. The core is of fine bamboo basket-work, coated with lac, or with lac mixed with the ashes of straw.
When the lac is dry, the basket is turned on a very simple lathe, the
wheel of which revolves backwards and forwards, the principle of the
crank being apparently unknown. In place of the more scientific ap-
pliance, the workman uses a treadle, which turns the wheel one way,
and it is brought back in the opposite direction by a long bamboo which
acts as a spring. The tool employed for smoothing is a bent chisel,
sharpened at the end and sides of the bend. After the process of shaving
has once been performed, fresh lac is applied, and it is shaved again;
for the finest work this is repeated as many as twenty times. After
being turned, the surface is polished with a piece of fine-grained reddish
stone of a sandy texture. The natural colour of the lac when dried is
black. After the coating has reached a sufficient thickness, the required
design is drawn on it by means of an ordinary double-ended graving
tool, and lac coloured red with vermilion is rubbed into the pattern
thus obtained. Finally the completed article is polished by covering it
with a mixture of lac and vegetable oil; the polish is simply smeared
over with the finger and left to dry. The drying takes place on a shelf
closed by a curtain, and the vapour of water is not, as in Japan,
considered necessary. The lac is obtained from a tree which is certainly
not the Rhus vernicifera, and I am inclined to believe that the process
and the materials employed do not differ from those used in the similar
manufacture which is carried on in Burmah. For my own part, I
consider the Burmese article to be superior to what is produced in
Chiengmai. One of the workmen who was engaged on a cylindrical
box about eight inches diameter and three and a half inches high said
that he would receive a rupee and a half for his labour, but that the
completed article would fetch ten rupees in the bazaar. The designs
are drawn from memory, and consist mainly of conventional flowers
and leafage, with sometimes a bird introduced, the peacock appearing
to be a favourite.

I am sorry that I could not find time to visit the silver-smiths who live
in the same part of the city. Their work is of two sorts, incised and repoussé.
The latter is said to be produced by hammering on the outside of a thin
sheet of metal formed into the required shape and filled with rosin, and
the pattern is thus brought out by a process of indentation. But it will be
better not to accept this without reservation as a correct account.

On the **15th of January**, I dined with the chief, who had courteously allowed me to fix the hour. I chose seven o'clock, but as the word had previously been passed to the cook to have everything ready by six, we found all the dishes cold when we sat down, except the soup and Siamese curry. The other guests were Gould, Archer, the Siamese Commissioner, and Luang Suriya, the Judge of the International Court, and some younger members of the chief's family. We sat on chairs at a long table, arranged in the European style, and were provided with knives and forks. The natives eat with their fingers as a general rule, but this was a special occasion. Fried wafers of cow and of buffalo-hide were served with a sauce composed of fermented tea-leaves, pork fat, onions, and a fourth ingredient which I do not recollect. A pile of these wafers was placed between the chief and myself, and we dipped by turns into the same sauce-bowl. He was evidently pleased to find that I could eat them. You can offer no more delicate flattery to an oriental than to partake of his native food. Europeans, or at least Englishmen, generally turn up their noses and call it "beastly", which is undiplomatic conduct to say the least of it. Though rather greasy, these preparations of skin were not unpalatable, especially a spongy variety which was well toasted.

The conversation was heavy, until someone started the subject of Burma, and the chief's eyes glittered with delight as he called to mind how his people had pursued a Burmese pretender, who appeared in Chiengmai some years ago, and killed one or two of the impostor's followers. The old man would not believe that the British forces had taken Mandalay; the whole story was too incredible. As if any European could have conquered the great Kingdom of Burmah, which had been too much for the Laos themselves a hundred years ago, with so little difficulty. Moreover our own Burmese subjects in Chiengmai disbelieved the rumour. It had been invented in Chiengmai itself by the foreigner who sat in a hut at the end of a wire and pretended to be in communication with Bangkok. Everyone knew that it was impossible. After dinner we admired his collection of gold boxes and basins of repoussé work, kept in a series of glazed cupboards at the back of the room, many of them very large and heavy, and probably ancient. They are the handsomest things of the kind I have seen in Siam, and the intrinsic value of the mere metal must be several thousand pounds. His crown, a gift from the King of Siam, was also produced.

It is a pyramidal arrangement, like that of the King, only wanting (I was told) certain feathers, and is covered with small rubies and other precious stones.

Another day I rode out with the chief commissioner to the woods at the base of Doi Su-thëp in search of orchids. Passing through the town we issued from the Patu Suen-dok on its western side. This gate is named after a pleasure garden of the chiefs of Chiengmai situated about a mile from the walls, which has been allowed to run to waste. As we emerged from the gate, the great mountain, which had hitherto been concealed by trees, appeared close at hand, almost overhanging our heads. The road leads in the direction of a pagoda built half-way up the mountain side, and is broad and grassy as far as a small *sala*, where we branched away to the right across the now dry terraced rice-fields. At the edge of the wood we were met by a hale old man, who is the "governor" of the mountain, accompanied by four or five men carrying baskets to hold the plants we expected to collect. The path ascended over the sparsely wooded spurs, and wound along to a beautifully cool and romantic spot on the banks of a torrent called Huei Më-chang-khien. Here we found a white clematis, *dok niu*. Our luck was pretty good, and we succeeded in finding a dozen or more varieties of orchids, which seem to prefer trees that are more or less decrepit and decayed. One of these had a pretty white flower, touched with mauve and pink and giving forth a pleasant fragrance; it is not much admired by the Laos, who have given to it the name *dok-uang ki má*, which in English had such a malodorous sound that I will leave it untranslated. On our way back we crossed the fields in a different direction to the north-west angle of the city, and then along the north wall to the river side road. Some of the fields were being broken up for a winter-crop of rice.

One morning we received a summons to the chief's house to be present at the presentation of the tribute-orchids already mentioned. The ceremony took place in the audience hall. We all sat on chairs ranged in a semi-circle, the chief wearing his everyday dress. The Lawas from Mu'ang Yuom were introduced by an old Lao who has served under seven successive chiefs of Chiengmai. They brought with them a tazza full of amaranths, which this old man handed to the chief, repeating first a long exorcism, during which the chief held up his hands as if in prayer. Next, a long joint of bamboo full of arrow poison and a few skeins of cotton yarn were offered to him. Then a small stone mortar full of pounded ginger, was handed to the chief, who put some in his mouth, chewed it and spat it out, to symbolize the fertilization of the ground for the reception of the rice-seed. The orchids were there, stuck into two sections of a tree, but apparently no reference was made to them. The whole business was got over very quickly, and was of the simplest possible character. I should mention that at the end the chief lifted up his voice and delivered himself of a short oration, of which I cannot give the contents, as no one thought it worth translating, but what impressed me most was the informal and 'fine-old-English-Gentleman, all-of-the-olden-style' manner he assumed. The chief stuck an orchid through the hole in his left ear-lobe, and gave us each a sprig to do likewise, but not being provided with those useful apertures we had to put them behind our ears, which is after all quite as elegant as the native manner of wearing a flower. We then adjourned to a raised shed to hear some music performed by women on a sort of three-stringed lute having three frets, which was placed on the floor in front of the player. An ivory pencil is used for striking the strings. The performers were two women, who played in unison, and the music was of the same simple monotonous character as that which we had heard at Phrë. There were a number of bamboo harmonicons and sets of small gongs lying about the room, which seemed to be of Burmese origin. The native Lao instrument is the bamboo flageolet.

During the whole of my stay in Chiengmai, I constantly longed to ascend Doi Suthëp, and ascertain its height, but business at first, and afterwards an unseasonable period of three days persistent rain frustrated my hopes. I managed however to get as far as to the pagoda, which is approximately 2,200 feet above the city. Leaving the Vice-Consulate one day about a quarter past nine, I walked my pony through the city, and out by the Patu Suen-dok, reaching the deserted garden by ten. This place is supposed by some of the foreign residents to be the site of an earlier town. But it is much smaller, by ten or twelve times, than the present city, and if it was ever surrounded by a wall, nothing now remains but an earthen mound. Immediately opposite on the south side of the road, are the remains of a Buddhist temple, standing in a square enclosure, pierced on the north, south and east sides by arched pyramidal gateways, nineteen feet thick. Inside of this is a smaller enclosure, at the west end of which rises a lofty circular *phra-chedi* on a square base, having a smaller *phra-chedi* at each corner, and a steep flight of laterite steps on each side at the top of which is an arched gateway. These eight structures on the outer edge of the base have sharp pyramidal pinnacles, while the coping of each flight of steps is formed by a five-headed *naga*. The *wihan*, which fronts towards the east, has four graduated roofs, the highest end being next the *phra-chedi*, its interior consisting of a nave and two aisles. At the west end is a colossal sitting Buddha, some twenty four feet high, of brick and mortar, freshly gilt. Back to back with the *wihan* stands a small but massively constructed shrine, decorated with stucco ornaments and containing a small sitting Buddha, apparently quite new. The doorway of this shrine is curious, being a mere longitudinal slit, as it were, in the wall of the building; or rather, it looks as if the wall with all its mouldings and other ornamentations had been divided vertically in the centre and then pulled apart to show the image in the interior. Gateways on this principle, which look as if a small *phra-chedi* had been cut in two, and its parts set up on either side of the passage-way, are however not infrequent.

Between the city and this garden are dotted here and there several tall *phra-chedi*, of which scarcely anything now remains but their brickwork core. Nothing however can be inferred as to their having been included within the walls of an earlier city.

A quarter of an hour's ride beyond the *sala* where we had diverged from the road on a previous occasion brought me to the foot of the mountain. Here I left the ponies, as the path was too rough for them, and began to ascend the foothills, which are covered with scrubby trees now almost denuded of their foliage. Further on the path divided, on the right ascending a sunburnt clayey spur through sparse forest, the left following a purling stream amongst densely growing umbrageous trees and over damp black soil. This contrast would seem to suggest that it is want of moisture, and not cold, that causes most of the trees in the Laos to shed their leaves during the winter. Close to this spot a delicate dwarf bamboo, having stems no thicker than ordinary grass, and reaching a height of about two feet, was pretty abundant. At a height of about 2100 feet above the sea acorns were lying in the pathway. They had fallen from large trees with lanceolate leaves of rather thin texture. There was also what I took at first to be the fruit of an oak, but may perhaps have been a diminutive chestnut: it was covered with prickles, and most specimens had only one kernel. The shell split naturally into three parts. It is certain, however, to judge from acorns which were afterwards shown to me in Chiengmai, that there are five, if not six, distinct species of oak on Doi Suthëp. Ten minutes below the summit was a green swampy glade, where a party of men and women were gathering the flower *dok un* which the latter wear in their hair. To represent the pronunciation of the second syllable to the eye, it should be printed half a letter higher than the first. Such a system of noting the tones of these mono-syllabic languages would, if practicable, be far more effectual than the use of accents or other diacritical marks, which are so easy to forget. For you must know that in Lao as well as in Siamese it makes all the difference in the world whether you pronounce a syllable with a rising or falling inflection of the voice, with a combination of both, or with no inflection at all.

The pagoda stands at the top of a detached knoll, and is approached by a long flight of steps at the back, on either side of which stands a row of lofty pines, evidently planted there, for although the tree can be seen in abundance on the summit of the mountain, there are none growing in the woods which surround this knoll. The leaves are three in a sheath, and the cone is from two and a half to three inches long. It is possibly the Pinus known in Burma. On the slopes Pardanthus sinensis, an Irid sometimes met with in the neighbourhood of certain mountains in Japan about 1000 feet above the sea, is common enough.

At 12 o'clock I reached the temple, which stands 3600 feet above the sea, and 2200 feet above Chiengmai, according to my calculations. On the south side of the hill there were bushes of a large white Bauhinia, which sent forth a delicious fragrance. The plain was almost enveloped in mist at this hour, so that the mountains on its further side were indistinguishable. Down below the thermometer was probably 85°, while at this elevation it marked only 72°. I sat patiently waiting for my luncheon to arrive, and enjoying the fresh air till a quarter to two, when the pangs of hunger began at last to make themselves felt, and as there were no signs of the basket's approach, I resolved on descending in search of it. About half-way down I met one of my men slowly toiling up the steep path, and no doubt he would have explained the delay to his own satisfaction at least, if I could have understood what he said. But all I could make out was that somebody else was to blame. Just below was the junction of the two paths, so I hastened down and enjoyed my meal in the cool shade, while the servants hunted for orchids. From this spot it took me half an hour more to the place where the ponies were waiting, and I got back to Chiengmai about the hour that it was expected I should have reached the pagoda.

On the **21st January** after many pros and cons as to the best excursion to be made in the immediate neighbourhood, I started to make the circuit of Doi Suthëp, if it should be found feasible with elephants. Dr. Cheek of the American Mission, the Rev. Mr. Webster, who is a missionary to the Karens and belongs to the Mission in Burma, and Archer were my companions. We started on ponies, the baggage being carried on nine or ten elephants, including a few spare ones for riding on in case it should turn out impossible to take the ponies across the ridge at the back of the mountain. Leaving the Patu Suen-dok about eleven, we struck at once into a track leading across the parched rice-fields to the south-west, and in about half an hour's time reached the village of Phông Noi on a streamlet called the Huei Sai. Beyond this we crossed undulating stony ground covered with thin forest, and came down upon the Huei Më-hia. Across the stream rises precipitously a pretty wooded hill named Doi Kham, on which the sun shone brilliantly, lighting up the scarlet tints of the dead foliage. Following this stream for some distance, we at last began to ascend a long horizontal spur that runs out from Doi Suthëp in a southerly direction, descending on the other side to Ban Phông on the right bank of the Më Thachang, a swiftly flowing rivulet several yards wide and about a foot deep. Siamese and Laos are alike averse from long journeys, and the chief's people in conjunction with the King's Commissioner, when settling the itinerary, had fixed upon this place for our first encampment; but as it was only one o'clock when we got to Ban Phöng, the more active western blood rebelled against the arrangement, and we determined to go on a bit further after having our lunch. Besides, the *wat* which was destined for my accommodation was by no means a comfortable building to pass the night in. I forgot to mention that the chief had lent me his best elephant to ride, besides several others, and had moreover sent with me a *Chao* or prince to act as chief of the escort and make things generally comfortable. Dr. Cheek had four of his own elephants, if not more, and we should have made an imposing cavalcade altogether, but for the dislike of the elephant for his cousin the horse, which forced us to travel in two separate bodies. There were of course a crowd of followers on foot, besides the cook, servants, grooms, and mahouts.

We left again at half past three and followed the bed of the stream for about a mile through a shaded rocky gorge, fording it pretty frequently until we emerged into a flat-bottomed little valley cut up into terraced rice-fields. The scenery here is soft and friendly, and recalls many a bit of Japan; on every side rose steep knolls covered with trees, whose brilliantly red foliage was lighted up by the sun now sinking in the west.

Keeping slightly away to the right in full view of the long ridge which extends westwards from Doi Suthëp, we climbed a steep hill, which we supposed to be a spur dividing the side valleys of the great mountain, but to our great surprise came down again on the same stream, to ascend once more to the top of a still higher hill on its right bank. Crossing this, we descended once more, and passing through a tract of forest, found ourselves at five o'clock still on the right bank of the stream, where we waited for the ponies to convey us across the muddy ford. The general character of the country hereabouts is that of open cultivated valleys [each] divided from the other by constrictions of the hills through which the stream has cut its way. After another half hour's ride the valley opened out into a huge amphitheatre, with rice-fields rising one above the other like broad rows of seats, in the centre of which stands the hamlet of Mu'ang Ha. We got here at half past five and found the *wihan* of a little *wat* prepared for occupation of Archer and myself. Dr. Cheek and Mr. Webster, the latter of whom now caught us up, after having been behind all day, pitched their tents on the opposite side of the stream.

Howdahs were taken off, and the elephants turned out to feed, while the natives lighted fires all round to cook their rice and to lie by during the night. I imagine that they mostly slept in the open air, wrapped up in their cotton blankets, and at this season of the year there was probably no danger in their lying on the ground. Height above the sea 1660 feet. The southern summit of Doi Suthëp bore E.N.E., so that we had already performed more than a quarter of the circumference, since from the Vice-Consulate it bears W.N.W.$\frac{1}{2}$ W.

January 22. The thermometer at 6.30 indicated 56°. We started on foot at half-past eight, and traversing the terraced rice fields quitted the valley at its further end. After crossing a steep hill covered with forest, we again descended to the stream which we had followed all yesterday afternoon, and after crossing and re-crossing several times finally left it behind us. Its source is evidently somewhere on the southern flank of Doi Suthëp. We now climbed a steep ascent over stiff red clay to the top of a knoll called Doi Nyung, which we reached at 9.20. From the rising ground to the right of the path we took bearings of the principal points. The southern summit of Doi Suthëp bore nearly due east, while the *wat* where we had passed the night lay to the south-east. Beyond it we could see a portion of the Chiengmai plain and of the range of mountains which borders its eastern side. The northern summit of Doi Suthëp bore east by north. A long pine-clad ridge running towards our left was seen extending like the sharp back of some emaciated animal from a point about 600 feet below the summit. So clear was the atmosphere that with the naked eye we could easily distinguish the form which is distinctive of the coniferous order. The altitude of this spot was approximately 2000 feet. It would perhaps not be impossible to reach the nearer summit of Doi Suthëp from here in one day, but the ascent would be long and toilsome, as there is no path, and finding one's way up a mountain side by the mere aid of the compass is no easy task.

We waited for the elephants and ponies to overtake us, and continued our journey at half-past ten. The path lay through undulating forest for three quarters of an hour, till we reached a small open space that seemed conveniently situated for luncheon. On our right were the spurs which stretch down north-westwards from the mountain, while to our left the country seemed to consist of hills and valleys extending in the direction of a plain that was however invisible, and perhaps may exist only in our imaginations. We had walked a good [deal] faster than our baggage animals, and it was more than an hour before they came up. Then we had to lunch and smoke a cigar, so that it was one o'clock before we were again under way. By this time every one of the party had walked quite enough for one day, and we got into our howdahs, the sole merit of which, in my opinion at least, is that they make you so uncomfortable that in a short time you feel going on foot to be less fatiguing.

The track ascended first to a height of about 2150 feet, and then wound for a couple of hours round the deep ravines on the steep flank of a lesser mountain, descending rather rapidly at last to a teak forest, where a party of men were working under Dr. Cheek's Burmese contractor. Probably it would be more exact to say Peguan, but this is a distinction that is seldom observed in Siam, although it is not without its significance. The forest occupied a tract of almost level ground, and the timber that was still standing or lying about ready to be dragged was consequently not of first rate quality. Leaving this valley we crossed a low ridge, and a few minutes after four o'clock reached the hamlet of Ban Samöng, where we put up as usual at the *wat*, but not this time in the *wihan*, as there were some long open sheds outside that promised more light and air than the dark and unventilated church. This village which lies at about the same altitude as Mu'ang Ha, contains 87 houses, which would give a population of about 500 persons. They belong by descent to a people named Lü, that is to say to the Shans of Chiengtung, whence their forefathers were probably transported some few generations ago, after a successful raid made on that place by the Chiengmai Laos. They have by this time become completely naturalized, the only difference between them and the pure Laos being in their intonation of the language.

January 23. The real object of our trip was to visit a teak forest, in order to get an idea, from actual inspection, of the manner in which the timber business is carried on. These forests exist all over the five northern Lao provinces, and many of them are worked by Asiatic British subjects under contract with the chiefs and other owners, in some cases by lease for a period of years, in others upon annual agreements, the usual terms being a royalty of three or four rupees a log, besides the presents in the nature of a premium that are given in order to obtain a lease. The lessees seldom or hardly ever are men of capital, but obtain funds at a high rate of interest (generally three per cent a month) from the Indian money lenders at Maulmein. A lessee will work part of a forest himself, another part will be sublet, and a third part will be handed over to contractors, who undertake to deliver logs at a fixed price at the bank of the stream by which they are to be floated down. The original lessee is bound to pay the royalty on each log before it leaves the limits of the forest on its way down to Maulmein or Bangkok, and to him the owner is entitled to look for payment. But sometimes he recognizes the sub-lessee by consenting to receive the royalty from him direct.

The foresters, being mostly men of straw, as a rule do not pay the royalty on taking away the timber, and in order to remove it have to give a promissory note for the amount due, with interest again at three per cent a month, and they often assign by way of collateral security some indefinite number of logs still lying in the forest or so many elephants, which are not in any way identified; this sort of document they are in the habit of styling a mortgage. Everything goes smoothly enough if rain falls every year in sufficient quantity to float out into the rivers the logs which have been dragged to the bank of the stream. The forester then sells them at Maulmein or Bangkok, or perhaps on the way to either of those places, and having got his money is in a position to redeem the note he has given for the royalty. If he is honest he gets on all right, but many of them are of extravagant habits and prefer spending the cash on women or temple building, the two kinds of luxury to which the Burman or Peguan is chiefly addicted. He gives fresh notes to the lessor, and the debt continues to grow at compound interest until all hope of its ever being discharged is given up by the parties. Then the owner tries to come down upon the lessee, sub-lessees and contractors, he lays violent hands upon all the logs lying in the forest and upon all the elephants he can find, no matter whose they are, and in entire disregard of the rights of the men who have by their labour given to the timber nine-tenths of the value which it now possesses. And a pretty crop of law-suits is the result.

Another source of dispute in past times has been the practice in-dulged in by some of the chiefs of granting away the same forest to two different individuals, or of giving the lease of a forest to one man after he has already accorded to another the right of cutting timber, in spite of a special treaty dating so far back as 1874 by which the Siamese Government undertook to put a stop to these proceedings. In another article of the same treaty it was provided that a court should be estab-lished to try all cases between British subjects and Siamese or Laos, but it never heard or decided a single action. A fresh treaty was negotiated in 1883 which, as far as can at present be seen, promises to produce better results under the constant supervision of the Vice-consul who resides at Chiengmai to look after the interests of the numerous British subjects scattered over the Northern Lao States.

The teak from the Western part of Nan, the State of Phrë and from part of Lakhon comes down the Më Yom past Sawankhalôk, while a certain quantity descends from Eastern Nan and the provinces of Phichhai and Phitsanulôk by the Menam Phô. A small quantity of inferior timber is obtained from the provinces of Sawankhalôk and Sukhothai also. The two rivers unite a short way above Paknamphô, from which place the rafts pass down the Mënam. That of Western Lakhon, Northern and Eastern Chiengmai and Lamphun finds its way by the Më Ping to Paknamphô and so to Bangkok. The Siamese provinces of Mu'ang Thön (Tern) and Rahëng also yield a certain amount. On the west of the State of Chiengmai is the well known forest of Mu'ang Yuom, the produce of which finds its way to Maulmein by the river Salween, as does likewise that of the Thoungyeen valley, the opposite sides of which belong respectively to Burmah and the Siamese Province of Rahëng. Further north contributions are received from Mëhong-son, which belongs to Chiengmai, the valley of the Më Hang and even from the banks of streams which lie in the Western districts of the State of Chieng-tung.

A curious circumstance is the great difference in the prices obtained at Maulmein and Bangkok. At the former port the rates for the finest logs are from eighty to one hundred rupees, while at the latter they sell for no more than thirty-five. One explanation I have heard offered is that in Maulmein there is a considerable market for shingles cut out of the "slabs" or outsides of the logs, while in Bangkok these are almost of no value, and hence the exporter cannot afford to pay as high a price for the rough logs as the teak buyers of Burmah are ready to give. Logs at Chiengmai, on which the royalty of three to four rupees has been paid are worth, say, about fifteen rupees, and the average cost of transit thence to Bangkok is eight rupees, half of which is for elephants "ounding" them over shallow places down to the rapids and thence to Rahëng, where they are made up into rafts, the balance being for rafting to Bangkok. At Chhainat a duty has to be paid to the Siamese government which averages another four rupees. So that with the high interest on the capital embarked in this trade, the profit to the forester is a very uncertain thing. If he is lucky in getting his timber out quickly, he will make money, but if a succession of dry seasons intervenes, he loses heavily. Three years is probably the least time in which a log can be cut and brought down. The fluctuations of the market at home, which of late years have been severe, must also be taken into account, and it is a matter for surprise that any man should think it worth his while to embark in such a business.

We spent the morning in visiting a teak forest about three miles up the valley. The walk thither was delightful, now alongside the clear

fresh stream, now by a path over some projecting bluff [under] a brilliant sky. A cool breeze and the sight of tall pine-trees fringing a hill
about three hundred feet above us contributed to elate the spirits of the
party. After a prolonged sojourn in a tropical country the mere presence of vegetation which recalls more temperate climes is in itself a
source of joyousness. At last we came to a spot where some eight hundred
massive logs, many of them over three feet in diameter and thirty five
feet in length, were lying densely packed in the narrow bed of the stream,
their lower surfaces just wetted by the flowing current. Beyond this
was the forest where they had been cut. Some elephants were brought
round from the opposite bank where they were engaged in dragging
timber, and we saw them harnessed to logs. The gear is made of twisted
bark, and is of the roughest description, passing round the animal's
chest, and attached to the log behind by a chain passed through a hole
cut at its thick end. Rough stems of young trees are placed underneath
as rollers. The elephant on being started by the mahout, moves forward
at what is a great pace for him during a few moments, and then stops
for an equal space to take breath, for the clumsy band across his chest
impedes respiration, so that continuous effort is impossible. When urged
forward again he utters loud cries of indignation, but with a great effort
soon renders obedience to the voice of his driver.

In the forest of Ban Huei Samöng the teak trees are mostly near the
stream, but in some parts of the Lao States the timber has to be dragged
as much as ten miles, and the labour required to get it to the bank of the
stream is enormously expensive. The elephant seems to do little work
in proportion to his huge size; for three days he drags timber up to
noon, and then has a five days rest. The logs are felled during the rainy
season, when they are less likely to be split by the fall, as the ground is
then soft. One forester cuts a single log per diem, but three usually
work together, and cut the same number of logs. They use a heavy long
handled axe, in preference to a saw. We saw several pine trees lying
there which had been utterly ruined by splitting, for ropes are not employed to break the force of impact on the earth. The woodmen no
doubt try to direct the fall of the tree so that it may come down clear of
its neighbours, but they are not always successful, and then the trunk
comes crashing down through the surrounding branches, damaging itself and sometimes seriously injuring the men who have miscalculated
the effect of their blows. Before being felled the trees are "girdled",

that is to say the bark is roughly hacked through with the axe at a height of about four feet from the ground, so that the tree dies, after which it is usually left standing for three years to dry. But sometimes the lessee has a larger number of trees "girdled" than he can cut during the term of his agreement, and they may then be left to dry for several years, which much impairs their value. A custom appears to exist of allowing the outgoing lessee to exact from his successor a rupee for each tree girdled and left standing. This right should not be recognized by the courts, as it leads to waste, and the price thus paid for girdling is far in excess of its value. There is no written law to regulate this industry, and the judges have therefore the opportunity by carefully considered decisions of giving the stamp of legality to those forest customs which common sense approves, while refusing to recognize those which are detrimental to the public interest. But what am I doing in assuming such a motive of action as regard to the "public interest" in a country where there is no public, and the people are regarded as existing for the sole benefit of their rulers?

There are of course no laws or customs having the conservation of the forests for their object, and in a few years more all the timber that is worth cutting will have been exhausted. The teak tree is self-sown, and if the forests are allowed to lie fallow for twenty years or so, the business will again revive. A regulation has been proposed by which the foresters would be heavily fined for each log felled that is of less than a certain diameter, but regulations are of little use when the officials cannot be trusted to enforce them. The unpopular system of government reserves which exists in Burmah would be even more difficult of application here.

January 24. This morning about six o'clock the thermometer marked 50°, an increase of three degrees over the temperature of the preceding day at the same hour.

We left Ban Huei Samöng on elephants about eight o'clock, and taking a path through the village to the right of that which leads to the teak forest we visited yesterday, were soon engaged in the narrow bed of a mountain torrent. Here for the first time I saw an elephant refuse a bank which his mahout ordered him to ascend. Although the track, steep as it was, had been passed by nearly all the other animals, mine could not by any means be induced to take it, and I had therefore to go round by a longer but easier way. When the path at last quitted the gully we found ourselves on some steep hills, which we crossed into the valley of another small tributary of the Huei Samöng, and continuing to mount upwards, we reached, after travelling an hour and a half, a small clearing laid out in rice-fields by a colony of Lü from Ban Samöng. We asked a middle-aged man when his forefathers first came to these parts, and received in answer the information that his parents had migrated from Chieng-tung into Chiengmai territory about twenty years ago, before he was born, displaying thus the utter disregard of dates which is characteristic of people who keep no records. According to his data, his age would be little more than eighteen, although he must have been at least forty five years old. He said he knew nothing of the Lü language.

The rice-fields which lay in the immediate neighbourhood of the cottages had just been prepared for sowing, and the soil seemed a rich black loam. Under a shed some of the women were engaged in weaving white cotton cloth in a loom which consisted of little more than four posts held together by a slight framework. The people here wear a sandal of thin bamboo strips plaited together as in the accompanying sketch, and it is worthy of notice that it is held on  by a thong passing between the big toe and the next, exactly in the same manner as the foot-gear of the Japanese. I cannot help suspecting that this contrivance is of Chinese origin. The Lao name for this sandal is *köp*. The position of this tiny isolated clearing, so far above the village, was extremely picturesque. Steep densely wooded hills surrounded it on every side, except at the narrow pass by which we had ascended, and seemed to shut if off from the outer world. Lower down we had passed one of the deserted clearings of the Karens. These people, who in Siam at least live together in small communities, have no settled villages. They constantly move about among the hills, and cut down the forests to plant their crops, migrating to some fresh site after a year or two, which time suffices, it would seem, to exhaust the capabilities of the soil. Height above the sea about 1,600 feet.

After waiting here half an hour for the elephants, we proceeded on foot up a deep shaded dell now by the side of the stream, now above it, along its bed and crossing it frequently. I could have easily imagined myself in some remote part of the mountain districts of Japan. In forty minutes Mr. Webster and myself, who though not entitled to claim rank as pedestrians, went better afoot than the rest of the party, had reached the last spot where water was attainable. The height here was 2,500.

Another half hour's toil brought us to the summit of the pass. Just below grew at least two species of oak and a tall lily, bearing large ripe capsules. A knoll on the right seemed to invite us to climb a little further, and in ten minutes more we were rewarded by a magnificent view of mountains on every side, and of Doi Suthëp rising high above us about E.S.E. But deep intervening densely wooded ravines forbade any attempt to reach it. S.W. in the direction of Mu'ang Yuom we saw the great mountain that is also visible from Chiengmai. Far away below us, almost due west we perceived the rice fields of Ban Huei Samöng, while through a gap on the opposite side we could discern other fields in the Chiengmai plain, which the guides seemed to think must lie near Ban Katsa, the hamlet we were to reach on the following day. The ridge we had attained was covered with tall pines, and a kind of dwarf palm was common on its steep, almost precipitous sides. It was just the spot for a picnic. A guide was sent back to stop the elephant which carried our lunch, and we waited there enjoying the view and otherwise idling the time away till half past one, when the beast at last appeared. This will give an idea of the slow rate at which elephants climb as compared with a man on foot. Neither Mr. Webster nor myself was in proper training: he had only just recovered from a somewhat severe attack of malarial fever, and I had injured a knee by too much tennis. We had however taken only an hour and ten minutes to make the ascent which had occupied the elephants three hours. My Japanese servant who carried the aneroid had unfortunately gone on, not knowing that we were on the knoll, and therefore I was unable to determine the height, but we may fairly add a thousand feet for the half hour's climbing, which would give 3500 feet above the sea for the top of the pass.

We quitted this delightful spot at a quarter to three. The path at first winds round the top of a pine-clad spur stretching towards Doi Suthëp, and then plunges down a steep declivity in a N.E. direction, bringing us to the hamlet of Pong-Yeng. Just at the bottom of the hill we passed a plantation of *mieng* or Lao tea. The natives call these plantations *pa-mieng*, or tea-forest if *pa* be rendered literally, and this causes it to be generally supposed that the *mieng* grows wild. Laos tell you that it is found growing in commixture with other trees, which are cut down leaving the tea tree to benefit by the additional air and sun.

But this account seems doubtful. It is possible that the Laos of Chiengmai, when the country was resettled, found old tea-trees growing in this way, and cleared them from the jungle which enveloped them, but the arrangement of the trees is too regular to allow of our supposing that they were planted by the mere hand of nature. Many were twelve to fifteen feet high with stems two and a half to three inches in diameter, and they were evidently not pruned. Some were in bud or flower, and others bore the half-ripe berry. The leaf is longer and more pointed than that of the Japanese tea-plant, and the foliage is less dense. But of its being a species of tea there can be no doubt whatever. The Laos do not drink the infusion, but prepare the leaf for chewing by burying it in pits, and it is one of their indispensable luxuries. You see a man put a lump of the fermented leaves in one cheek, which he leaves there while he proceeds to chew betel or smoke a cigarette, looking for all the world as if his face were distorted by the mumps.

The village of Pong-Yeng is situated in an extensive amphitheatre surrounded by hills, and having for its area a series of terraced rice-fields rising from the centre. Here three brooks unite to form the Më Sa. Northwards, above the nearer hills, rises Doi Kwamlong, where a hero of local legend lies buried below a precipitous rock near the summit. He is said to have determined the site of Lamphun by shooting an arrow from the top of Doi Suthëp, and on the spot where it fell the city was founded. He must have used a very long bow on this occasion, since the distance is about twelve miles as the crow flies. He afterwards removed his abode to a place on the west bank of the Salween and died there. His corpse was brought home to be buried either at Chiengmai or Lamphun, I forget which, but arriving at Pong-Yeng, could not be got to pass the spot where it now lies, and the rock which is pointed out to you from Pong-Yeng is "alive to this day to testify of it".

As usual, we put up at the village temple, and passed the evening sitting round a wood fire, smoking and drinking whiskey punch by moonlight, while the doctor who speaks Lao like a native, entertained some of the guides and ourselves with an interchange of marvellous sporting stories of rare animals and fish bigger than whales that are believed to haunt the waters of the Më-Khong. The Laos take care to place the locality of these wonders as far away as their geographical knowledge permits, and if you doubt what they say, you can go there and see for yourself.

January 25. The barometer shows the height of the Pong-Yeng to be about 2000 feet above the sea, while the thermometer at sunrise marked the same as yesterday morning, namely 50°. We started at a quarter past eight, and crossed the rice-fields to the point where the Më Sa makes its exit through a narrow gorge. Here is a good-sized tea plantation in a shady spot. A little further on we were requested by the *Chao* to dismount from our elephants, as we were approaching a dangerous precipice high above the left bank of the stream, where there was a possibility of falling over. But the peril was much exaggerated, and the animals passed safely along. In fact there was no danger at all, but if anything had happened, the *Chao* would have [been] rendered responsible on his return to Chiengmai, and he did not like to run the risk of having his head taken off for allowing the little finger of a 'distinguished foreigner' to get scratched. It was a pleasant walk, continually descending by a rocky path, and generally in sight of the roaring torrent. We rested half an hour at a romantic spot where a fallen trunk formed a natural bridge, near a pool that filled us with regret at not having our towels with us. Shortly afterwards we forded the stream, which having now descended nearly to the level of the plain, was taking its ease under overhanging branches. Then we climbed again up a hillside and descending again, entered a teak-forest, where the direct path to Chiengmai seemed to diverge to the right among the trees. We were in no hurry to get back there, and so kept on our way to Ban Katsa. Mr. Webster and I were in advance, the others having returned to the slothful discomfort of their howdahs. By twenty minutes to twelve we reached the edge of the cultivated plain, and lay down under a tree to wait for our companions, who came up just an hour later.

From here it was a ten minutes walk across the rice-fields to the village. Here the *Chao* wanted to lodge me in the *wat*, but as there was a stream not far off, it seemed better to migrate to its banks and pitch our tents among the trees. A capital spot was found in a grove, and while we made ourselves comfortable in the shade, the Lao guides busied themselves with the construction of a bamboo bathing-house out in the stream, so that we could enjoy a bath in the clear cool running water.

During the evening an alarm was raised in the camp by news of an elephant in 'must' that was supposed to be about to make a rush upon us. When the male is in this state he is usually isolated, and the elephant in question, which belonged to the chief, had been sent out to the neighbouring jungle to be kept quiet until the fit was over. Somehow or other he had got wind of our party, and was reported to be coming down. His mahout was not to be found. Our *Chao*, who is the chief's principal keeper of the elephants, had a double source of anxiety. If the infuriated beast were to charge the camp, one of us might be trodden underfoot and killed; and it was possible that a fight would occur between the elephant and some of our animals, which would be equally productive of disaster. He begged earnestly that we would go back to the *wat* and place ourselves in safety within its walls. I consulted Luang Suriya, who was of the party, and found him by no means alarmed; he thought that it would be rather good fun if the elephant did make his appearance. My other companions were of the same opinion, and we united in resolving to run the risk. In the meantime a number of men crossed the stream with torches to drive the elephant back in case he should seriously attempt to get near our animals, while others went in search of the mahout, whom they luckily found at last. Tranquillity was therefore restored, and we congratulated ourselves in having stood firm. In such a matter a foreigner is bound almost to be guided by what a native, speaking with authority, tells him, and if the *Chao* had been alone probably I should have taken his advice, but as Luang Suriya hinted pretty clearly that the *Chao's* warning proceeded from the excessive caution of which an example had already been given during the morning, we were justified in disregarding it and in consulting our own inclinations.

We were now some ten or twelve miles from Chiengmai and as ponies had been sent out by Gould to meet us, the Doctor and Archer rode gaily in on the following morning. Mr. Webster, who felt his walking powers were completely restored, preferred to go in on foot. Having hurt my side by falling over a log a couple of days before, I had to have recourse to my elephant, and as it was a level road, and the mahout probably was willing to get home as quickly as possible, he urged the animal to its utmost speed, so that we actually covered the distance in three hours and a half. This, you will perceive, gives him a maximum rate of 2.857 or 3.428 miles an hour according as you take the lesser or greater estimate of the distance; and he is one of the largest elephants owned by the chief. Slow and steady should therefore be the motto of the traveller by this kind of conveyance.

PART 7

FROM CHIENGMAI TO BANGKOK

From the 31 January to the 3 February inclusive, we had rain almost without intermission, not of the usual tropical sort, but like a succession of gentle showers. On the mountains however it must have rained somewhat heavily, for the river rose a couple of feet and inundated a considerable part of the vegetable-gardens that had been constructed with so much care and patience by the women of the suburbs. The thermometer never rose above 74° during the day, and ranged mostly between 70° and 72°, while at night it went down to 57°. After dinner it usually became so cold that we should have been glad to light a fire, if that had been possible in a house constructed chiefly of bamboo and matting.

The date when I should have to commerce the journey down the river was fast approaching, and I was compelled to abandon my cherished plans with regard to the ascent of Doi Suthëp. Some matters of business which it was unfortunately necessary to discuss with the King's chief Commissioner prevented my taking advantage of the rise of the water, and by the 9th it had fallen again to its previous level. There were still three months to the beginning of the rainy season, and the longer I delayed, the more time would be consumed by the journey. The chief, who was indirectly involved in the questions under discussion, showed his resentment by making difficulties about finding boats and crews for me, although it was well understood that I was to pay their wages, and in spite of his being the absolute ruler of the country at whose disposal every inhabitant is bound to place his person and property. Had it not been for the friendliness of the Doctor who was going to Bangkok to fetch his wife and children, and consented not only to take the trouble of hiring the men but also to place a couple of his own boats at my disposal, I should probably have been delayed much longer.

It had been arranged from the commencement that I should go part of the way on elephants, which the chief was requested to furnish as far as Chorm-tong distant only two or three days march. He did not venture to refuse, but gratified his spite by sending one amongst the rest, which was undersized, ill-shaped and deformed, together with a how-dah that was unfit for a cook to ride in. The Commissioner however made him change the animal, but being unable to procure another how-dah, good-naturedly let me have his own. Archer had to remain in Chiengmai to take charge of the Vice-Consulate, while Gould went on a trip in the north of the state, so I arranged with Dr Cheek that we should travel down together. This was both convenient and agreeable, as he is thoroughly conversant with the language and an extremely amiable com-panion at all times.

We quitted the Vice-Consulate at eleven o'clock on the morning of the 10th of February, striking across the rice fields to the south-west, until we hit the road to Mu'ang Hôt (Hawt or Hort) which leaves the city by the gate called Patu Changmai. The boats had started a couple of days earlier with the major part of our baggage, so as to reach Chorm-tong at the same time as ourselves. The highway over the plain exists only during the dry season, but that is a matter of small consequence, as no one travels during the rains if he can help it, and the country-people are accustomed to finding their way along the 'bunds' which intersect the swampy rice fields. We lunched about half past twelve under the shade of a large tamarind tree near some cottages situated in an enclo-sure surrounded by bamboos, a pretty situation, from which we enjoyed a good view of Doi Suthëp. The Lao houses are as a rule dirty and uninviting, and the open air is always preferable. There are as you already know, no inns in Siam or the Lao States, and the poorer traveller has to sleep under a tree or in one of the temple *salas*. Europeans of course use tents if they have them, but the chief when he travels has a temporary hut of bamboo and matting constructed at every stage, and it was in one of these that we put up at the end of the first day. He had chosen the same time as myself to leave Chiengmai on a trip to some sacred spot lying a little to the right of the main route, and had fortu-nately preceded us by a few hours, so that when we got to the hut the coast was already clear.

After an hour's rest we went on again, crossing almost immediately the dry bed of the Më Hia. The course of this stream can be traced for a long distance across the plain on both sides by the bamboo clumps and plantations of areca palms and bananas which line its banks. The scarlet masses of the Butea fringe the woods on the foot-hills behind which lie Ban Phông, where we were a few days ago during our excursion round Doi Suthëp. At twenty minutes past two we passed another stream, of which I could not learn the name. It probably rises on the nearer side of the foot-hills, and at this time of the year the current was still flowing. Shortly afterwards my eye was suddenly caught by a beautiful tree covered with pink and mauve blossoms, which stood on the edge of some plantations we were passing. It resembled from a distance one of the lovely pink and white peach trees which are the delight of Japanese landscape gardeners, but it was impossible to believe it to be that. It is a good rule in travelling to find out everything for yourself by actual inspection, rather than to trust to guess work or what the natives may tell you, especially if your knowledge of the language is imperfect. I have known a foreign savant in reliance on the name given to him by his guide for a tree that he saw in Japanese forests 3,000 feet above the sea, to be betrayed into the statement that the tropical Lagerstroemia was a native of the temperate zone, while an English lady travelling in Yezo, misled by a superficial resemblance that she did not take the trouble to put to the test of examination, had no hesitation of recording that she found the maiden hair tree (Ginko biloba) growing wild in the forests on the eastern coast of that island. * Mindful of their example, I directed the mahout to go closer, right up to the plantation, and then I discovered my tree to be a Bauhinia, which the Laos call Sió Ka-lúng. There were hardly any leaves on it, and the flowers gave forth a delicious scent. Its being in bloom at this season is perhaps exceptional, as the other Bauhinias I had hitherto met with in the north, with only one exception, were all in fruit and full leaf.

At three o'clock we came to the banks of the Më Thachang, many miles below the spot where we had met it on the 21st January. Here it was a gently flowing stream, which in passing through the intervening country had been deprived of much of its water for purposes of irrigation. The opposite bank was occupied by a grove of teak, very little of which appeared to be fit for timber. This tree seems to grow much better on the sides of the steep hills than on the level ground of the plains. We installed ourselves in one of the two huts prepared for the chief, and made ourselves extremely comfortable. It consisted of an inner room some twelve or fourteen feet square, and an outer hall of the

* [Presumably Mrs Bird-Bishop, on her visit to Hokkaido in 1878. See her *Unbeaten Tracks in Japan* (London, 1880)].

same size with a broad verandah on the south and west sides. There were sheds for bathing and cooking and others for his numerous following scattered irregularly about. A few yards further up stream was a second hut of similar arrangement and dimensions, which perhaps had been occupied by the female members of his family.

We crossed the stream by a dam just opposite, and walking through the teak-grove discovered a considerable village concealed behind it and, like all Lao villages, embosomed in trees. A yellow hibiscus without any dark centre and having a hairy calyx was pretty common (*dok chi chók-khún*) as was also the purple creeper that abounds all over Siam and is known as the Thunbergia (*dok num në*). A large tree called *dok som-súk* (probably the Asoka Jonesia) bears flowers resembling those of the Ixoras which are so plentiful in gardens at Bangkok, Singapore and Rangoon *Má ta-sua* (*luk yoh* in Siamese) is the fruit of a low dense shrub, bearing shiny green lanceolate leaves about eight inches long, the fruit being shaped like a fir cone. It is not edible, as far as I know. *Dok sëo phrë* is a shrub bearing bunches of white flowers which remind one of jasmine. A tall tree with yellow flowers shaped like a wide mouthed trumpet is called *dok kë hangkang*. These Lao names were given to me by Dr C's "Teacher", or as he ought more properly to be called 'intendant', a charming old man full of varied knowledge about his own country and its productions, and they may be relied on as correct.

This day we travelled during four hours, one of which was spent under the taramind tree, and the distance we got over was certainly not eight miles. Yet no one seemed to think we had wasted our time, or that we ought to have done more. If we had stopped several miles nearer Chiengmai the Laos and Siamese in the party would have been perfectly contented. Sometimes I fancy there are indications of a similar indifference beginning to infect the doctor, and almost dread to succumb in my turn to the pervading sleepiness of temperament that is characteristic of the people. Plenty of sticky rice to eat, plenty of *mieng* to stuff the cheeks with, plenty of betel and tobacco, with plenty of time to sleep and plenty of nothing to do - there you have a Lao ideal of, not happiness, because that implies a certain amount of active sensation, but the nearest approach in this life to the conscious unconsciousness of perfect bliss which is the Buddhist Nirvâna.

February 11. Thermometer 52° at 6 o'clock a.m. We began the day
resolutely on foot, leaving the elephants to dawdle along behind. For
the first half hour our way lay across dry rice-fields, and then rose
slightly on to dry sandy ground among sparse brushwood, which wore a
parched-up withered look, as if a long period had elapsed since it last
had an opportunity of quenching its thirst. The sky was of a dull hazy
bluish tint, and Doi Suthëp, which lay behind us to the north, looked
flat and featureless like a smoky wash on a grey ground. After an hour
of this the scene entirely changed, and we came to the Mëkung, an
abundant stream which by means of numerous artificial channels is made
to feed the rice fields on either side of the road. These are now
being ploughed over to be planted a second time with rice, and the
stubble remaining from the last crop is still to be seen here and there.
We sat down to rest, and waited for forty minutes in expectation of the
elephants, without whose help it did not seem possible to cross the
pond-like puddle which filled up all the road. But as they did not make
their appearance, we had to circumvent the water as best we could,
and after much tentative exploration of the fields right and left of the
road, at last got safely to terra firma on the other side, though not
without trespassing on the privacy of several cottage enclosures and
provoking the hostility of sundry ill-tempered dogs.

We wandered on for half an hour, talking and neglecting our surroundings until we got into a shady lane bordered by lofty trees, which
invited [us] to repose on a damp green bank, and we lay there till ten
o'clock, when the head of the caravan overtook us. After a two hours'
walk with the temperature rapidly rising, we were not sorry to climb
into our howdahs. The road soon left the damper lower ground, and
ascended almost imperceptibly on to a sandy tract through forest, where
the leaves had fallen off from lack of moisture, so that a shady place
for luncheon was altogether not to be discovered, much to our regret,
for of all forms of social enjoyment there is nothing to be compared to
a tête-à tête picnic in the woods, no matter what sex, age or persuasion
one's companion may own to. On and on we went, our eyes parched
by the heat reflected from the dry soil, until the road began to descend
rapidly, and we soon came in sight of deep ditches connected with the
Më Kan. A few yards beyond lay the river itself, its course dammed up
above to fill the irrigation canals, and flowing away to the left in shallow winding channels where the lightest dug-out could scarcely float.

The village lies on both banks, and on its hither side we found a large *wat*, where the tables and chairs were speedily placed under the shade of a wide-spread umbrageous banian. Close by was a well some thirty feet deep to the surface of the water, in which the branches above it were reflected as clearly as in a mirror.

It was a quarter to twelve when we got to this place, and if there had been any available accommodation we should probably have ended the day there. But the priest's quarters were dirty and uninviting, and after all one does not quite like to turn a church into a bedroom, unless there is a *chao* to assure you that it is all right. There was nothing for it, but to mount the elephants again at one o'clock and struggle on-ward through the rice-fields, which in this district seemed to be everywhere in course of preparation for sowing. The fields which are cultivated at this season of the year are called *na doh* in Lao. Here and there a Butea in full blossom relieved the dull monotony of the landscape. After about an hour's constant plashing through the deep mud, we turned to the right through a belt of trees, and crossed the stream to a dilapidated building on the right bank. Here our men urged us to stop for the night, falsely alleging that there was no water on ahead for several hours. But experience had taught us to distrust their statements about the road, and we pushed on with determination. Ten minutes had not elapsed until we met with a perfect network of canals full of water on the opposite side of a dry field, and crossing them we got into a rice-swamp, where we continued to splash along in sight of a line of cottages half hidden by trees, until about three o'clock we reached the bank of the Më Ping a few hundred yards below its confluence with the Më Kan. The latter stream flows in a southeasterly direction from the ford where we had crossed it.

It was a pleasant surprise to find ourselves again close to the broad river, after wandering among innumerable attenuated streams, whose generous current had been drawn off to feed the insatiable rice-fields. We wound now along a narrow path over-hanging the river, which in the rainy season is perpetually engaged in undermining the banks and carrying off the soil to heap up new stretches of fertile bean-field below, till we arrived about half-past three at Wat Song-Kwë. There was no *sala*, and we were driven to occupy the *wihan* in violation of our own feelings, as the tent we had with us was unluckily only big enough for a bathroom.

February 12. Thermometer marked 56° at the usual hour this morn ing, the rise showing that we are getting further south. Intending to walk to Chorm-tong, reported to be only ten miles distant, we started alone at seven o'clock along the river bank, while the elephants and servants took a shorter course inland. The brilliantly coloured tree of which we had noticed so many on nearing Wat Song-Kwë turned out yesterday afternoon to be the Bombax malabaricum, or so-called 'cotton tree'. It grows to a great height, and has opposite branches at regular intervals. The flowers are collected by the natives and used as an ingredient in their curries. It is all blossom just now and quite bare of leafage. The Butea has a flower of a more vermilion tint, and grows somewhat irregularly, one part of the tree often being covered with dense foliage, while the rest is a mass of blossom. From the latter tree a considerable quantity of stick-lac is obtained. Not far below Wat Song-kwë we passed Ban Taphi, well known as a leper village. But many of the inhabitants present no evidence of the disease. For a long distance beyond this place there are no signs of cultivation on or near the banks.

At 8.20 the path passed between the river and the foot of a low rocky tree-clad hill called Doi Loi. There is a second hill in this neighbourhood called Doi Noi, on the top of which stands a *phra-chedi*. We had noticed it yesterday afternoon and again early this morning, but as we passed without seeing it, it probably lies hidden in the forest some way from the river. Further on we came to a village inhabited by refugees from Rahëng, who are said to have migrated into Chiengmai territory in order to escape the excessive burdens imposed in that province, under the name of 'government service'. Once over the boundary line they are beyond the oppressor's reach. About half-past ten we began to think that Chorm-tong could not be much further off, as we had already done more than the ten miles. Just beyond Wat Thali, a temple which forms a prominent land-mark for travellers by boat, we reached a village surrounded by vegetable gardens, where we had to quit the shady forest and proceed along the sandy bed of the river in the full blaze of the scorching sun. It was beginning to be more than we had bargained for in the way of a day's constitutional. Seeing a boat passing down the stream, the Doctor hailed her, and shouted to the steersman to take us on board, but he did not even turn round to see who was calling. We had been walking at a fair pace for over three hours, and as the elephants had taken a different route, there was little hope of falling in with them.

We made a dive into the forest, but saw no signs of them anywhere. At last we were fortunate enough to find an empty canoe lying on the edge of a sand bank, of which we at once took possession, and the Doctor good-naturedly undertook to punt it down stream with a bamboo pole. The current runs here about four miles an hour, and at a quarter past twelve we got to the landing place at Chorm-tong, miserably exhausted and in a state of incipient sun-fever. I should not advise any future traveller to follow our example, unless he is in first-rate condition and impervious to heat. But we forgot our fatigue on seeing our little flotilla of boats tied up alongshore, all ready for a start on the morrow.

Luang Thoranen, whose existence I had almost forgotten during my stay in Chiengmai, had presented himself at the Vice-Consulate a few days before my departure, anxiously inquiring about my movements. He probably obtained the information he wanted, and was now lying here, having left a day to two before me. As he was more likely to be an obstruction than a help, and I was now under the wing of an experienced traveller on this river, it seemed unnecessary to invite any communication from him, while he on his part entirely abstained from trying to see me.

The baggage animals did not make their appearance until two o'clock, and after lunch we started on elephants for the temples of Chorm-tong, of which so much had been said. It was but a forty minutes ride across swampy rice-fields, which were being ploughed preparatory to sowing. The plough used by the Laos has a broad share, square at the lower end, and curving upwards in the direction of the handle. It is drawn by a single buffalo, which is usually driven by the ploughman, but sometimes the animal is guided by an additional man. The edge of the share being drawn along the soil, shaves off its surface in thick ribbons, which fall irregularly to one side. Rice is not sown in furrows, and the plough is of little use in turning over the soil, which has to be done by buffaloes driven in to churn up the mud with their hoofs until it becomes thick and slab. These fields were not cultivated last summer, owing, it was said, to deep floods which had rendered the usual operations of agriculture an impossibility. They were dotted here and there with small clumps of trees, among which the Butea was conspicuous. Chorm-tong, which lies on the high road from Chiengmai into Burma via Mu'ang Hôt and Dahgweng, stands at the edge of low sandy foothills, immediately behind which rise mountains covered to their summits with forest, and attaining an apparent height of from three to four thousand feet. One of these is called 'Tiger' from a fancied resemblance to the shape of that animal. It is a very holy, but shabby-looking place, and from a foreigner's point of view is scarcely worth visiting. It boasts a dilapidated double *phrabat* and an old temple behind which rises a *phra-chedi* said to contain a relic of the Buddha's body. There are no signs of antiquity about any of the buildings, which are constructed of brick, and it commands no view. In consideration of the sacred character of the temple the villagers are exempted from both taxation and forced labour, and one can easily imagine that other Laos of Chiengmai must envy the inhabitants of this place their happy condition.

A strong south west wind blew during the afternoon, and at night long lines of burning forest were seen on the hills to the south a mile or two down the river. This was a sight that almost daily repeated itself, and we soon got accustomed to expect it as part of the evening's entertainment.

February 13. Thermometer at 8 a.m. 67°. Here begins the voyage down the river, about which there is not very much to be said, since being in a boat nearly all day we were shut off from communication with the people, and the incidents of the journey were few in number. We usually got under weigh about six or half past, and travelled till the middle of the day, when we foregathered under the bank in some shady spot for lunch on board my boat. After lunch, the boats moved on again. Sometimes we played a game or two of chess or talked till three or four o'clock, when the doctor would go back to his own boat. At half-past five or six we tied up at the edge of a sand-bank, and perhaps went for a short walk. I used to take my bath just before dinner, to which we sat down at seven o'clock. Generally to bed at ten, to read or sleep as one felt inclined. We had five Lao boats, almost as large as that in which I had travelled up the eastern branch of the Menam to Phichhai. Each of us had a boat to himself, which makes two, then there was the kitchen boat, one was loaded with my baggage and the fifth was empty. Dr. Cheek has induced some of his men to row in the Bangkok style, that is, standing up with their faces to the prow, and backing the boat along. In this way he easily outstripped my boat, which was rowed in the Lao fashion. The men, generally four in number, sit down on the deck of the boat before the house, with their backs to the bow and with their knees more or less raised up in the air. They use no stretchers, and consequently are unable to pull with proper effect. As the boat floats along at a fair rate with the current they probably imagine themselves to be doing a great deal of hard work, and are quite unconscious that they are simply dipping their oars in and lifting them out again.

I have said before that the water was exceptionally low this year, which means that in many places it was not deep enough to float a boat drawing two feet of water, though in the rainy season it rises fifteen to twenty feet above the winter level. Five minutes after casting off from the shore at Chorm-tong my boat runs aground in the middle of the stream. The boatmen immediately plunge into the water up to their knees, with their clothes tucked-up, some one way and some another, to find a passage. This is soon done. They regain the deck, and we proceed gaily on our voyage, to ground again after a minute or two. All in the river once more, twisting the boat from side to side with strenuous shouts of *Ao! Ao!, Ao!* until she works herself a passage through the sand, and glides over into deep water, that is, water just deep enough for her to swim in. This sort of thing happens to each boat in turn with annoying frequency, and at one especially difficult curve in the river we were delayed for a whole hour, where a very obstinate bed of sand seemed to forbid all progress.

About noon we passed some hills on the right bank which came down close to the river. On anchoring for the night I landed and walked a short distance inland through the forest, which here is rather sparse, the soil being sandy and incapable of effective irrigation owing to its undulating character. The ground above the banks of the river declines landwards everywhere, instead of inclining towards it as one would naturally expect. This fact seems to be due to the deposit of sediment by the river floods as soon as they come in contact with tranquil accumulation of rainwater in the interior. Rice cultivation is the least troublesome of all methods of causing the earth to give its increase, and so long as there is plenty of swampy land still unutilized, the ground near the river is not likely to be converted to the purpose of agriculture. But it is the great highway of the country, and by far the larger part of the population lives on its banks in scattered hamlets, with long uninhabited stretches between them, so that a traveller journeying along in his boat is apt to look on the country as little better than a sterile desert, and wonders how it can support even the small number of inhabitants he sees.

On the following day about three in the afternoon we passed the confluence of the Më Cham. This river is almost as broad as the Më

Ping, and its rapidly flowing current adds largely to the volume of water on which we are borne forwards, so that we stick on sandbanks much less frequently than before.

February 15. The thermometer both yesterday and to-day marked 57° at half past six. We started at six o'clock, and were not long in coming to Pa-wing-chu, the Rock of the Lovers' Leap. A streamlet falls in here, issuing from between two bluffs, the lesser of which is seventy or eighty feet high. At this early hour the eastern sun shines right across its hard face of red sandstone, casting deep shadows. The upper portion is marked in a peculiar manner with deep perpendicular scorings, so that it resembles a multitude of slender columns grouped along the face of a wall. Overhanging these is a mass of darker rock, resting lightly as a feather cushion on the red cliff, so deeply have atmospheric influences worn away the seam between the two. The boatmen have a legend to tell of a pair of young people who, eloping from tyrannous parents, and galloping across country on the back of a horse, suddenly found their flight arrested by this precipice. Here the youth's heart failed him, but the girl, who doubtless felt she had most at stake, drove their steed to take the leap which promised to place them beyond the possibility of pursuit. The horse and his riders were dashed to pieces, and the fragments, borne down the stream, were cast up here and there, thus forming the rocks which obstruct navigation to this day.

An hour later we reached Mu'ang Hôt (Hawt or Hort), a village on the right bank, where the road to Maulmein branches away westward over the mountains. Here are to be seen the ruins of a temple consisting of several isolated buildings. The most interesting of these was a small octagonal shrine, which seems to have been covered by a dome with pyramidal ceiling. Its diameter is six feet, the height from the floor to the apex of the pyramid having been about twenty feet. It contains a considerable number of well modelled bronze Buddhas, mostly with the right hand hanging across the left, which lies palm upward on the knee. I saw only a single example with the hands crossed. All these buildings are constructed of brick, and decorated with elegant stucco mouldings. As usual, they were much overgrown with trees, which have contributed not a little to their dilapidation.

This morning we have enjoyed several fine mountain landscapes. Only a man who had descended the river with his eyes shut could say

that this part of it is lacking in interest. In the immediate neighbourhood of Mu'ang Hôt rises a sharp-peaked mountain, which appears
and disappears repeatedly as the boat rounds the numerous curves, until
you begin to fancy that some spell has been cast upon you which prevents your escaping from its vicinity. About ten o'clock we passed a
long sandstone bluff on the left bank. Some of the mountain ranges
seemed to run at right angles to the course of the river, especially just
above and below Mu'ang Hôt, while on the left bank the foot-hills appeared to close in upon our course. Everywhere the banks are brilliantly decorated by the blossoms, " in two shades" of scarlet, of the
trees already mentioned for their striking beauty of colouring. At Ban
Nong I-pum, which we reached half an hour later, there were a consid
erable number of huge water-wheels arranged in pairs for irrigating the
areca orchards that surrounded the peasants' cottages. They are constructed very lightly, and present a broad surface of floats to the stream.
Sections of bamboo a couple of feet in length are fastened diagonally to
that half of the tire which is nearest to the bank, which filling themselves as they dip underneath, discharge their contents into a large trough
as they come up again; a narrower trough or bamboo-pipe buried in the
bank conducts the water to the orchard, where it is distributed through
a multitude of channels so as to give a due share of refreshment to each
tree. Wherever the river as it subsided had left a convenient patch of
sand, the industrious villagers had sown rice, which was now about a foot
high.

On the following day (**16 February**) the thermometer marked
56°at seven o'clock. We started at six, and soon afterwards reached
Thadua, a substantial looking village on the left bank. At a quarter to
nine we passed Pha Hip (the Box Rocks), high and much broken bluffs
of sandstone. At eleven we were off the mouth of the Më Hat, on the
upper waters of which is situated a teak-forest. The stream was quite
dry when we passed, but must present a fine head of water in flood time.
The scarlet-blossomed Bombax was a prominent object in the landscape, relieving gratefully the arid brownish green of the ordinary forest trees. About half an hour's slow pulling brought us to some sandstone bluffs on the left bank, having conglomerate strata interposed
containing a large proportion of small pebbles, the strata being somewhat dislocated; the natives call it Pha Phiap. In another hour we were

at Mutka, also called Mëka, where we lay to for the special pilots to come on board, who alone know how to steer through the rapids. We fastened our boats off the mouth of the Më Lai, a tributary stream falling in on the right bank, which, although draining a large tract of country, now appeared to be quite dry. Ahead of us we could see mountains sloping upwards from both sides of the apparent course of the river, which lies hidden by the cocoanut palms and other trees that line the left bank. An hour and a half sufficed for all the arrangements, as Dr Cheek is well known here, and the people are willing to serve him. Off we go at a quarter past three with the liveliest anticipations (on my part at least) of shooting like an arrow past the wonderful precipices of this celebrated region.

The very word "rapid" seems to affect one's general conception of what lies before him. But this illusion in soon dispelled. Instead of rushing along with the speed of a mill-race, the stream gently deposits my boat on a sandy shoal which stretches under the water right across from bank to bank. The oarsmen plunge into the water and try unavailingly to push her over, but after wasting a quarter of an hour, and affording one more illustration of the familiar proverb about lazy people, they finally have recourse to the wooden scraper which every boat carries. These resemble in shape the scavenger's mudrake, but are three times as big. Attached to one surface are a couple of cords to which a long crossbar is fastened. One man seizes the scraper by the handle and plunges it about six inches into the sand, whereupon three at the crossbar tug with all their might until a space of two or three feet wide is cleared. Then they move on a little and repeat the process, until at last a channel is formed, not deep enough to float the boat, but just large  enough for the crew to push her through by main force, and on we go again. Often, as we took our evening stroll on the sand bank by the edge of which we had 'tied up' for the night, we came across these long furrows smoothed by the round bottoms of the boats that had slid along them, now left dry by the falling of the waters, and looking like the trail of some huge worm. I don't know exactly why, but they used to remind me of Longfellow's jingling lines about "footprints on the sands of time" from which some forlorn and shipwrecked brother is to derive consolation, not however as he is walking along the shore like ourselves, but as he sails on the main.

Before two hours had passed we were already floating along to the rhythmic but almost idle movement of the oars, in a narrow gorge between limestone mountains rising steeply and even precipitously on either hand. We did not get clear of this wonderful cleft in the hills until the morning of the 20th, so that the passage of the rapids took us nearly four complete days. When the river is full, it can be done in half that time or even less. The distance from Chiengmai to Bangkok has been accomplished in nine days, not, it is true, without risk in descending the rapids, and travelling part of the way at least during the night. But it all depends upon the depth of the water. It took me four weeks from the 10th February to the 10th March, and as the river continues to fall until the beginning of May, the journey must frequently be even longer. The distance is about 300 miles as the crow flies, and is probably not more than 450 when a liberal allowance is made for the windings of its course. So that gives an average of about seventeen miles a day, for the combined result of current and oars, deducting one day which I spent at Rahëng.

We stopped on the first night at Pha Hua-hok, where the river's breadth is not more than fifty or sixty yards, the hills sloping down almost to the water's edge, leaving but a small patch of sandbank on one side. We are still above the rapids, and the river lies calm and smooth in the light of the full moon.

February 17. We started at 6.15. The thermometer stood this morning at 58°. About seven o'clock we passed a small rapid, where the stream was contracted between rocks emerging from the river bed. A short way further rises a fantastic cliff about fifty feet high, called Pha Om, where the water pouring down from the limestone and clay-slate rocks above has formed stalactites of every possible shape, and of a reddish hue. At half past seven we were abreast of some huge copper-coloured rocks lying on both sides of the channel; the mud marks on them seemed not more than four feet above the present level of the stream, and yet there can be little doubt that the rise of the river in these narrow gorges must be nearly ten times as much. I landed close by on the left bank and ascended the hill for a short distance. The red soil, derived from disintegration of the clay-slates, discolours the trunks of the trees for ten to twelve feet above the ground, having to all appearance been carried up by the white ants. The occurrence of this coloured earth, which gets washed into the Mënam by the heavy rains of summer, may perhaps account for the peculiar red tint seen for a few days in the water at Bangkok when the river begins to rise shortly after the commencement of the rainy season. We stopped here for three quarters of an hour while the men had their breakfast. A path runs through the woods along the left bank, and we saw a few people passing with baskets suspended at the two ends of a bamboo pole carried on the shoulder. This is the common method of carrying burdens on flat ground through-out the East, but in the mountains it is more usual to use the back. It is only in Japan, and there not very often, that you see burdens borne upon the head. The scene constantly changes as we float along. Mountains rise on either side of the rapidly winding stream but never cliff opposite to cliff. If one bank is perpendicular rock, the other is a talus of fallen fragmentts overgrown with trees, slender bamboos, and grass. Excepting close down by the water's edge the vegetation is dry and leafless.

At nine o'clock we passed the village of Ban Umpë and at eleven that of Ban Kô (or Kaw), near which a streamlet called the Huei Kô falls in. At half past eleven we lay-to for lunch, which took fifty min-utes. By ten minutes to one we were off a rocky precipice named Pha Patip, the height of which I estimate at from 100 to 120 feet; it is pictur-esquely covered with stalactites. At half past one our progress was stopped by the rapid called Këng Kon. A small stream running in here has in the course of ages brought down a quantity of boulders, which have spread themselves to the right and left and extended across the river bed, forming an almost complete barrier. Above it the river is banked up, so that for a considerable distance it flows along smoothly and silently, but overflowing runs rapidly down the incline on the other side. It is too shallow to float the boats which have to be pushed and hauled along, two or three crews being required to perform this labour. It is for this reason, and also for purposes of mutual defence against gangs of robbers (dacoits) that boats usually descend the river in com-pany. Just below the rapid is Ban Katá.

At half past two we passed the mouth of the Huei Ompát, and a quarter of an hour afterwards the village of Ban Kokinu. By four o'clock we were at Ban Choliöm at the mouth of a stream. It took us three quarters of an hour to get the boats over the rapid here. Half an hour beyond we came to Këng Puang, a rapid at the mouth of the Huei Puang, and by a quarter to six were drifting past Pha Mëo (Cat Rock), a precipitous wall of rock some 300 feet high rising from the top of a wooded slope and extending along the river side for a third of a mile. At the lower end some remarkable stalactites overhang the current. These precipices are generally marked by vertical bands of black, red, yellow and even white, which however do not indicate a dislocation of the strata, as you would at first sight be disposed to conjecture. They are the natural painting of the rock, done by the water which falls over the cliffs during the rainy season. Indeed, there are few signs of distortion and the huge fissure in the mountain mass through which the river finds its way, far from owing its origin to volcanic violence, has probably been produced in the course of ages by the action of water flowing out of the great basin in which lie the states of Chiengmai and Lamphun.

Many fragments of the rock exhibit laminae scarcely thicker than millboard, with sandy deposits interposed. Other boulders are perfectly homogeneous, or are marked by veins of quartz.

During the night the air was so hot that a blanket was no longer endurable, and at six o'clock on the following morning the thermometer marked 62°. A quarter of an hour after starting we reached Këng Changhong, the most difficult rapid yet encountered. Here the boats had to be pulled through a shallow channel formed by removing some of the smaller boulders, while part of the crew held on by way of drag to a stout rope tied to the "fish-tail" behind. It took forty minutes to get our little fleet over, and we at once entered a picturesque gorge formed by a succession of steep mountain slopes descending to the water's edge on either side alternately. On the right hand rose a precipice of red rock called Pha Mân, with a wall of bushy dark-green trees opposite. Here the strata at the base had an inclination varying from forty to seventy degrees out of the horizontal line. It is crowned with innumerable tall yucca-like dracaenas, with a smooth brown spongy stem (*ton chan*), and arboreal euphorbias that at first sight look like cacti. The latter have a ligneous stem from which a milky fluid exudes when an incision is made in the bark. The branches are jointed and concavely four-sided, like a string of hog's puddings turned inside out; thorns and small pale yellow flowers extend along the edges. Both these plants are pretty common in the south of Siam, for instance on Koh Sichang, the island where the Hongkong steamers take in part of their cargoes during the south west monsoon.

A little further Doi Pha-këo (Mountain of Crystal Rock) suddenly appears in front as we round a corner; a precipice descending halfway from the sky-line, then a wooded slope, with a second precipice below it plunging sheer into the river. We hurry round another corner, and pass below Doi Pha Miu of which a rough sketch is given on this page. It is a lofty isolated rocky tower sparsely overgrown with euphorbias.

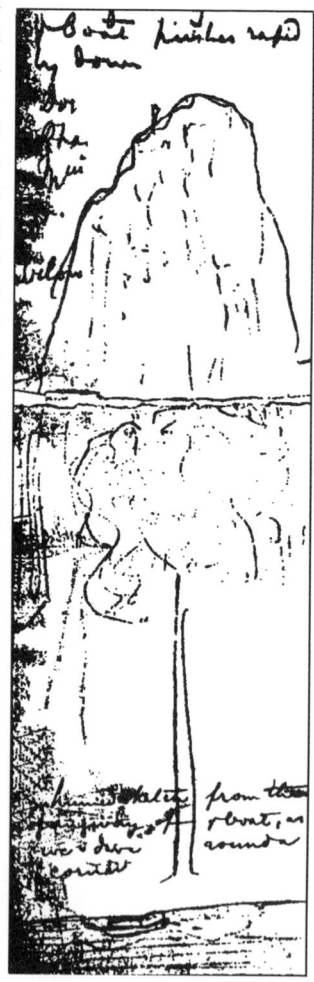

In two minutes it is out of sight, so rapid is the stream and so abrupt the turnings in its course. At half past seven we pass Pha Nguang, a precipice covered with remarkable stalactites, of which perhaps the most curious is one shaped like a huge overhanging apron. Just here were some newly planted fishing stakes extending across from one bank to the other, and we met a couple of boats close by whose crews were occupied in cleaning the fish they had just caught. These were fifteen to eighteen inches in length, with silvery scales and salmon-coloured flesh. The fishermen had also captured a big fish about four feet in length, stout in the body and having a wide gaping mouth provided with two rows of molar apparatus in the upper jaw. It did not look an inviting article of food, but Dr Cheek nevertheless bought it for his men, and we saw them afterwards making a good dinner off huge chunks of its coarse flesh.

At twenty minutes to nine we passed Këng Chang, a rapid formed by an arête extending along the middle of the river with the aid of boulders that have evidently been washed down from some higher point, as there are here no lateral streams which could have supplied them. On the right hand the hills have momentarily retreated from the neighbourhood of the river. The boats were easily handed over by their crews, and a straight reach half a mile in length brought us to the redoubtable Këng Soi in half an hour more. Here we were delayed nearly three hours, as there were a full dozen of ascending boats already engaged in the channels. An almost unbroken precipice rises on the left bank to a height of at least four hundred feet, above which is a slope, crowned by a second precipice. The bed of the river is occupied by a wide waste of limestone and granite boulders collected here in the course of ages from the lateral streams on the right bank. Tradition says that a city once stood here, and the ruined foundations of temples are thickly scattered about in the forest. On a low hill close by, not more than two hundred feet in height, stands a small brick and stucco pagoda, commanding a view up the river back to Këng Chang. The fringe of green vegetation along the water's edge contrasts in a striking manner with the arid-looking leafless trees that cover the mountain sides above. Here I found a tall straight-stemmed tree, with rough bark like that of an oak, and obovate leaves, bearing bunches of sweet-scented pale-primrose-coloured flowers, called *dok kë* by the Laos. The blossom is trumpet-shaped, the edge being divided into five lobes wrinkled like crape.

We got under way again at noon, and in forty minutes were off Doi Umlu. Here on the left bank a series of precipices and steep rocky walls rise from the water's edge to a height which may be estimated at 2000 feet. Opposite are two sharp pyramidal rocky peaks that seem to keep watch over a tributary streamlet which passes between them into the main river. I climbed up the nearest, in defiance of the fierce heat reflected from the bare black limestone rock, to look for dracaenas, but found only the euphorbias before described. It took us an hour to get over the rapid here, which is one of the most difficult. At two o'clock, we pass the Këng Chut Tu'n, opposite to the mouth of the Më Tu'n, a fine broad sandy stream flowing into the river from between steep densely wooded hills; it is now almost dry. The rapid is so easy that we shoot it without the usual business of landing the crews to haul the boats over. Just below are some huge rocks in the river-bed which reduce its width to a little more than three yards; in flood time they are no doubt covered with water.

An hour below the Më Tu'n is Këng Ap-nang (Rapid of the Maiden's Bath), so named from a dirty stagnant streamlet that flows in on the right bank. The heap of boulders which caused the rapid stretches so far across the river that only a very narrow channel is left, and the boats have to pass under an overhanging mass of rock from which a steep-sided hill rises for several hundred feet. The boats descended one at a time, and as mine went by I espied the bunches of fern adhering to the roof of the rock close by an ever dripping spring, which the Siamese Commisioner at Chiengmai, himself a lover and collector of ornamental plants, had told me to be on the look-out for. My men could not get near enough, but on arriving at the bottom of the rapid, I sent some of them back in a smaller boat to procure specimens. It turned out to be Adiantum, closely resembling our English maiden-hair fern. The roots unfortunately did not survive the journey to Bangkok, and I had no means of drying specimens. Nothing did I more regret on this journey than my having neglected to bring apparatus for preserving plants, by which an opportunity was lost which I can never hope to regain, of obtaining a very considerable number of species, which if not new, at any rate have not yet been recorded as occurring in Siam. The botany of this country, as far as I know, has not yet been investigated, and nothing seems to have been published on it, if we except a few scattered papers and notices by the late Sir Robert Schomburgk.

At a quarter past five we reached Fa Pin, the 'Sky Reversed'. This is the name given to a lofty precipice some 800 feet high, surmounted by a slope, which is crowned by a second precipice. Perhaps the total height is 1600 feet. The brilliant red rocks lighted up by the westering sun were a magnificent sight, and looked almost volcanic, but they were nothing else than limestone or clay-slate. In the bed of a stream which falls in on the right bank opposite to Fa Pin granite boulders abounded, this being only the third place where I had observed them during my journey, the first being Doi Suthëp and the second, one of the rapid-barriers already passed. On the whole it is not a common rock in Siam, compared for instance with limestone. We 'tied-up' for the night at Wun Wing, a deep bay on the right bank a mile further on, where there is a very powerful eddy. I amused myself with dropping pieces of paper into the water over the gunwale of the boat, and watching them as they described a wide circle which eventually brought them back alongside; by the morning they had all got ashore on the sand bank near which the boat was fastened.

On the **19 February** the thermometer marked 70° when we started, about six o'clock, which showed a considerable rise above what we had hitherto been accustomed to. It seemed evident that for the rest of the voyage the heat would be far too great for comfort, as the roof of the boat was thin, offering little more protection than an umbrella, and the reflection from the surface of the stream would be even hotter than the direct rays of the sun pouring down overhead. And later on we suffered a good deal from the heat, so much so as to have feverish attacks, and to feel at noon as if our heads were on the point of blowing up.

Yesterday we met over twenty boats ascending the river and today we passed fifteen. Some of the statistics of the number and size of the boats which annually pass up and down between Rahëng and Chiengmai would be useful in considering a plan for improving the navigation of this part of the river. As the barriers which form the rapids are the accumulation of no one knows how many centuries, it seems not unreasonable to suppose that a broad channel deep enough for the largest boats to pass through might be maintained with little trouble. In most places there would be no blasting to be done, and the boulders are seldom too large to be removed by manual labour. There is however a point where the river-bed forms one gentle but continuous slope for two or three miles, and here it might be necessary to construct a canal on one side with locks at the required distances. We discussed the question pretty frequently, and came to the conclusion that a moderate toll on every boat that ascended would yield a fair rate of interest on the capital required. The time saved would shorten the voyage considerably, and diminish the freight on goods in proportion, besides stimulating trade. A railway up this gorge by the riverside would be quite impracticable, except at an enormous expense for bridges to carry the line over from bank to bank in order to avoid the constantly recurring precipices on either hand. But the Siamese are destitute of all enterprise, and the Laos have no interest in the removal of what they consider to be an important series of defences against invasion from the south. Perhaps the project of a railway by way of Lakhon and across the mountains to Chiengmai may become an accomplished fact one day, and then whoever rules at the mouth of the Mënam will hold direct sway over these northern states, which although not further from Bangkok than Edinburgh is from London, are at present a full month distant in time.

Shortly after we start the river makes a sudden bend to the north, and we see the sun rising over the right bank, whereas it ought to be on the other side, since we are going south. You know how to find your bearings in travelling if you happen to have left your compass at home.

By turning your back to the north you have the west on your right hand, your left points to the east and the south is straight ahead - the rest being of course perfectly easy. But to have the sun in the west, that is on the right, early in the morning when you are travelling down a river which rises in the north and discharges into the sea at its southern end is truly a perplexing circumstance when you are taken by it unawares. The reverse happens when you ascend from the mouth of the Mënam to Bangkok, after coming over the bar with the morning tide. At first the sun is on your right hand, and on your left of course is the western bank of the river. You have come on deck in your night-dress, as it is still early, but after a while, becoming conscious of the fact that you are approaching a great capital, and that it behoves you to present yourself decently clad to its multitudinous inhabitants, you retire for a few minutes into your cabin to change your clothes. On returning to your former post of observation you see the star of day apparently rising where he ought to be setting twelve hours later. It does not occur to you that a civilized river can do anything but run straight, and you consequently begin to fear that some sudden and unperceived cataclysm has upset the solar system. Far from standing still like Joshua's sun on Ajalon, the luminary has in a few minutes leapt over 180 degrees of arc, and seeing his mistake is coming back again the way he went. But on consulting the chart you find that nothing so terrible has happened. It is only the course of the river which here makes almost a complete circle, and during your absence down below you have got round to the other side of it. After a while things come right again and the sun reappears in his proper place without the intervention of miracle.

In the same way our boats descending make the circuit of a semicircle, first to the left and then to the right, after which we go on straight again. The river appears to be issuing from the gorge into a wide basin of which the mountains form the rim. Deer are said to be plentiful about here, and Dr Cheek, who is an ardent sportsman, landed with some of his men to get up a drive. For my part, I preferred lying down on the dead leaves under a tree alternately enjoying a book and a cigar. After being absent for a couple of hours they returned without having had a shot, though numerous footprints of more than one species had been seen on the sand drifts by the shore. Travellers speak also of another kind of large game sometimes met with on the rocky precipices which overhang this part of the river. A story is told of a man who shot one as it was putting its nose out of a cave 400 yards above the stream (a good shot), but it fell headlong into the water, so that he did not get his quarry. From the description given and authentic horns which I have inspected it would seem to be the sheep-faced antelope (Antilopa crispa) which is found on the mountains all over Eastern Asia, and notably in Japan.

The sportsmen having got over their disappointment, we started again at a quarter past nine and immediately afterwards shot the Këng Chum Rapid. Twenty minutes more brought us to the Këng Song-Kwë, or Rapid of the Two Channels, which is rather shallow. It took us nearly an hour to let down the boats, which was done by the aid of a stout rope. Këng Song-Kwë is one of the bigger rapids, and seems to be formed by the mere inclination of the river-bed, as there are no side-streams to block it up with boulders. It is here that a canal with locks will have to be constructed, if the plan of improving the navigation to which I have already alluded ever comes to be carried out. At a quarter to eleven we reached Këng Pha-môn (or Maun), where we took an early lunch under the shade of the high bank, starting again at half past. A series of almost continuous rapids now succeeded, and it took us nearly three hours to pass them, though the distance to be overcome was not great. We were now through the wearisome basin, and entered upon a second rocky defile cut through its further edge. Perhaps "wearisome" is an unfair epithet, for the scenery is very fine, surpassing even that of the Elbe above Dresden, but I was suffering from an attack of sun-fever, and the perpetually intrusive rocking motion imparted to the boat by the crew in pushing it over shallow places was extremely irritating under the circumstances, so that one must be excused for taking a pessimistic view. At three o'clock we are below Doi Tahëo, a mountain on the left bank. Far up its side stands a small chapel build over a *phrabat* or Footprint of the Buddha. Two hours later we turn a corner below a lofty blunt needle-shaped rock, almost bare of trees, whose summit is 400 or 500 feet above the river. The Laos call it Kan Bët, or Fishing Rod. The rough sketch on the next page will give you some idea of it. We rowed on till six o'clock and then stopped for the night.

February 20. The thermometer at six o'clock marked 71°. Almost immediately after starting we grounded in a shallow place where a large number of sunken rocks necessitated very careful steering. This part of the river would perhaps be the most difficult to render navigable at all seasons, as the channel would have to be cleared by blasting. The mountains on the right bank seemed to have receded to a considerable distance, while on the left hand they are still pretty close to the river. It looks as if we were getting clear of them altogether, but it turns out after all that we are only passing through a basin, and towards half past nine we begin to approach Doi Luang, or the Big Mountain, which rises on the right bank opposite to the continuous chain which has followed us on the left since we started this morning. As we float past, a series of magnificent precipices begin to develop, somewhat in the form represented in the sketch. We reach its southern end about

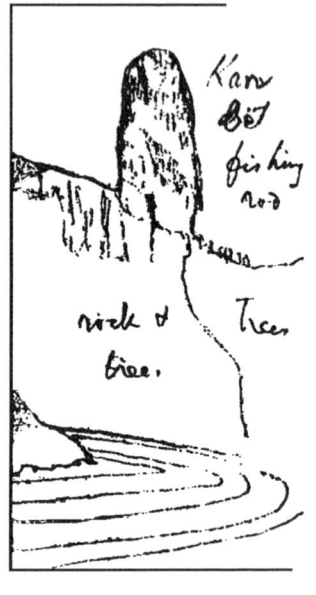

ten o'clock. The summit forms towards the south a precipice, at whose foot lies a slope, beneath which the vaster mass of perpendicular rocky wall extends far to right and left above the brown sparse woods that slope away down to the river's brink. Blackish brown is the prevailing hue of the rock, here and there accentuated by the shadows thrown by the south-eastern sun, and enlivened by scattered patches of pale yellow and red. Owing to the advantageous point of view, this is the most picture-making mountain on the whole course of the river, and its total height cannot fall far short of 2,000 feet.

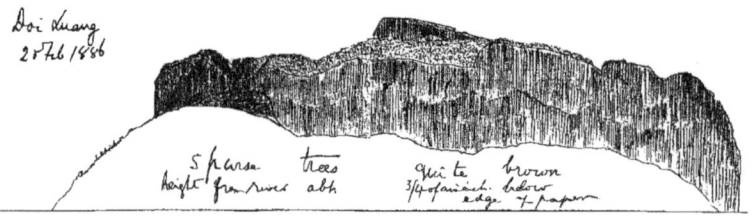

We are now in the plain, which henceforth widens out continually on either side, and stretches for a couple of hundred miles as the crow flies in a southerly direction towards Bangkok. The first village is Ban Tung-cha on a level bit of the left bank, backed up by peaked mountains, between which a deep valley runs eastward. In the centre of the village a gilded *phra-chedi* forms a conspicuous landmark. An hour later we pass Ban Thadua on the right bank; a wide valley stretches away behind it as far as the eye can see. We now begin to meet with cocoa-nut and sugar palms, bananas and tamarind trees, and the river spreads out far and wide over its alluvial bed. Ban Na-luang and Ban Na-pak-huei, where the steersmen taken on board at Mutka leave us, are two villages a short way below. At three o'clock the river narrows again between sloping hills, at a place called Ta Pui. This was a famous spot in past times for the exploits of gang-robbers, who came chiefly from Mu'ang Thön and Më Pik in the northern part of the province of Rahëng. More recently the comparatively energetic measures taken by the local authorities have for a while caused this plague to cease out of the land. We pass a bluff, halfway up whose face are three large Buddhist figures carved in relief on the reddish rock. *Sam ngao* is its name, from three miraculously persistent shadows to be seen there, which in the course of ages were transformed by supernatural agency into stone images. At six o'clock we stopped at Wang Namdip. Tonight for the first time since I left Phitsanulôk it was necessary to sleep within mosquito curtains.

On the following day the river was very wide and shallow. Our progress was slow, owing to the frequent grounding of the boats, which necessitated constant recourse to the channel-scraper. We passed twenty-four boats going upstream. At half past twelve we stopped for lunch near the confluence of the Më Wang, the river on which stands the town of Lakhon. Its mouth was almost blocked up with the sand brought down by the more powerful current of the Më Ping, but the volume of water issuing from it was nevertheless considerable. The mountains are now far away behind us on the northern horizon.

In many places the huge clumps of bamboo which predominate over other forms of tree life are in flower, and when seen from a distance they present a parched-up appearance. This inflorescence invariably precedes the death of the stem on which it occurs. Since noon tokens of occupation appeared here and there along the river, in the shape of palms and fruit trees. The *mai yang* or dammar oil tree has again become a conspicuous object in the landscape, the Butea is less common though by no means rare, while the bombax is plentiful, but its blossoms are beginning to fade. We passed Ban Talingsan, a good-sized village, about a quarter past five, and soon afterwards stopped for the night. Some mischievous persons had kindled fire in a bamboo jungle, which spread rapidly from clump to clump, devouring one tall parched stem after another, and causing a noisy conflagration that continued long after we were in bed. In the morning nothing was left but blackened stumps and white ashes covering the ground. Henceforward for many days we looked every evening for these jungle fires, which are not without their cheering influence in a region where there are so few signs of life.

February 22. Thermometer 70° at six o'clock. For several days past it has risen as high as 93° in my stern-cabin at noon, continuing so for two or three hours. We made but slow progress, owing to the shallowness of the stream, and it took us two hours to get out of sight of the place where we had passed the night. About one o'clock in the afternoon the river narrowed again between low hills, and we got along faster. The scenery is more like what we saw on the upper waters of the Mënam Phô, palm trees and huge spreading tamarinds line the banks, overshadowing the houses which stand each in its own neat enclosure. At half past five we passed a large and respectable-looking village, with a considerable number of boats lying off the sand bank in front of it. In fact, the riverside is inhabited almost continuously from here to Rahëng, which we reached on the following morning about nine.

Rahëng, as may be seen from the map, lies about halfway between Chiengmai and Bangkok. It is the principal town in the northern part of Siam proper, and the province of which it is the capital immediately adjoins the Lao States of Lakhon and Chiengmai. Mu'ang Tâk is the official name, Rahëng, by which it is best known to foreigners, being as far as I have been able to ascertain, its original Lao appellation. On the west the province of Rahëng is conterminous with Lower Burmah, and the road hence to Maulmein is much frequented by traders, who take about five days to perform the journey. Where traders go, dacoits are pretty sure to abound, and cases of gang-robbery are not uncommon on the frontier. The ringleader in these crimes was until recently a certain subordinate of the Governor of Rahëng, named Phra In, who, owing to subterranean connections with the Palace at Bangkok, has hitherto managed to evade the penalty of his misdeeds. He has however been at last arrested, and will no doubt be put on his trial in company with two of his accomplices who have been extradited for that purpose by the British Authorities in Burmah, whither they had fled to escape justice. A line of telegraph has recently been constructed between Rahëng and Maulmein, doubling that which already exists between Bangkok and Tavoy.

Trade here seems pretty brisk, and there are a large number of boats lying in front of the town. It is the custom for travellers descending the river to change here both boats and crews. We escaped the former necessity, as we had Dr Cheek's own boats, but my men went ashore, and I shipped a fresh lot.

The Governor is a fine-looking man between fifty and sixty years of age, with a bushy grey moustache and perfectly black eyebrows, which give him a distinguished air. * His manner is modest and yet dignified. Among Europeans he has the reputation of being one of the best officials in the Kingdom, firm, energetic and honest, as officials go in Siam. I can only judge of his outward appearance, and have no hesitation in saying that he is the handsomest man I have met in this country. He very civilly placed at my disposal a large floating-house which lies at the steps in front of his official residence. The latter is a brick building constructed to a great extent in European style, and plastered white, as are all brick houses in Siam. My mail was waiting for me here, and I had so much to do in the way of reading letters and newspapers that I found no time to explore the town, but the description in Carl Bock's book shows that there is little or nothing worth visiting, and the heat was too great to be encountered out of doors during the day. On the following morning I paid the Governor a visit at his house on shore to transact some business matters, and we left the place about eleven o'clock on the morning of the *24th February.*

The river at Rahëng is fully a mile wide from bank to bank, but at this season of the year much of its bed is occupied by bare sand banks, the channels [through] which wind considerably. From here to Kamphëng Phët is perhaps the worst part of the Më Ping. We often

---

* [Phraya Sucharit Raksa (Cheua Kalyanamit). Ed.]

started down what seemed to be a fairly deep channel, and after descending for half a mile or so, would find ourselves in a cul-de-sac, where it was necessary either to pole back up stream or cut a way for the boat with the aid of "scrapers". It was a toss-up which would take most time, and the crews generally preferred the latter alternative, which had at any rate the merit of visibly advancing us on our way. On one of these occasions we were passed by a small boat with a crew of five men and one woman, who was the most active of them all. She took the command, ordered the men about, pushed and shoved with untiring energy. In fact she almost carried the boat over the sand-bar on her shoulders. An ugly, fish-wife sort of a woman, [she was] typical of her sex as it exists in Siam, devoid of all physical attractions, and exceedingly masterful. The sand-banks shift so constantly that where a deep channel existed a month ago, to-day you will find a bare patch high out of the water. On the second day we got a respite from these troubles near a range of small hills on the left bank called Doi Padang, where the river narrows considerably and is consequently deeper. The jungle which lines the banks is parched up, and but little overgrown with climbing plants, while the banks themselves are not more than twelve to fifteen feet high. We had a succession of somewhat cooler nights, the thermometer marking only 68° at sunrise, but the heat during the middle of the day was intense, and in fact continued so for the rest of the voyage.

At four o'clock in the afternoon of the *27th February* we landed at Ban Nong Pling, the Village of the Leech Pond, situated on the right bank not a mile above Kamphëng Phët. Here are the ruins of a temple called Wat Phra thât, consisting of a lofty *phra-chedi* of unplastered brick, evidently occupying the site of an older building of the same form. Adjoining it on the south are the remains of a *wihan*, which was constructed of laterite blocks, many of which are scattered about what was once the floor. The lower portions of one or two octagonal pillars built up of laterite blocks still remain *in situ*, while those which once formed the outer wall have been carried down to the river bank, to be used in the construction of a jetty.

A walk of about twenty minutes brought us to a ruined *phra-chedi*, of which I add a rough sketch, as the upper part has a somewhat unusual form. It is of brick, but close by lay a few scattered blocks of laterite, which I conjecture to have belonged to an adjacent *wihan*, whose

very foundations have disappeared. The egg-shaped portion above the plastered pedestal is rarely seen in these structures, and it has been suggested that it is a mark of Burmese influence. Ten minutes beyond, in a jungle of tall trees on the opposite side of the telegraph track is a deep circular well, long since disused, six feet in diameter, the lining of which is regularly built up with bricks. Just beyond this again is an enclosure formed of upright blocks of laterite fifteen inches square, crowned with a heavy stone coping, in the same style as at Old Sawankhalôk. In the centre stands a ruined brick-built cella with an entrance portico. The interior of the building was much crowded with trees, growing almost on the very base of what had been a sitting figure of the Buddha. On either side is a large block of laterite about three feet each way, which may perhaps have been used as a fireplace, but it is difficult to see why any one should have wanted to boil his rice inside a chapel. At the Wat Phra thât already described there is a similar block at the entrance of the ruined *wihan*.

In returning across the telegraph track I perceived some other ruins in the distance, and on approaching them found a *phra-chedi* much overgrown with bushes and climbing plants. At the base on each side there had originally been a cell containing an image. A smaller *phra-chedi*, much more dilapidated than the first, stands on the opposite side of a ruined enclosure, and the telegraph wire is stretched between the two. The walls are constructed of large well-made red bricks, the proportions of which are noteworthy, being thirteen inches long, six and a half inches wide, three and a quarter inches deep, by exact measurement.

We reached Kamphëng Phët next morning a little before nine o'clock. It is almost within view of Ban Nong Pling, but the position of the channels was such that we had to drop down below the town and then pole up again along the left bank before we could get alongside the landing place. Kamphëng Phët is close to one of the ancient historic sites of the Thai race, and I was anxious to visit the remains, which are said to be of similar character to those of Sukhothai and Sawankhalôk. Unfortunately Dr Cheek was suffering from an attack of fever, and I did not like to keep him lying off the town all day in the burning heat while went off on an excursion to the ruins. So I contented myself with a visit to the Governor, which had to be a very short one in consequence of my extremely slight knowledge of Siamese. I managed nevertheless to make out from him that the old city is surrounded by a wall, which, as well as the temple, is built of laterite procured from quarries in the neighbourhood. The ruins we visited yesterday afternoon probably date from the same period, which is at least anterior to the fourteenth century, if not much earlier.

The town of Kamphëng Phët, as seen from a short distance below, is picturesquely situated along a curving shore, the brown wooden houses being built on piles or on the bank, with a background of trees of various hues of green shading them from the morning sun. It is probably subject to floods, for the greater part of the narrow market street which extends along the bank is raised two or three feet above the ground and floored with planks.

We started at half past nine and by noon were out of sight of the town. During the latter part of the day we made better progress than usual. The river almost seems to cut up into a succession of bays, for as one looks either up or down its course, a series of wooded promontories are observed jutting out into the broad bed. At nightfall we stopped off at Wang Phra thât, near a lofty and somewhat dilapidated *phra-chedi* which shows its summit over the tall trees on the right bank.

The navigation continued to improve from this point, and the forest began to lose the parched appearance which had characterized it hitherto. The Butea is now less frequent than before, but the Bombax is still numerous. If it were not for the slow rate at which we were drifting along, and the consequent apparent monotony of the river banks, the traveller would be inclined to praise the scenery, for every now and then lifting his eyes from a book he perceives a clump of trees which is perfectly beautiful as regards colour and grouping, and in the early morning the play of light and shade admirably diversifies the rich green foliage. But just when he is enjoying this contentedly, the boat runs aground on a shallow sand bank, and disgust with the disgraceful condition of the river becomes for a while the predominant feeling. A light dredger running up and down during the dry season between Manorom and Ban Na would surely help to improve the channel, while a slight toll on boats would suffice to meet the expense. Whenever we are thus brought to a standstill one or more of the boatmen get into the water up to their knees and angle with a bamboo rod. One of them to-day got a bite from what was evidently a big fish, but after playing it for some distance to the edge of the shallow water, finally lost it. This man was a Lao whose legs were tattooed of a deep black, which recalled the prince in the Arabian Nights who has his lower limbs converted by magic into black marble. He was a good-tempered and finely-built fellow, and highly appreciated by Dr Cheek for his sturdy good qualities. It was with much regret that I heard of his death from cholera a few days after we arrived in Bangkok, where the disease had for a time assumed the proportions of an epidemic. Another method of fishing, which is rather a favourite with the Laos, is to throw into the water small balls compounded of rice and tobacco. These the fish greedily devour, and becoming half stupefied, they are then easily caught by hand. This sort of fishing our men used to practise nearly every evening at the edge of the sand-bank where the boats lay. They also wasted a good deal of time by stopping during the day to cut fire-wood as a provision for the lower part of the river, where it is not so readily obtained, but they might just as well have done this work in the evenings after the boat was tied up.

On *March* 3, we passed by Ban Sentô (or tau), named after the snags which abound in several places just above. An energetic governor would have them cleared away, as they are extremely dangerous obstacles to navigation. But in a country ruled like Siam no one has any disposition to undertake improvements for public benefit.

In the afternoon of the same day we caught sight of a small but picturesque group of hills, called Doi Kwang (or Mount Deer's Horn) by the Laos, and known to the Siamese as Khao Nô (Mount Rhinosceros Horn) rising over the hills to the east. At first only a single summit was visible, but as we approached nearer and got it on our right, it separated into two, presenting an appearance which I have tried to reproduce in the accompanying sketch made when we got opposite to them an hour before sunset. We stopped just above a village named Ban Den, and sent a man on shore to make inquiries about a path which we thought

probably existed. The messenger, one of those who in reply to our question had previously asserted that the distance was fully equal to a day's journey, came back with the information that the priests who live at the foot of the mountain were in the habit of coming every morning to the village to beg their breakfasts, and that an old woman who was going out at sunrise next day would guide us thither. So I cheered up, in spite of a feverish attack which had left me very weak, and we resolved to remain here for the night.

Rising early, we crossed the wide stretch of sand that intervened between our boats and the shore, where we found our conductress awaiting us. She was a fat, grey-headed old woman with close-clipped hair, resembling a venerable baboon rather than a human being. But her extreme good-nature more than compensated for the defects of her personal appearance. The path lay through a wood, and the distance turned out to be even shorter than we had anticipated, for we walked there and back besides climbing about over the rocks and visiting the caves, in two hours. The distance to the foot of the northern hill cannot be over two miles. As seen from the river the side turned towards us had looked like a wall rising above the forest, but on penetrating the latter, we found the base of the mountain to be an incline covered with trees for quite two thirds of the height. The rock is limestone, the stratification having assumed the vertical position shown in the sketch [missing]. The highest point is probably not more than 300 feet above the level of the river. At the end of the northern hill is a lesser pile of rocks containing several good-sized caves, some of which have been converted into shrines for countless small images, and one of them contains a recumbent figure of the Buddha eighteen or twenty feet in length. The [dracaenas] (*ton chan*) and arboreal euphorbias abound all over the rocks. But of greater interest than these was a handsome flowering tree called *dok kë sai*, with white trumpet-shaped flowers and primate leaves, probably of the same genus as the *dok kë* found at Keng Soi. Here is a sketch made from a specimen which I brought away. We  have a very fine example of this tree on the river front of the garden at Bangkok, which tradition says was brought from Chiengmai many years ago by Sir Robert Schomburgk, when it was still a young plant; but I did not [find it there?] and all my inquiries after it were [in vain]. *

That evening we reached a village on the left bank not far above Paknam Phô, of which I am not able to record the name. It was a wretched-looking place surpassing in squalor even the ordinary Siamese village. The day's work being over, a few of the inhabitants were lounging on the high bank under the trees. In answer to our questions, they said they had not been able to raise a rice crop last year on account of the deficiency of water, nor the year before last, owing to the floods. They complained of the hardships of the "government service", to which there appeared to be no limit. The native officials who travel on the river are allowed to impress the inhabitants to serve as boatmen, for which no pay is given. Life was not worth having, they said, so great was the oppression under which the people groaned. For the expedition to Luang Phrabang the government had required a levy of a hundred men from the district, but the local officials called out the whole male population and forced those who were not needed to pay for exemption. They were glad to see foreigners in the country, for they paid for everything they had, and did not take away the villagers to row their boats. There is no doubt that the administrative system in Siam is capable of being greatly ameliorated, and perhaps we might without much exaggeration call it very bad. It is even possible that the common people imagine they would be better off under the dominion of a civilised power, and would not fight very bravely in defence of their own King. But on the other hand, there is no government in the world that satisfies everybody, and grumbling

* [The words here in brackets fill in gaps in the original Ms. Ed.]

against the powers that be is a favourite occupation with people who have not energy enough to defend their natural rights or to insist upon improvement. And I do not think that the benefit we confer on Asiatics by relieving them of corrupt and oppressive rulers quite counterbalances the loss of their independence. But those only deserve to be free who can secure freedom by their own exertions.

Sugar-cane is planted here, and the juice is expressed in rude wooden mills of the same construction as elsewhere in the north of Siam. We found rice growing in patches on every convenient sand bank in the river bed, but Dr Cheek told me that he supposed that the inhabitants had adopted this plan in consequence of their having been unable to raise any grain during the preceding season in the ordinary way.

On the *5th of March* we reached Paknam Phô about half-past four in the afternoon, having made rather slow progress all day. I strongly suspected the boatmen of purposely running us on shoals and contriving other causes of delay, in order that they might pass the night at this centre of trade and spirit-drinking. But if this was their secret intention, it did not bear fruit, for I made my crew push on ahead and 'tie up' a mile or two below the town, and the other boats had to follow.

I have now brought my narrative back to the point where I left the Mënam on the journey northwards, and the rest of the voyage down to Bangkok was over the same ground, except for a short distance, where we had to make a circuit to the west, the channel by which I had ascended the river in December being now too shallow. I had telegraphed from Rahëng to have the launch sent to meet me at Paknam Phô, but it was unable to get so far, and we eventually fell in with it only a couple of hours distance above Angthong.

On the afternoon of the *10th March* we got into a creek leaving the main stream some way above Sikok, and stopped a short distance beyond Ban Kathi on the Bangsai creek. The country about here is perfectly flat and destitute of forest. On landing we beheld a vast rice-swamp plain, now absolutely dry, extending as far as the eye could reach to the north and west almost without interruption and dreary-looking like the Egyptian desert. From Paknam Phô southwards we had several times been grievously delayed by the strong breeze blowing from the south-west, which took the boats aback and rendered them quite unmanageable, and now as we approached Bangkok the flood tide performed for us the same disservice, so that we did not reach home until between seven and eight in the evening of the *11th March*. I had thus been a hundred and one days away, two-thirds of which time had been spent in actual travelling and after having been pent up so long in a boat, I was only too glad to return to a terrestrial existence at Bangkok, and the comfort of a leathern armchair.

Correspondence from the Satow Papers, Public Record Office, Kew, Series 30/33

Vol. 14/2

Satow to Sir Philip Currie,[1] 16 March 1886

My dear Currie,
    ... Things have not been going on at all well up there [Chiengmai]. It was very necessary that I sh[ou]ld make the journey & see things with my own eyes. I have now left there as Acting V[ice] C[onsul] a very intelligent young fellow named Archer, & started [E.B.] Gould off on a tour to the frontier to pick up what information he can ab[ou]t Chien[g]tung. The latter is an excellent warm-hearted fellow, but I am afraid his judg[emen]t is not always to be relied upon. I hope that the vacancies will speedily be filled up by the app[oin]tm[en]t of new students, for [E.H.] French & I are alone here, & when Gould comes down French must go home on leave. G[ould] is subject to attacks of intermittent fever, & I am afraid I have got malaria too as one result of my journey.

y.v.t.

Vol. 11/5

Satow to F.V. Dickins,[2] 4 April 1886

My dear Dickins,
    ... It is about four weeks since I returned from my journey up country. It was a highly varied experience, and gave me a knowledge of the country that I could not have acquired by years of residence at Bangkok. Of course I kept a pretty minute journal, but it would be inconvenient to publish it, and in fact it would need a good deal of work to put it in shape. I visited some old ruined temples which as yet are quite unknown to Europeans, but could not stay long enough to make them

out thoroughly. The northern country is much pleasanter to live in than the delta, but people accuse it of being more malarious. On the mountain, near Chiengmai, at about 3000 feet above the sea, grows a species of pine, probably the same as P[inus] Kasya[?] in Burma, and at least four species of Guercus[?]. I brought away cones and acorns, but am not within reach of a botanist who would identify them for me. Some of the trees have magnificent red flowers which during the winter-season blaze on the plains and river-banks. Most of the trees about Chiengmai with the exception of the oaks[?] & pine appear to be deciduous, and it is rather an unexpected sight to find the forests almost bare. Bock's account in ["]Temples and Elephants," though inexact in details, is on the whole a fair picture of the country and people. What he says about tattooing is confirmed by everyone whom I have asked. But the custom is said not to be natural to the Thai race; the Siamese and Eastern Laos do not practise it to any extent, while among the northern Laos and Shans who have at different periods of their history been subjected by the Burmese, it is universal. The conclusion is that the fashion was introduced by the Burmese ...

... I have begun at last to study Siamese, and am reading the history. It is an easy language, but the words are uncouth.

Yours ...

Vol. 11/3

Satow to W.G. Aston,[3] 22 April 1886

My dear Aston,
... My journey to the Northern Laos was on the whole a pleasant one, and proved to be very necessary from an official point of view. But it took a terribly long time. I am writing an account of it for my people at home, and feel as if it were impossible to condense what I saw into the pages of a letter. The Lao States are governed by mutually inde-pendent chiefs, who are more or less interfered with by the Bangkok Government. This however is a good thing. They belong to the same race as the Siamese, and ought to belong to her [sic], especially as they occupy the head-waters of the Menam. But the control of the King over

his out-lying provinces and states is very imperfect. Teak-forests are chiefly what take British Subjects thither, and they are mostly Peguans and Toungthoos from British Burma. We have a Vice-consul up there to look after their interests, but he has no jurisdiction, that having been handed over to the Siamese through the indifference of the Indian Gov[ernmen]t. I think it was a mistaken step, but try to make the best of it ...

Yours very sincerely ...

Notes

[1] Sir Philip Currie was currently the assistant permanent under-secretary at the Foreign Office, and the official Satow reported directly to. In 1889, he succeeded as Permanent Under-Secretary, and in 1894, was appointed Ambassador to Constantinople.

[2] F.V. Dickins was one of Satow's oldest Japan friends, as a naval officer serving in the Far East in the 1860s. He had returned to England in the meanwhile to take up a legal career, and in 1891, became Registrar to the University of London. Nonetheless, he maintained his Japanese interests, and in retirement taught the language part-time at Bristol University College.

[3] W.G. Aston was with Satow and Basil Hall Chamberlain, a member of the early triumvirate of British Japan scholars. In 1885, he had been invalided home from the British Legation at Seoul, Korea.

Index